IMAGES
of America

SHELTON

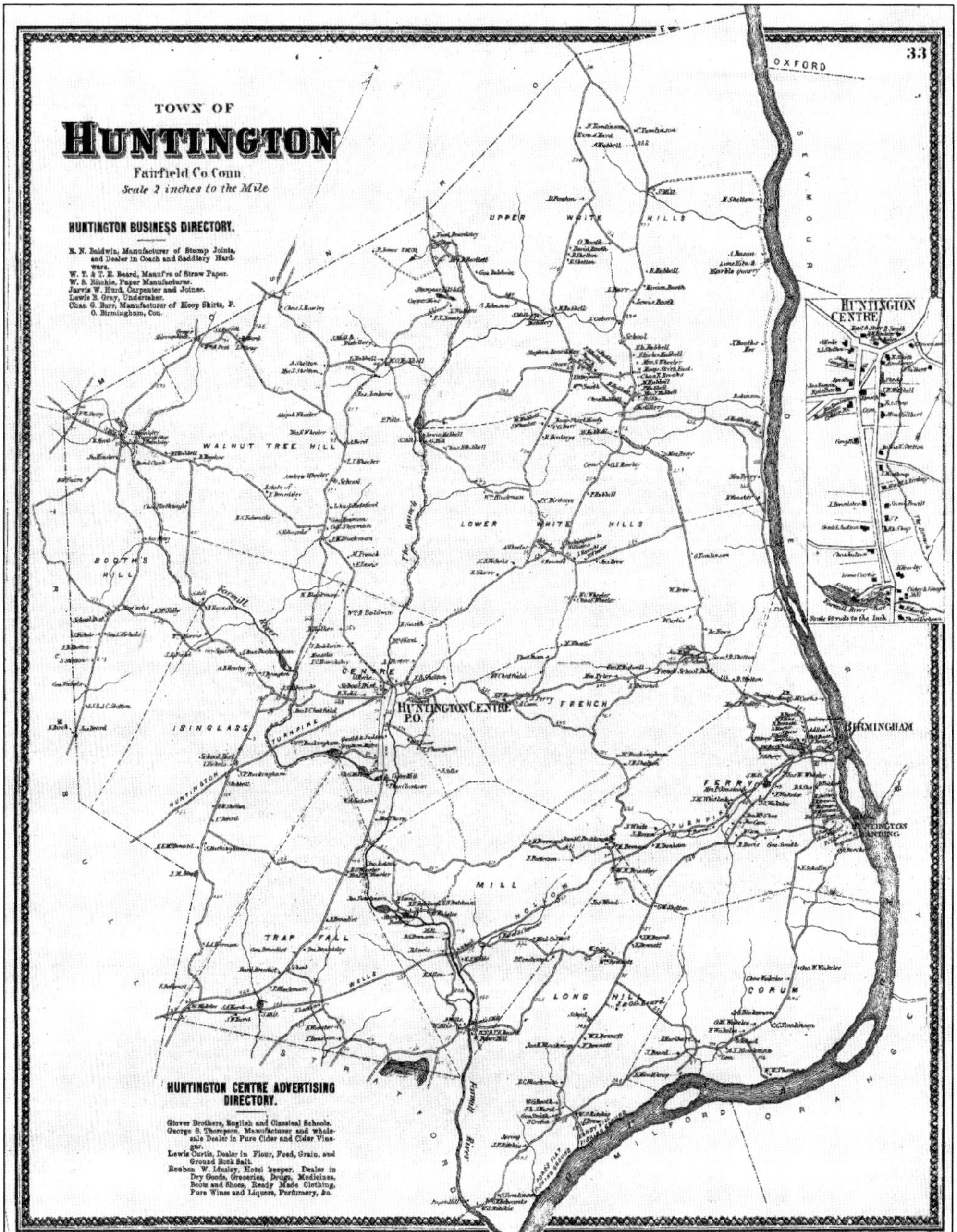

When this map was originally published in 1867, in *Atlas of New York and Vicinity,* by F.W. Beers, the city of Shelton was known as the town of Huntington. The map is divided by school districts. While most streets are not labeled, houses are marked and identified with the owner's name.

IMAGES
of America

SHELTON

Shelton Historical Society

ARCADIA
PUBLISHING

ISBN 978-0-7385-1066-8

Published by Arcadia Publishing
Charleston, South Carolina

Printed in the United States of America

Library of Congress Catalog Card Number: 2002106586

For all general information contact Arcadia Publishing at:
Telephone 843-853-2070
Fax 843-853-0044
E-mail sales@arcadiapublishing.com
For customer service and orders:
Toll-Free 1-888-313-2665

Visit us on the Internet at www.arcadiapublishing.com

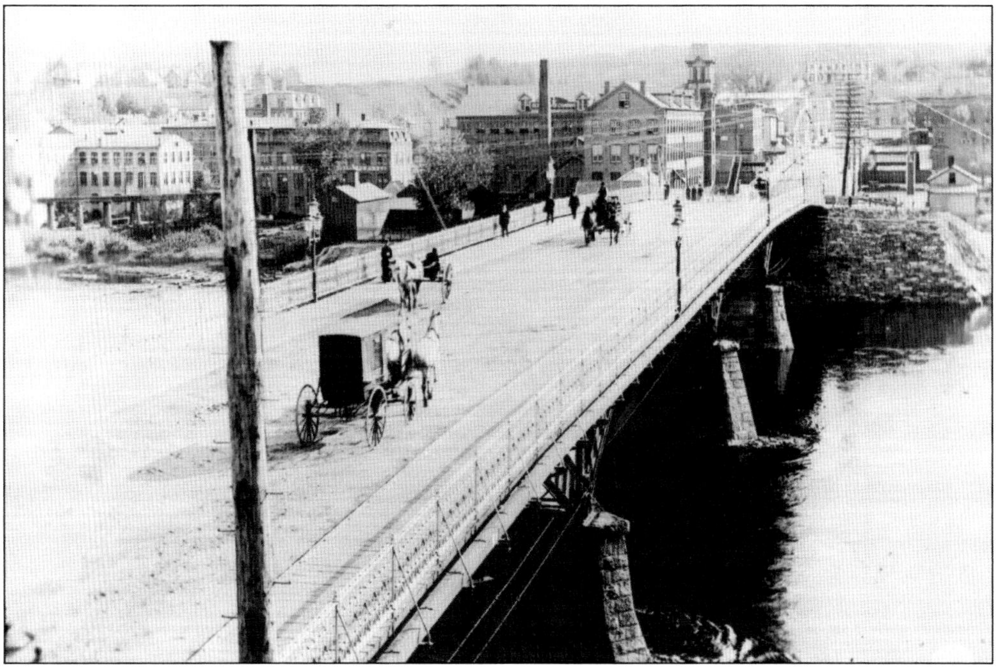

Taken *c.* 1891 or 1892, this photograph of the iron bridge between Shelton and Derby shows the daily traffic across the river, both on foot and by horse. The large building to the left of the bridge is the Derby Silver Company; the Birmingham Corset Company is next door. (Courtesy of Philip Jones.)

Contents

ACKNOWLEDGMENTS

The Shelton Historical Society sincerely thanks the committee who worked on this book: Deborah G. Rossi (chairperson), Paula Anthony, Marty Coughlin, Joe Hansen, Philip Jones, Lin Mulford, Heather Rhodes, Patricia Sweeney, and Tracey Tate.

As *Shelton* grew, so did the photographic archives of the Shelton Historical Society. The society has been able to supplement its collection of photographs from the hundreds of pictures that have been generously loaned or donated to us as work progressed on this book.

It was decided that this book should illustrate the chronological growth of the city of Shelton from its agrarian traditions through its industrial heyday, to the challenges it faced during the latter part of the 20th century. While each photograph presented to the committee deserved a place in *Shelton*, many deciding factors contributed to the selections. Picture quality, whether similar images have been previously published, identifiable locations and individuals, and the storytelling qualities of each photograph were taken into consideration.

The Shelton Historical Society thanks all the lenders to this book and the many people who have donated photographs to our collection over the years. We would especially like to thank Ray Allen, Zaida June, Paul and Lillian Kassheimer, Raymond Lavietes, Joyce Nelson, Charlotte Nesteriak, and G. Alton Russell for their photographs, which contributed immeasurably to this publication.

The committee would like to thank Tom Patsenka of Stockbridge Photo Lab in Shelton for all his hard work in reproducing the photographs contained in this book. His dedication and creativity saved many photographs from degradation and led to copy prints that were actually an improvement of the original images.

The committee also thanks the city of Shelton for its interest and support, as well as Jeanette LaMacchia, city historian, for her help.

The most valuable photographs reviewed were labeled with dates, locations, and names. Please label your photographs now!

INTRODUCTION

The area that became Shelton, Connecticut, was originally the home of the Paugussett Indians. Primarily hunter-gatherers, they also farmed corn, beans, and squash to supplement their food supply. The Paugussetts called the land along the Housatonic River "Pootatuck."

In the 1690s, English settlers in Stratford felt the pinch of overcrowding and began moving north, settling along the current Long Hill Avenue. They named the area Coram. By 1717, there were some 50 families in Coram who petitioned the Connecticut Colony for the right to form a separate parish. Ripton Parish was established by vote of the general assembly that year. The parish green became the centerpiece of a predominately agricultural community. Numerous saw, grist, fulling, and cider mills were built along the Far Mill River and smaller tributaries.

By 1789, Ripton Parish had grown large enough to re-form as the town of Huntington, which was named in honor of Samuel Huntington, a signer of the Declaration of Independence and then governor of Connecticut. According to the 1800 U.S. Census, which contained the first itemized listing for Huntington, the free white population of 2,616 was evenly divided between males and females. There were 143 people described as "all other free persons except Indians not taxed," which included indentured servants and freed slaves. There were also 33 slaves.

While the majority of Huntington residents were farmers, some branched off into other industries. The Leavenworth family, who owned land on the Housatonic River near what is now Indian Well State Park, began building ships in the late 1700s. The family built wooden sloops and schooners that sailed up and down the eastern seaboard and as far as the West Indies to trade lumber, livestock, and other farm products for molasses, sugar, and rum. The shipbuilding industry peaked around 1800 and dwindled following the War of 1812.

The population of Huntington declined during the westward migration period and remained around 1,500 until 1880. Farmers turned away from such grain crops as wheat, oats, barley, and rye and gradually began production of farm goods such as milk, butter, fruits, and vegetables, which were sold locally as well as in nearby Bridgeport, New Haven, and New York City.

The completion of a dam across the Housatonic River in 1870 altered the agrarian nature of the community. The Ousatonic Water Company, which financed the dam, aggressively promoted the area. Advertising touted the community's proximity to several major metropolitan areas, rail and water connections to markets, cheap power provided by the two canals associated with the dam (one in Shelton and a shorter one in Derby), and an available work force. The water company owned more than 260 acres of land below the dam and leased many sites to businesses. Factories were built on the leased property and harnessed the power provided by the canal. By 1896, there were more than 25 manufacturers located along the Shelton canal. Travelers who came along River Road from Stratford and Bridgeport were greeted by a large sign that read, "Welcome to Shelton—Home of a Mile of Factories."

With the growth of available jobs came an influx of immigrants. Settling primarily in housing along the river, immigrants from Germany, Ireland, Italy, and the Slavic nations increased the population significantly. The downtown area quickly grew into a borough of the town of Huntington and was named in honor of local businessman Edward Nelson Shelton, a leading proponent of the dam. Shelton became a legal borough of the town of Huntington in 1882. By 1919, Shelton was officially established as a city, and the town of Huntington voted to be incorporated within it.

As Shelton moved further into the 20th century, life near the river was dominated by the industries lining the Housatonic. People worked, lived, and shopped in the downtown area. In the hills, the farming tradition continued producing crops and dairy products for sale in nearby urban areas. After World War I, industries relied less on waterpower in favor of electricity and began moving south. Many of the businesses on Canal Street closed during the Great Depression, and while World War II provided some recovery, it was not enough to keep major manufacturing in downtown Shelton.

The opening of Route 8 in 1975 connected Shelton with the cities and towns between Bridgeport and Winsted. The new highway provided people who worked in cities such as Bridgeport, Stamford, Waterbury, and even New York a convenient way to commute between work and a suburban Shelton home. Residential and corporate development during the 1980s threatened the rural character of Shelton, which had motivated many people to relocate here. In the early 1990s, an open space plan was adopted by the city, resulting in hundreds of acres of land being set aside in public trust.

Shelton's historical past was also threatened by development. To address this issue, the Shelton Historical Society was formed in 1969. In 1971, the society purchased and relocated the c. 1820 Brownson House, which was slated for destruction. The house was moved to a one-acre site at the corner of Ripton Road and Cloverdale Avenue, which had been donated to the society by Dorothy and Wisner Wilson. Soon afterward, the 1872 Trap Fall School, a corncrib, and a three-person outhouse were relocated to the site. The c. 1860 Wilson Barn was restored in the 1990s, and in 1998, the exhibit "3 Centuries of Shelton: From Farming to Industry and Beyond" opened in the barn. The society has also been instrumental in the restoration of the Curtiss Memorial Fountain on the Huntington Green. Future projects include the reinterpretation and restoration of the Brownson House.

The primary mission of the Shelton Historical Society is to preserve the history of the city and to educate people about our city's engaging past. We hope that this publication will contribute to the fulfillment of these goals.

One

Farming

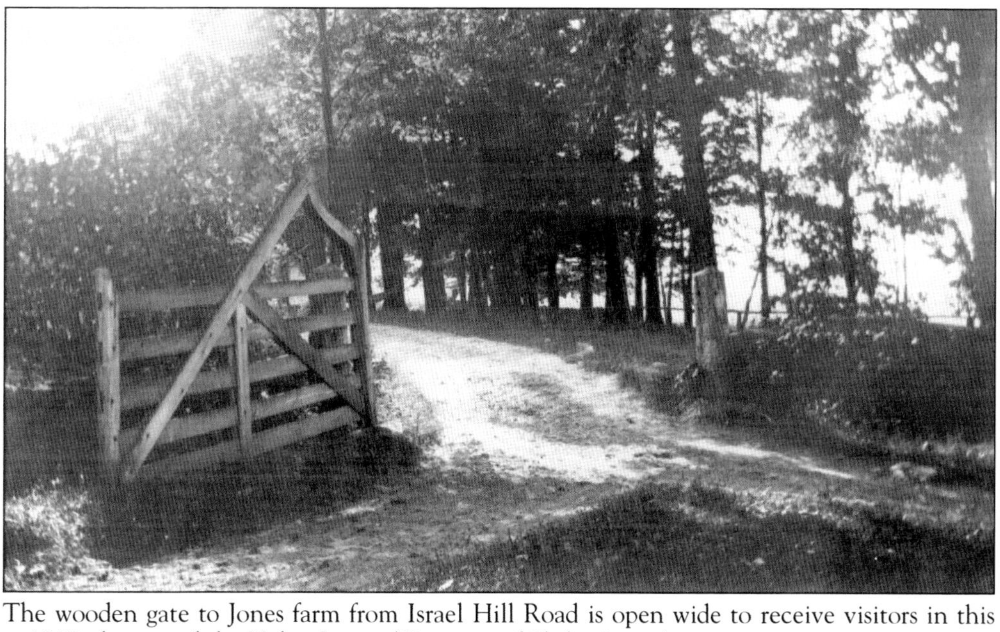

The wooden gate to Jones farm from Israel Hill Road is open wide to receive visitors in this *c*. 1910 photograph by Helen Jones. (Courtesy of Philip Jones.)

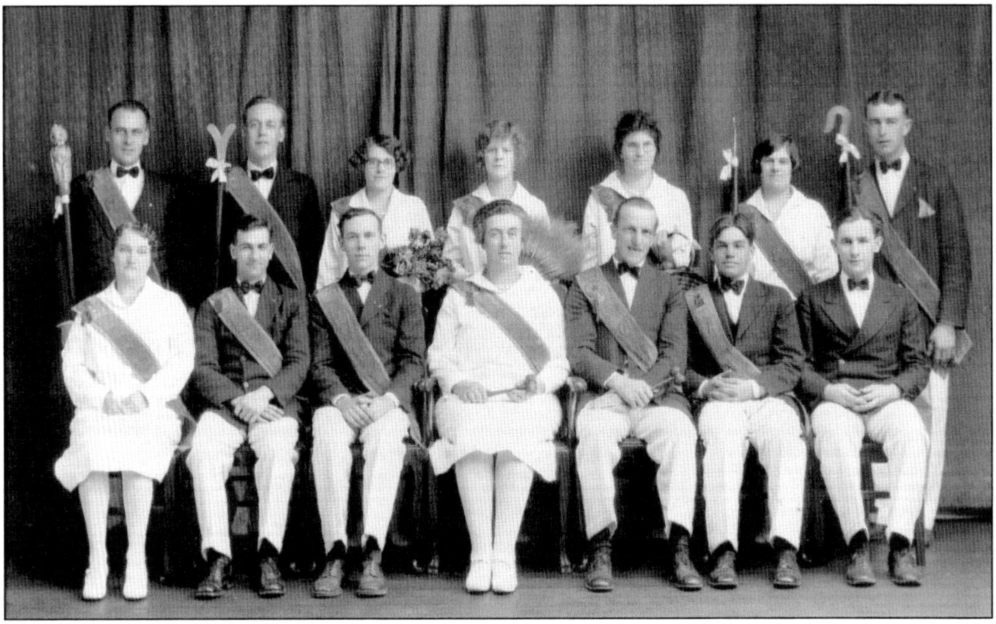

The Far Mill River Grange was organized in 1892 to improve the lives of rural families and their farms. The group sat for this portrait *c.* 1930. The members are pictured, from left to right, as follows: (front row) Emelie Birdseye, Charlie Goldspink, Edward Ferguson, Ina Goldspink, Stephen Tucker, Horace Webb, and A. Arthur Shepardson; (back row) Earl McConney, Lesley Baldwin, Ethel Baldwin, Gertrude Adams, Nellie Tucker, Annie McConney, and Earl Millard. (Courtesy of the Wells family.)

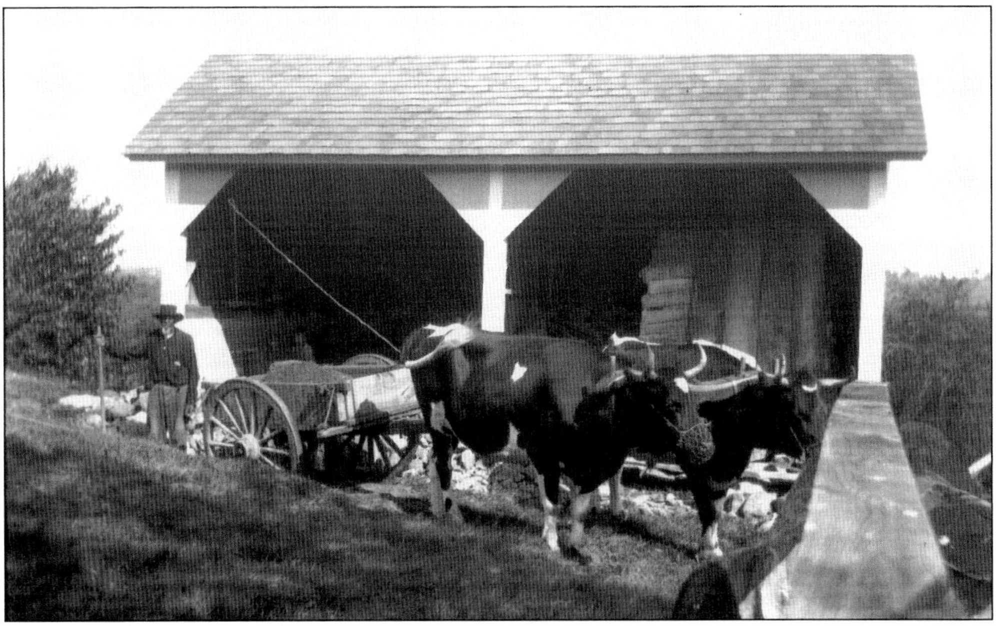

John Benson worked on Shelton's farms and made baskets for his friends. In 1914, Helen Jones photographed him excavating a driveway for the garage of her father, William Jones. Benson was a Native American and may have been a descendant of the Paugussett tribe, which once populated the area. (Courtesy of Philip Jones.)

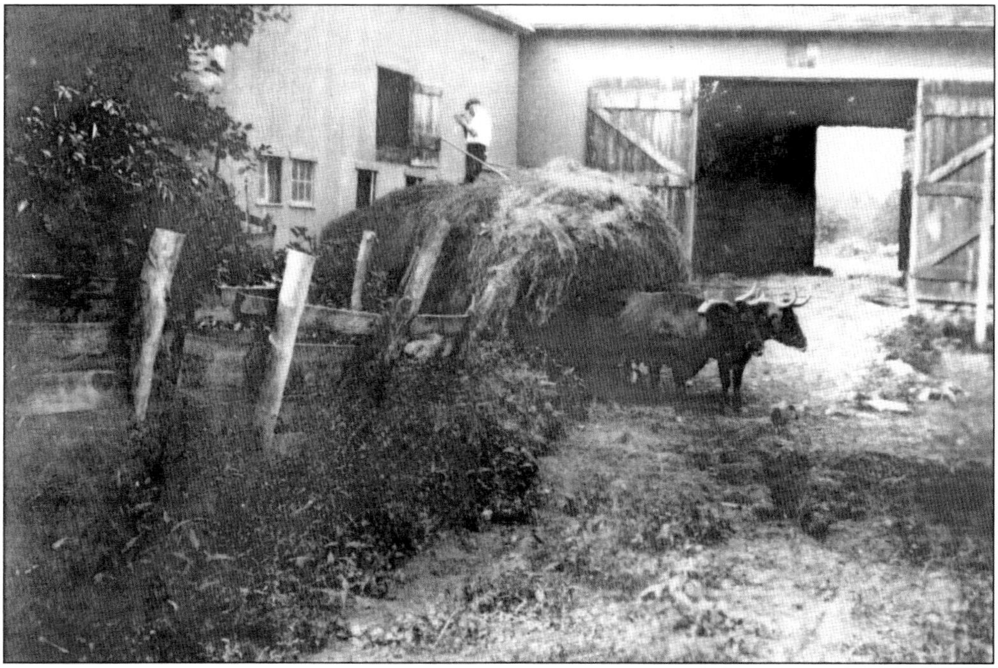

Before 1910, putting the hay away for Ben Wells was a hot, sweaty, and difficult project at the farm at 656 Bridgeport Avenue. Each cow, horse, and ox can eat several tons of hay over the winter season. (Courtesy of the Wells family.)

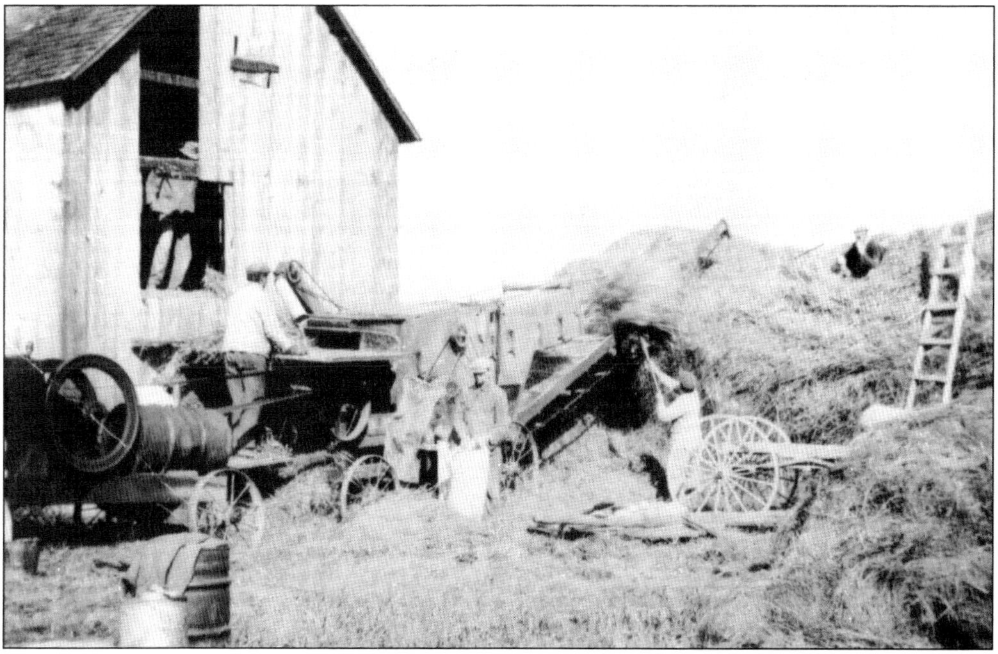

Only a few years later, most likely *c.* 1920, this photograph was marked "modern haying" due to the introduction of motorized farm equipment at the Wells farm. (Courtesy of the Wells family.)

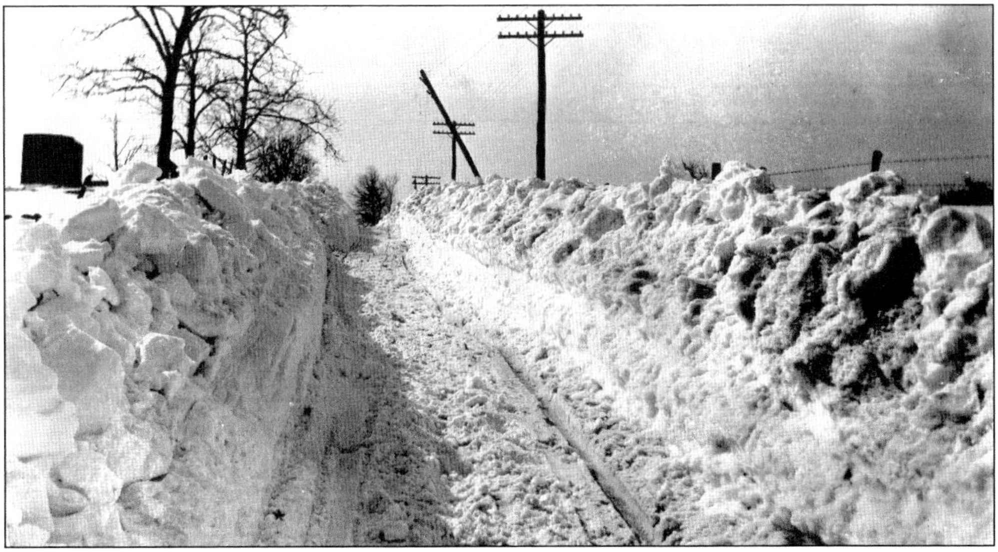

Rural life is dictated by the seasons. In 1922, Helen Jones photographed Nicholdale Road after a snowstorm. Neighbors gathered together and shoveled out the road by hand. (Courtesy of Philip Jones.)

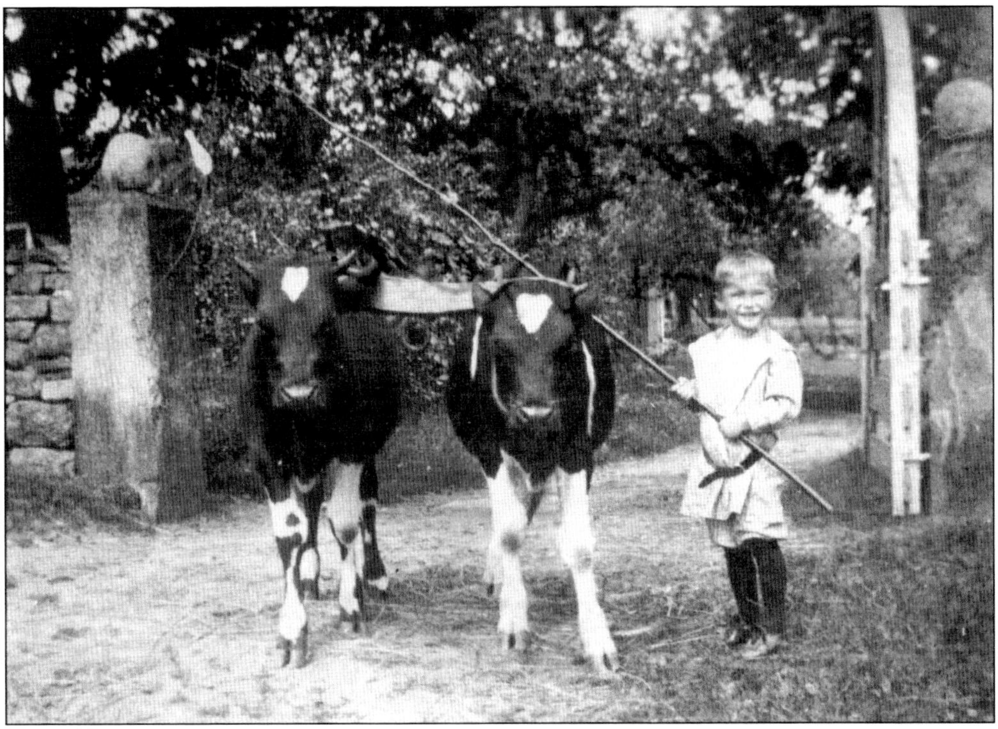

Andrew Fair is justifiably proud of his young ox team in 1908. They are at the gate of the farm of his father, James Fair, at Walnut Tree Hill Road. (Courtesy of Jim Fair.)

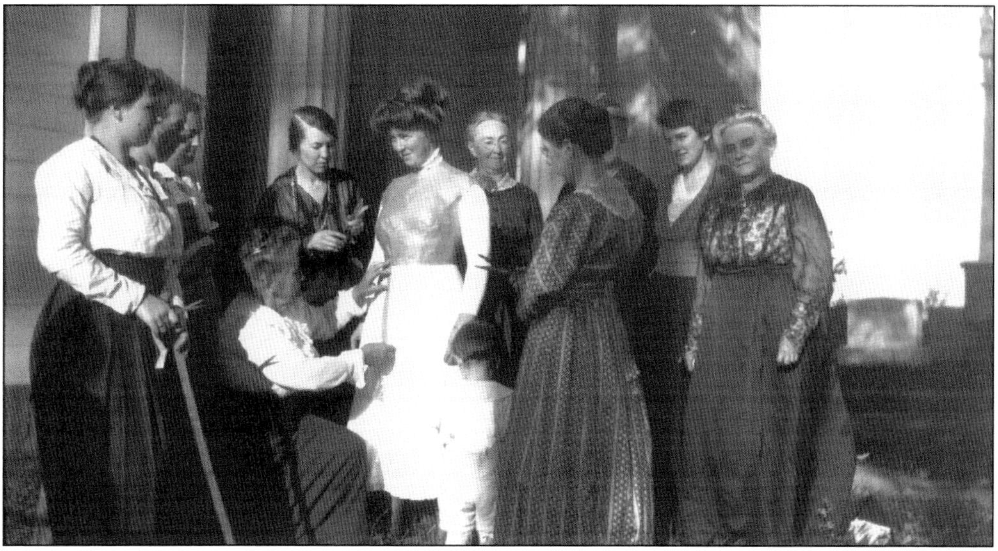

Pictured is a lesson in making a dress pattern at the White Hills Baptist Church in 1920. Helen Jones photographed her sister-in-law, Joan Jones, being fitted, while Joan's young son Newell keeps by his mother's side. (Courtesy of Philip Jones.)

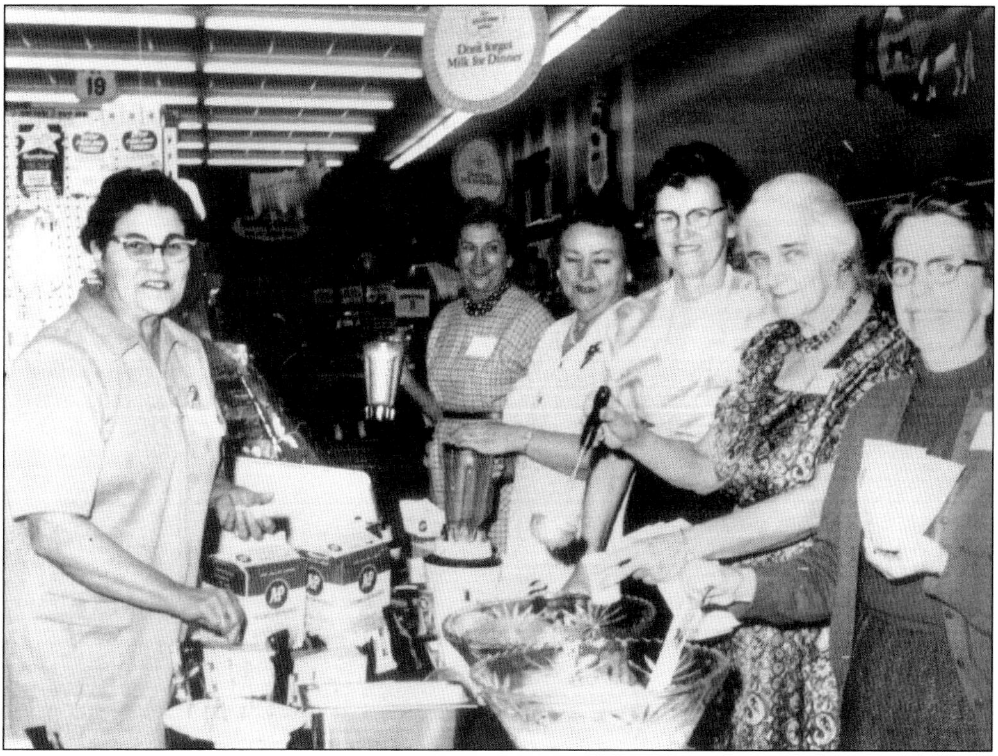

Like the Far Mill River Grange, the Farm Bureau worked to improve the lives of rural residents. A milk promotion at the A & P on River Road in April 1968 was one such community program that taught people about the nutritional value and availability of Shelton products. Pictured, from left to right, are Anna Bachkowsky, Martha Thornton, Edith Birdseye Wells, Evelyn Swendson, Dorothy Wilson, and Gertrude Wilson. (Courtesy of the Wells family.)

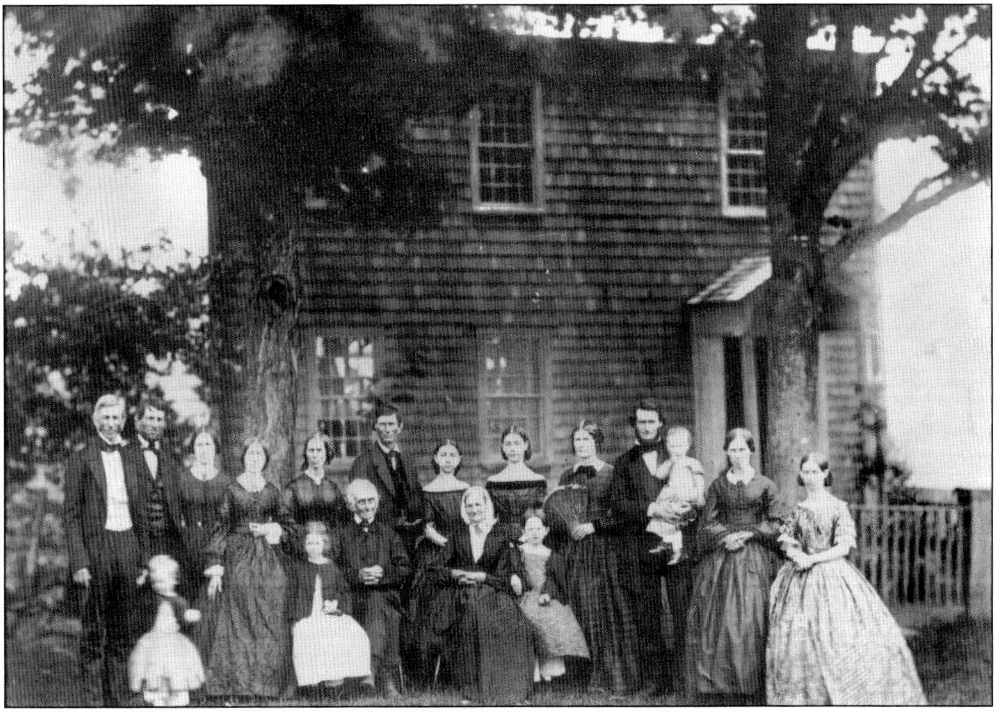

In this *c.* 1860 photograph, one of the earliest taken in Shelton, the Wells family gathers outside their home, formerly located at the corner of Commerce Drive and Route 8. Henry Shelton Wells is holding baby Frank Wells. (Courtesy of the Wells family.)

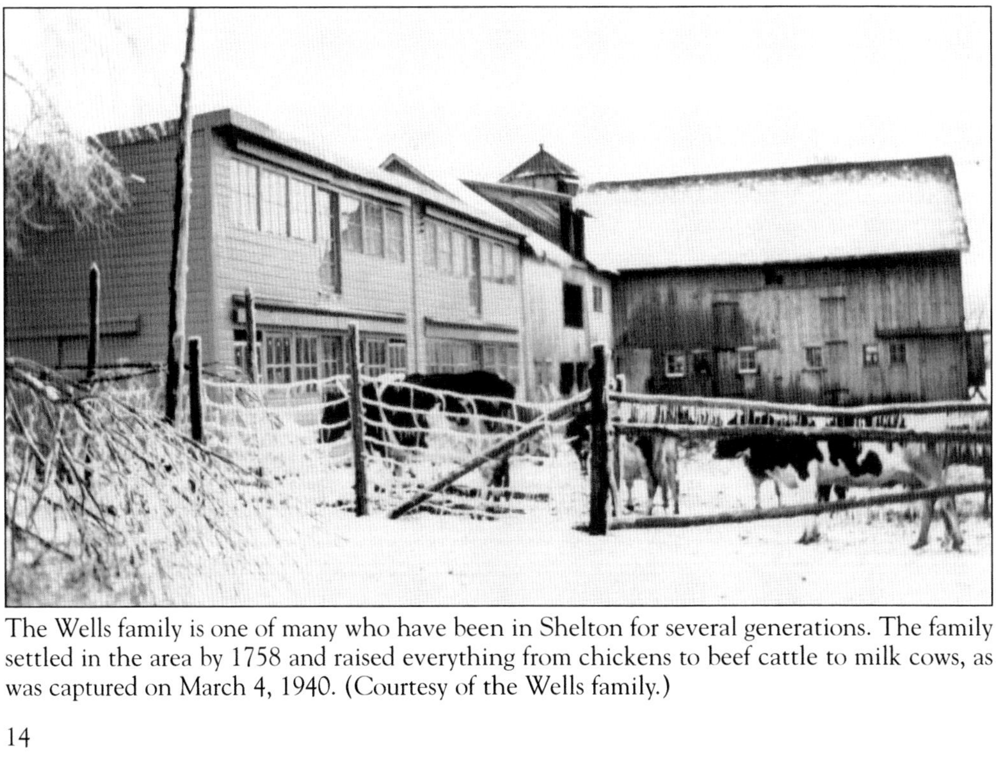

The Wells family is one of many who have been in Shelton for several generations. The family settled in the area by 1758 and raised everything from chickens to beef cattle to milk cows, as was captured on March 4, 1940. (Courtesy of the Wells family.)

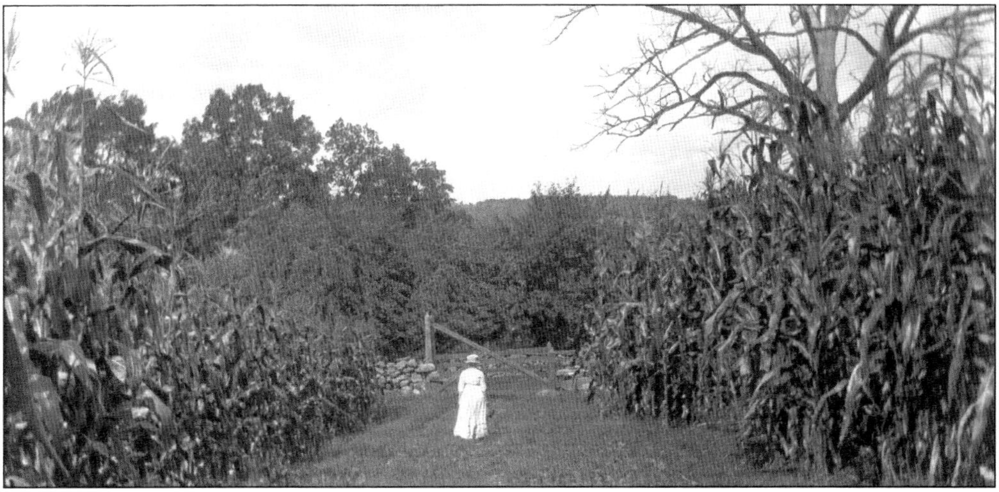

Israel Hill on the Jones farm was a cornfield when Helen Jones took this photograph c. 1910. The Jones family arrived in Shelton in 1859. Philip James Jones originally raised beef cattle and sheep. (Courtesy of Philip Jones.)

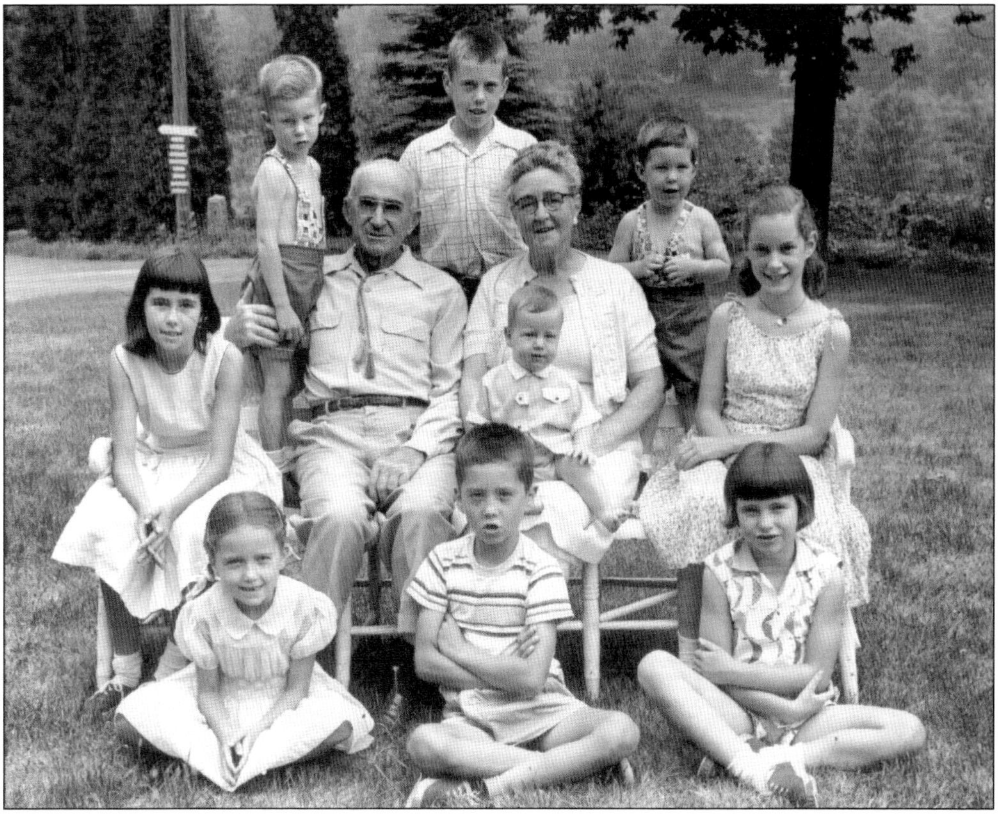

Nearly 100 years after the Wells family portrait, Philip and Joan Jones had theirs taken with their grandchildren in 1958. From left to right are the following: (front row) Rebecca Jones, William Jones, and Sandra Jones; (middle row) Melissa Jones, Philip Jones Sr., Daniel Jones, Joan Jones, and Lois Malarkey; (back row) Drew Glover, Terry Jones, and Timothy Glover. (Courtesy of Philip Jones.)

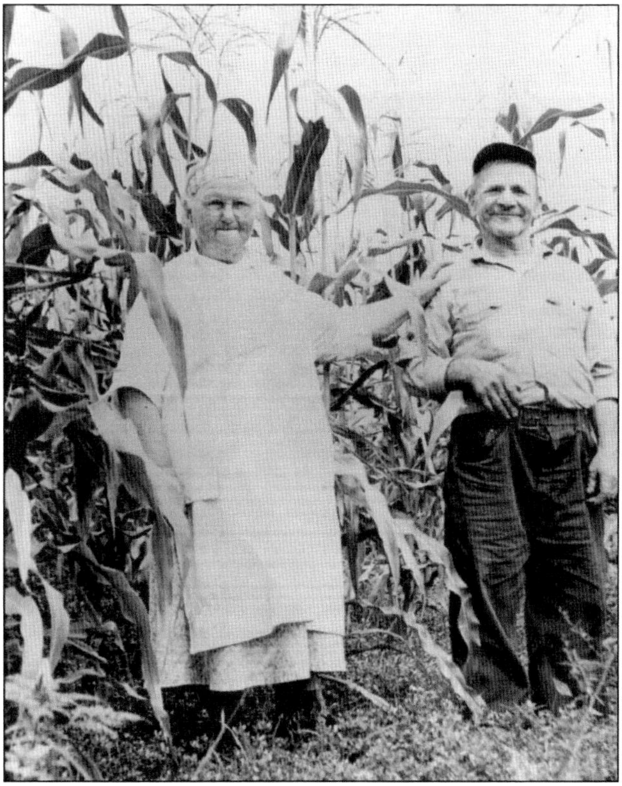

Mary and Alex Pacowta farmed vegetables and corn on 52 acres of land at 171 Meadow Street. This photograph from the 1960s originally appeared on the front page of the *Suburban News*. The Pacowtas had 11 children, and Mary lived to be 102. (Courtesy of the Pacowta family.)

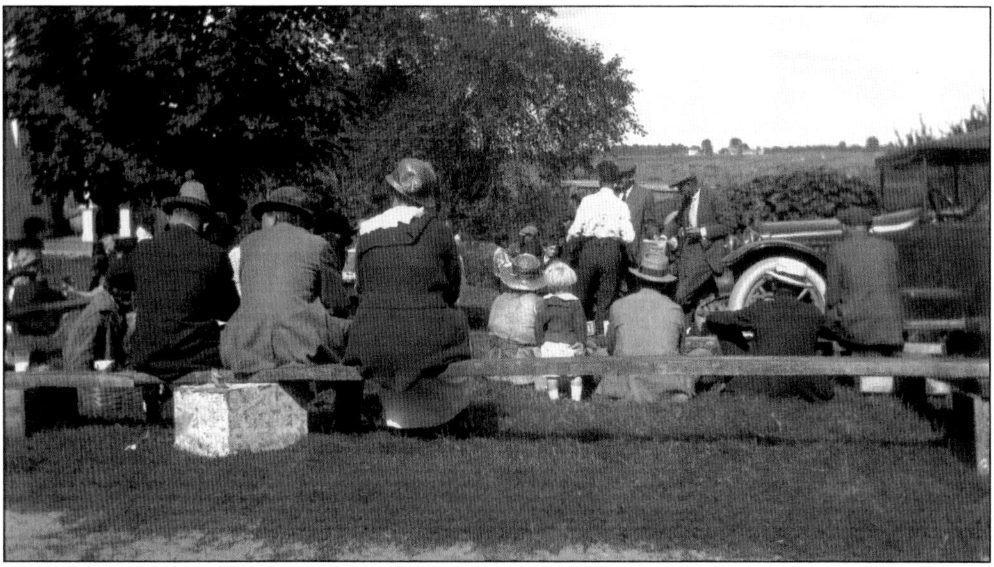

A Farm Bureau field day could include field crop studies, livestock seminars, or machinery demonstrations. This photograph, looking toward Pumpkinseed Hill on Beardsley Road, was taken at the Jones farm in 1920. (Photograph by Helen Jones; courtesy of Philip Jones.)

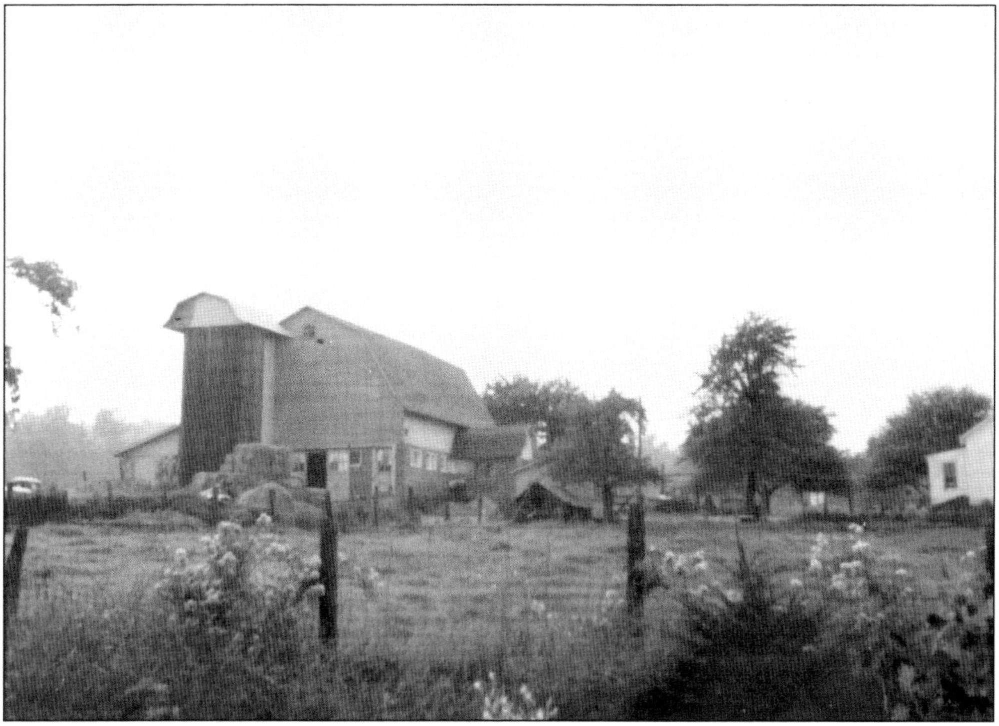

This silo, shown in July 1968 at the Wiacek farm at 152 Meadow Street, was originally built on the French farm on East Village Road. It was used to store silage, which consists of ground-up corn and stalks used to feed livestock. The Frenches' barn collapsed, leaving the silo. The Wiaceks needed a silo, so they dismantled and moved it to their farm sometime before 1955. The silo stood until *c.* 1985. (Courtesy of Elma Jean Wiacek.)

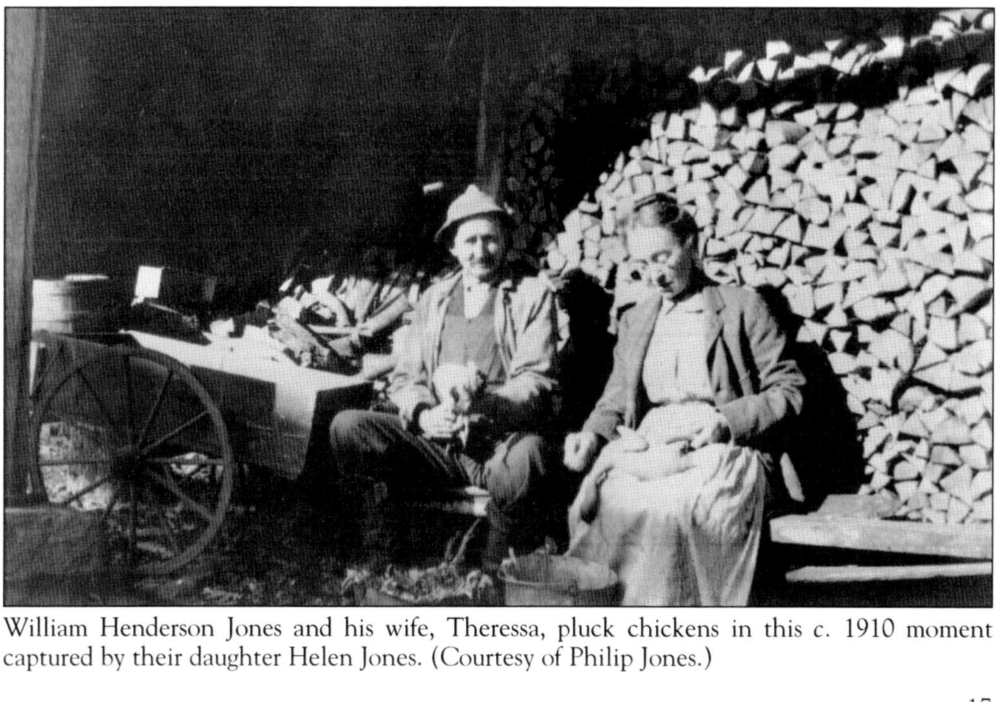

William Henderson Jones and his wife, Theressa, pluck chickens in this *c.* 1910 moment captured by their daughter Helen Jones. (Courtesy of Philip Jones.)

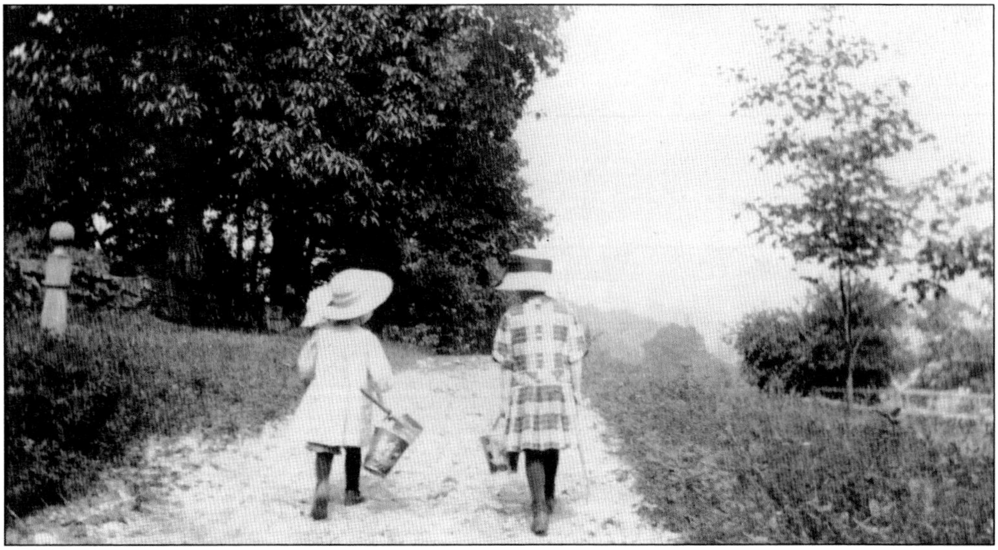

Local farmers cobbled together a living by combining farming, industry, mercantilism, and taking in boarders. People traveled from far away to spend quiet summers at farms in the country. Here, cousins of the Jones family from Chicago go off to enjoy their afternoon c. 1920. (Photograph by Helen Jones; courtesy of Philip Jones.)

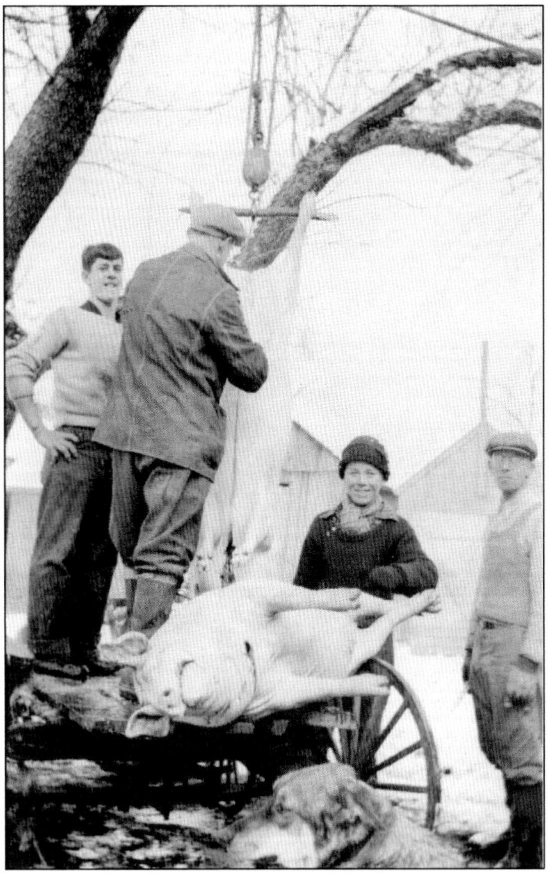

Raising and butchering animals was another way in which farmers literally put food on the table. Here, "Susie Q" is butchered on December 30, 1939, at the Wells farm at 656 Bridgeport Avenue. Two boys watch Lewis Twist and Henry Shelton Wells complete the job. (Courtesy of the Wells family.)

The caption for this image is "Henry and an egg eater." Henry Shelton Wells (1901–1995) began selling eggs for extra money during the Great Depression. He rode his bike to Bridgeport, often with no shoes, to deliver eggs. The eggs were stored in the cellar of the family farm at 656 Bridgeport Avenue, and the occasional varmint, such as this opossum in 1956, had to be killed. (Courtesy of the Wells family.)

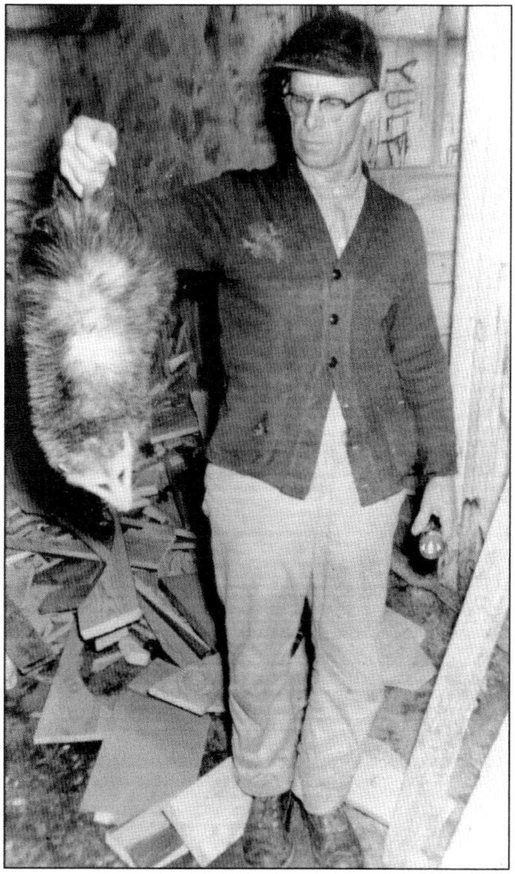

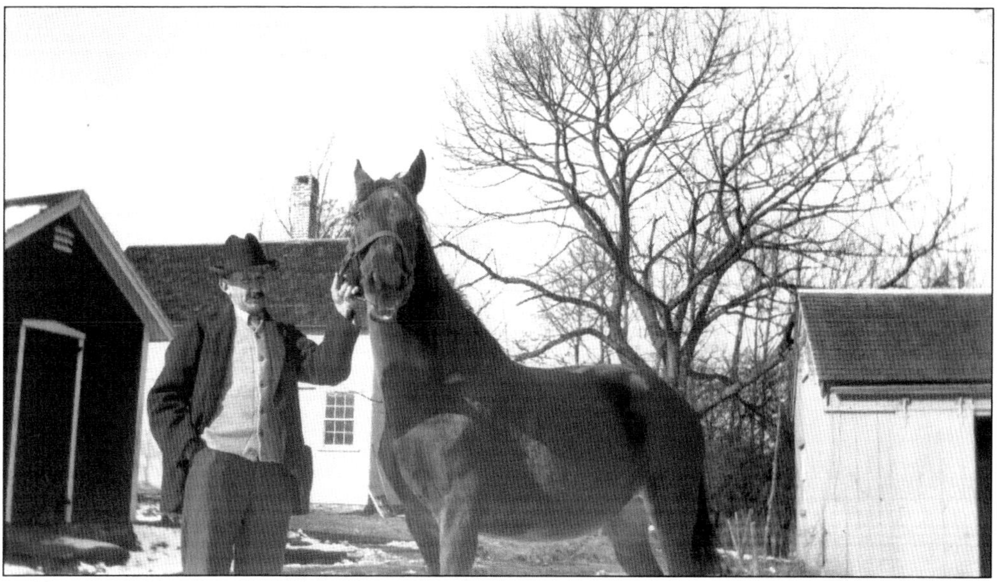

William Henderson Jones, shown here c. 1910, used to race in the Danbury Fair as a young man. Horse races were popular events, and both participants and observers looked forward to fairs and races. (Photograph by Helen Jones; courtesy of Philip Jones.)

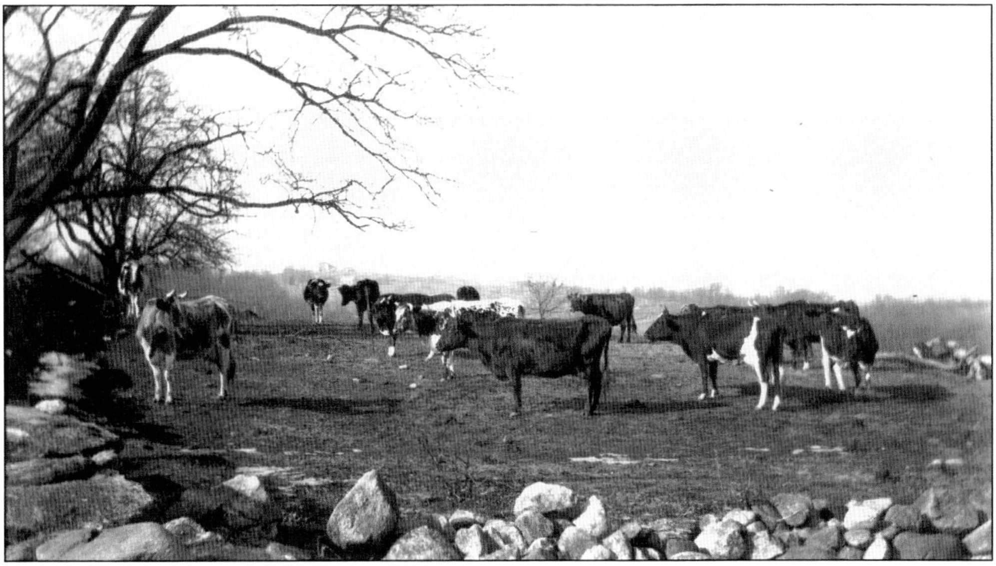

Before 1914, this field on the Jones farm was a pasture for the family's herd of milk cows. This is a herd of Holstein and Ayrshire cows. (Photograph by Helen Jones; courtesy of Philip Jones.)

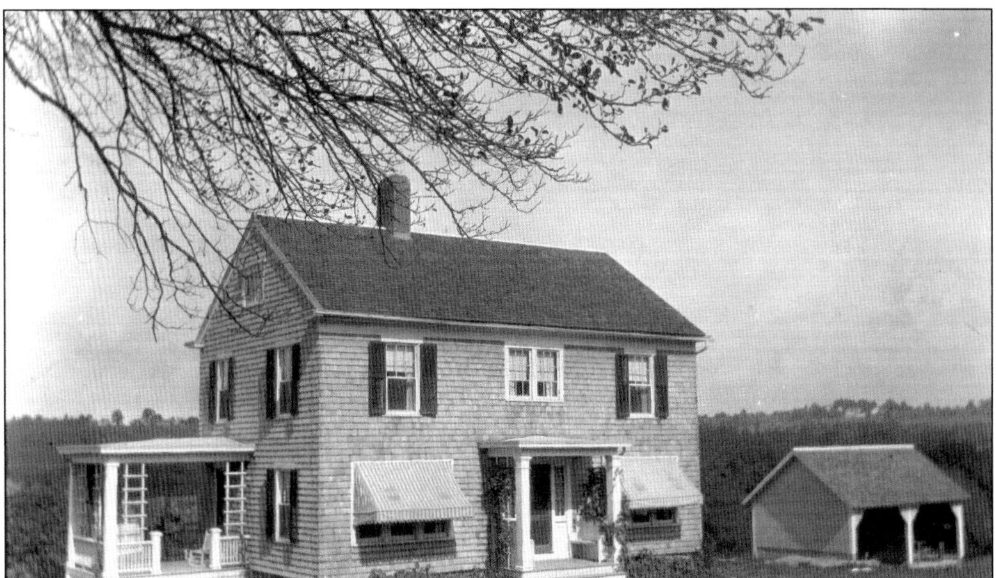

Change is inevitable. Built on the cow pasture in 1914 by William Henderson Jones and his wife, Theressa, this home at 605 Israel Hill Road still houses the Jones family today. It was built for the princely sum of $4,500. (Photograph by Helen Jones; courtesy of Philip Jones.)

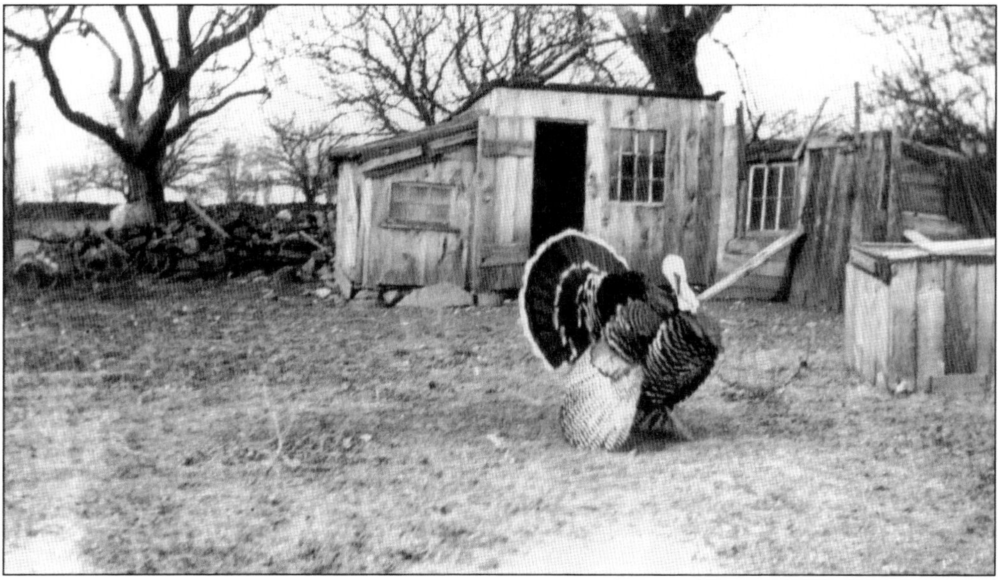

"Thomas Jefferson Turkey" awaits the Thanksgiving table at the White Hills Baptist Church parsonage *c.* 1915. He was named by Reverend Bickford's daughter, Fanny, who had a fondness for naming animals and cars after historical characters. Her first car was named Bucephalus. (Photograph by Helen Jones; courtesy of Philip Jones.)

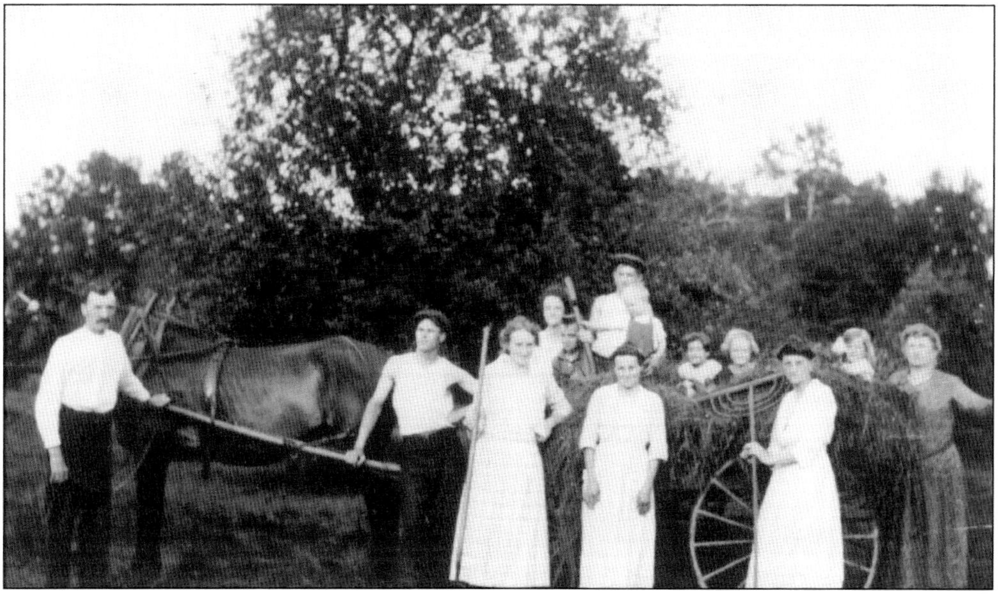

Activities such as haying were best accomplished by large groups of people. Here, the Ritter, Jones, and Bullwinkel families give H. Henry Ritter a hand at Sunnyview Farm on Maple Avenue in 1922. Pictured, from left to right, are H. Henry Ritter, William Jones, and Anna Ritter Jones. The rest are unidentified. (Courtesy of Randy Ritter.)

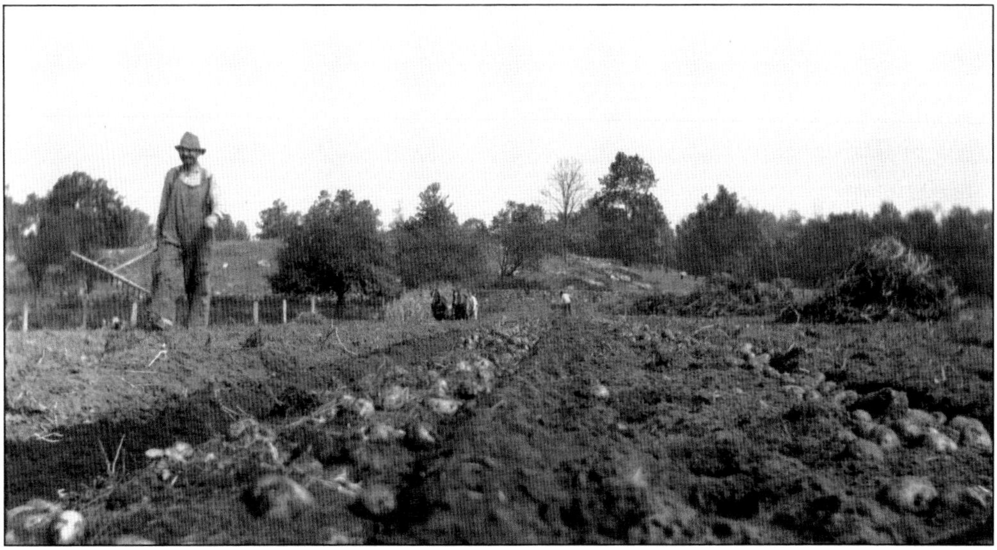

The Plains at Jones farm was a multiuse field. In 1917, the crop was potatoes. Hay and corn were also grown there. The field is now part of Strawberry Valley on Israel Hill Road. (Photograph by Helen Jones; courtesy of Philip Jones.)

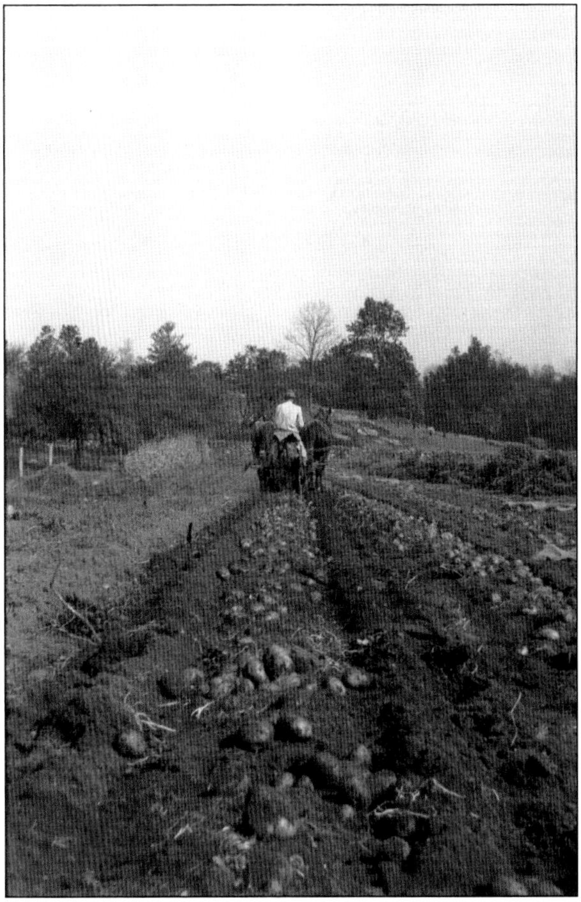

Fortunes could go boom or bust with a single crop. The 1917 potato crop from the Plains at Jones farm was so good that Philip Jones Sr. was able to buy a Patterson car with the profits. The Patterson was handmade in New Jersey and featured an aluminum radiator, control knobs, and dashboard. (Photograph by Helen Jones; courtesy of Philip Jones.)

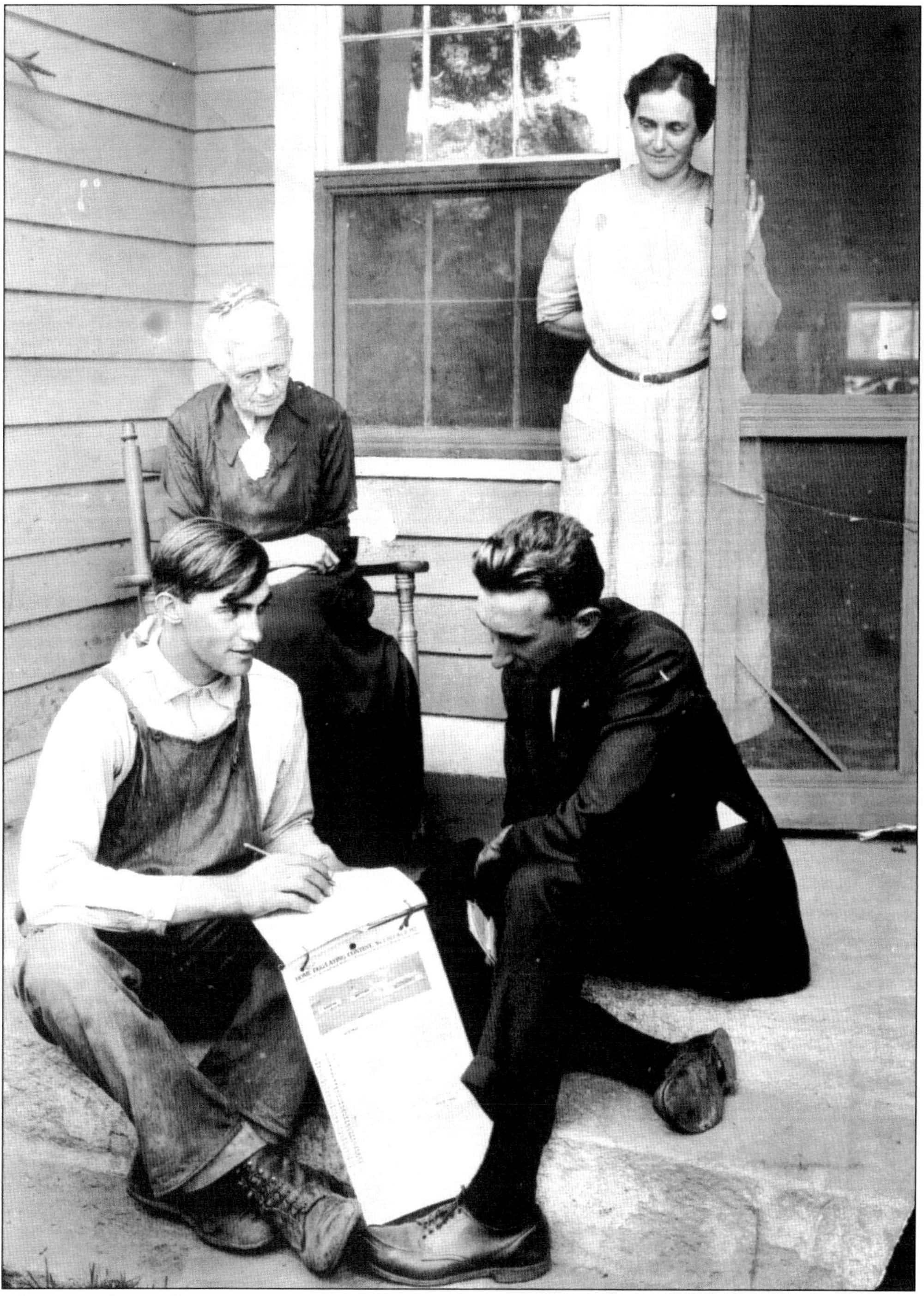

This view shows three generations of the Fair family. They are, from left to right, Andrew Fair, Eliza Jones Hubbell (Fair's grandmother), James R. Case (of the Farm Bureau), and Carlotta Fair (Fair's mother). Taken in 1925, the photograph may have been advertising for the Home Egg Laying Contest, which ran from November 1, 1924, to October 31, 1925. Fair is reviewing the tally sheet for the contest with Case. (Courtesy of Jim Fair.)

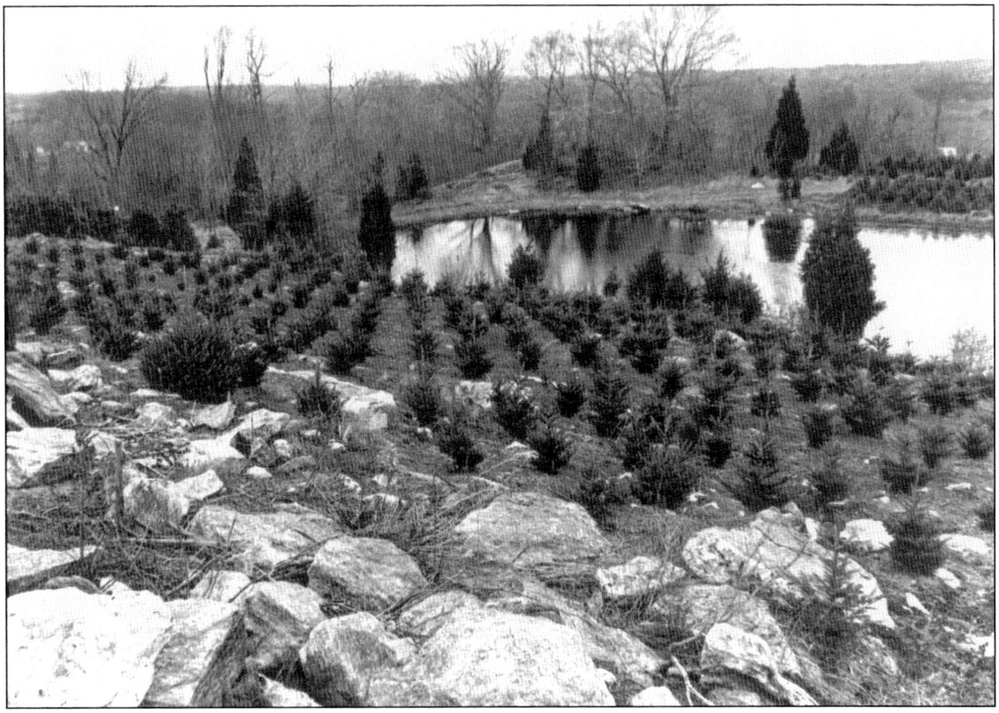

Philip Jones Jr. began planting Christmas trees in 1938 as a 4H project and moved the family farm away from the dairy business. Now, with more than 10,000 trees hauled away every November and December to households all over the tri-state area, Jones Family Farms has become a Shelton institution. (Photograph by Patrick O'Hara; courtesy of Philip Jones.)

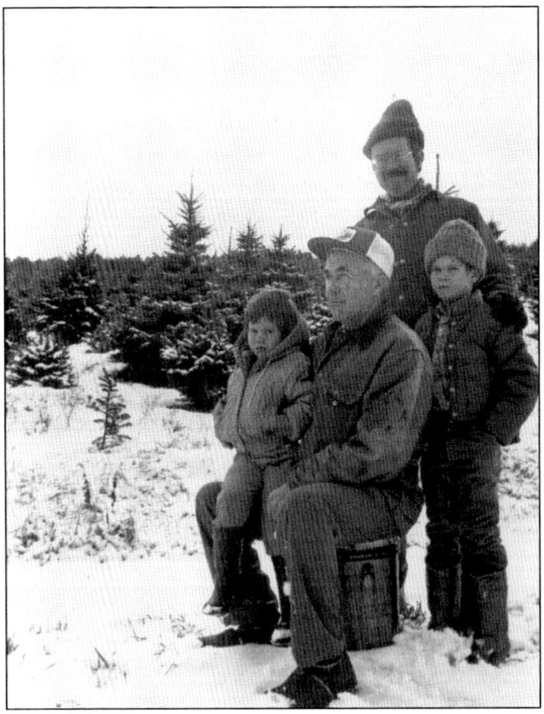

In 1985, three generations of Jones farmers gathered for a group portrait in one of the Christmas tree fields. Gwyn, Philip, Terry, and Jamie are the fourth, fifth, and sixth generations to work the same land. Philip planted the Christmas trees; Terry the strawberries, blueberries, and pumpkins; and Jamie is currently working on a vineyard. (Photograph by Patrick O'Hara; courtesy of Philip Jones.)

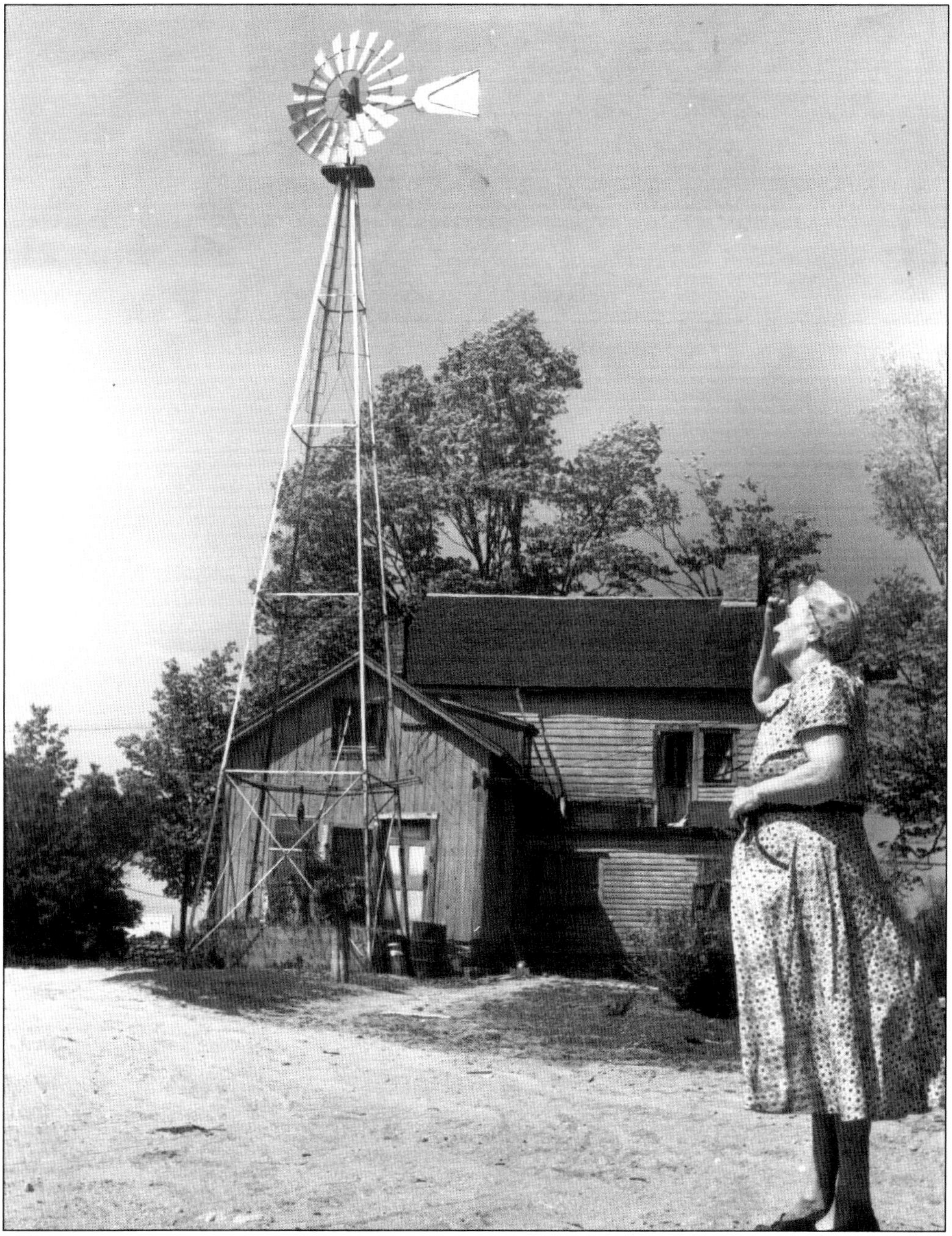

This photograph accompanied an article in the *Bridgeport Telegram* on June 1, 1957. Emelie Louise Twist Birdseye is pictured on her farm at 50 Mohegan Road. The article discussed the origins of the Birdseye windmill and how they were quickly disappearing from rural areas. The windmill was moved from a Nichols farm by George Birdseye in 1922 to pump water for his Mohegan Road dairy farm. He raised the 57-foot-tall structure with a block and tackle and a team of horses. Every morning, Emelie released the brake that kept the wheel from turning, and it pumped water for the barn and house. By the time this photograph was taken, the drive shaft had snapped. The windmill was eventually removed in the early 1990s. (Courtesy of the Wells family.)

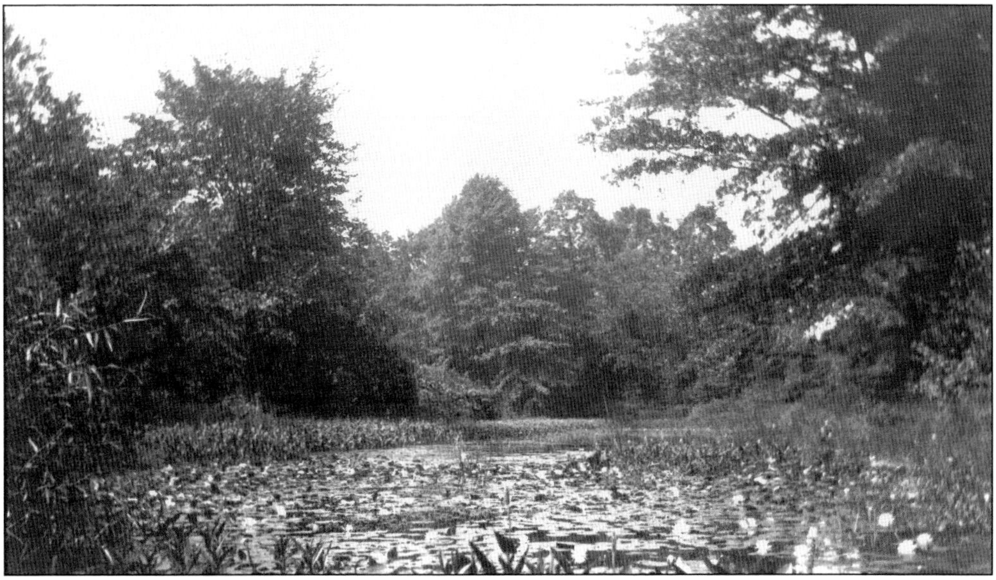

The beginnings of Shelton's industries can be found in the saw, grist, and cider mills that once dotted the countryside. Between 1676 and 1900, there were at least 30 mills along the Far Mill River alone. The pond on Sawmill City Road, photographed before 1918, served a cider mill and a sawmill. (Photograph by Helen Jones; courtesy of Philip Jones.)

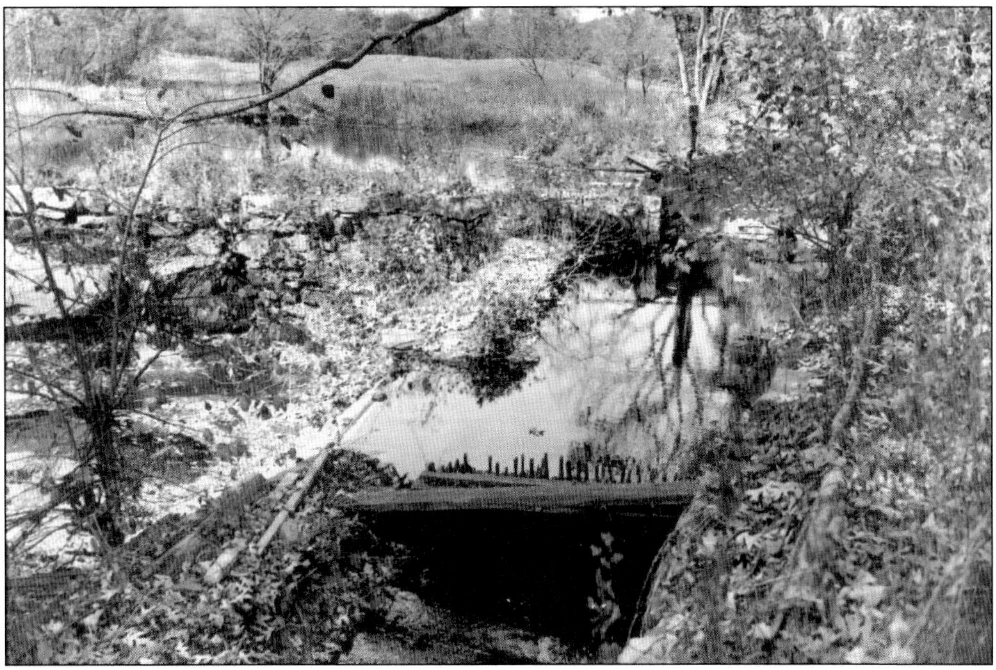

If not located right on the edge of a stream, river, or pond, a mill had to divert water over a wheel. By 1935, the canal that served Beard's sawmill on Beard's Sawmill Road was overgrown but still functional.

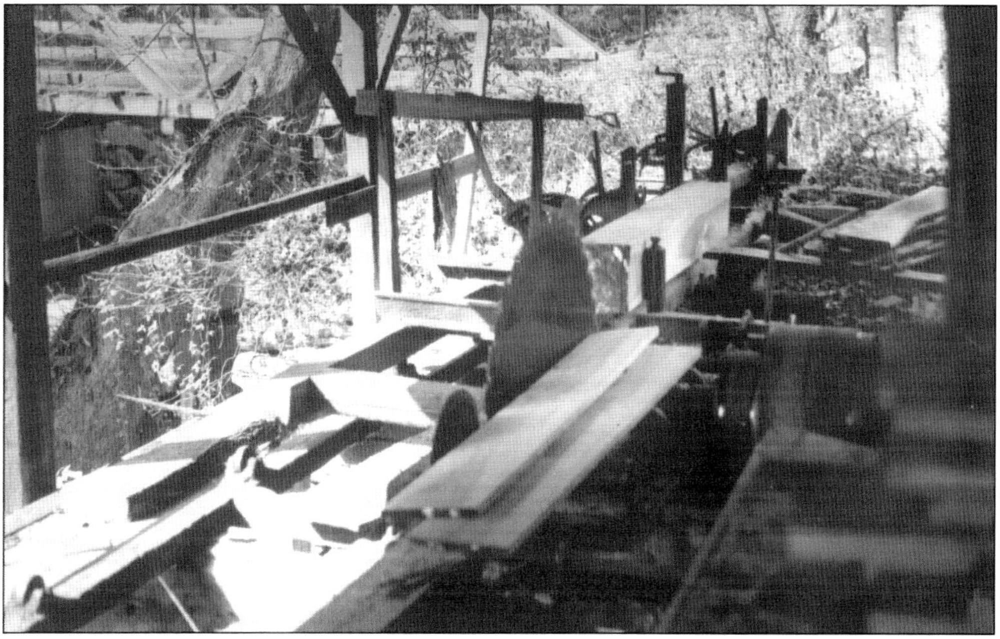

The Beard sawmill utilized a water turbine to power a 60-inch circular saw. The saw is in use in this 1935 photograph. It operated sporadically until the 1970s.

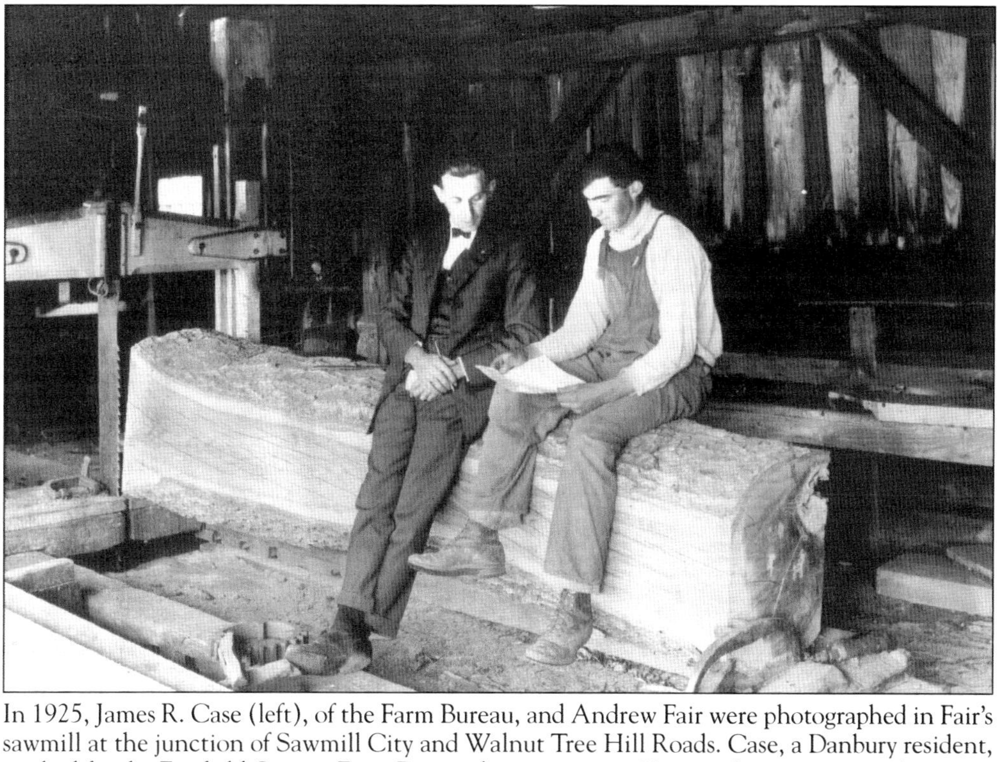

In 1925, James R. Case (left), of the Farm Bureau, and Andrew Fair were photographed in Fair's sawmill at the junction of Sawmill City and Walnut Tree Hill Roads. Case, a Danbury resident, worked for the Fairfield County Farm Bureau for many years. He was also a prominent historian for the Sons of the American Revolution and is remembered for his dedication to the education of farm children. (Courtesy of Jim Fair.)

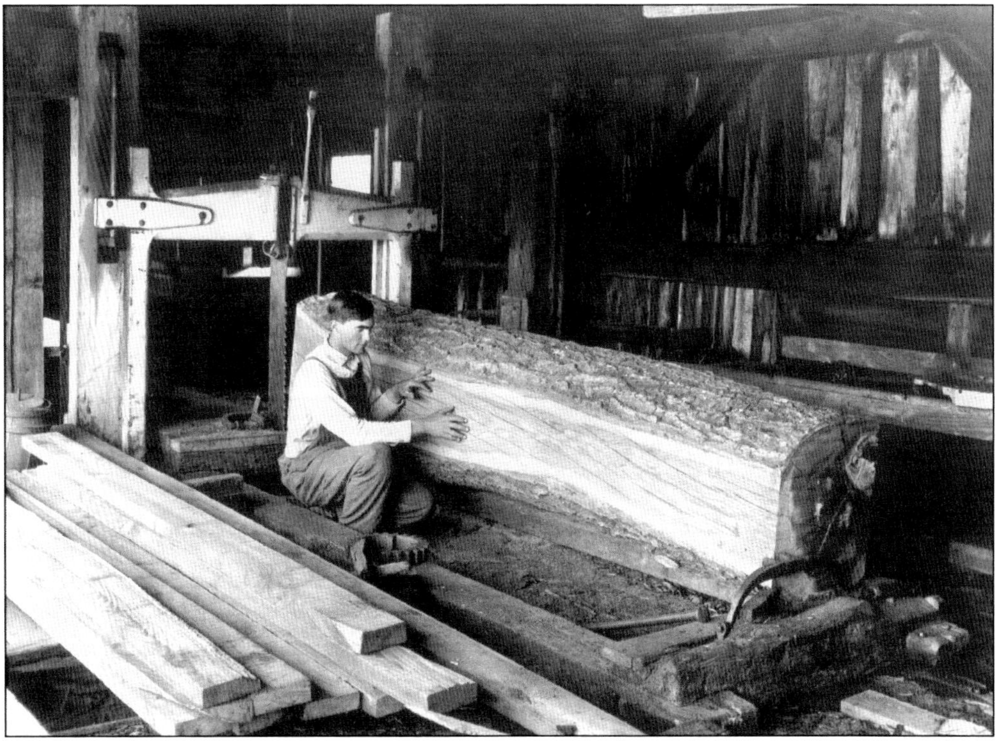

Built in 1876 by Theodore and Marcus Hubbell, this sawmill utilized an overshot flutter wheel. The wheel powered the up-and-down saw seen here, as well as a shingle saw, wood lathe, cider press, cut-off saw, and jig saw. The mill collapsed sometime shortly after the 1955 hurricane. (Courtesy of Jim Fair.)

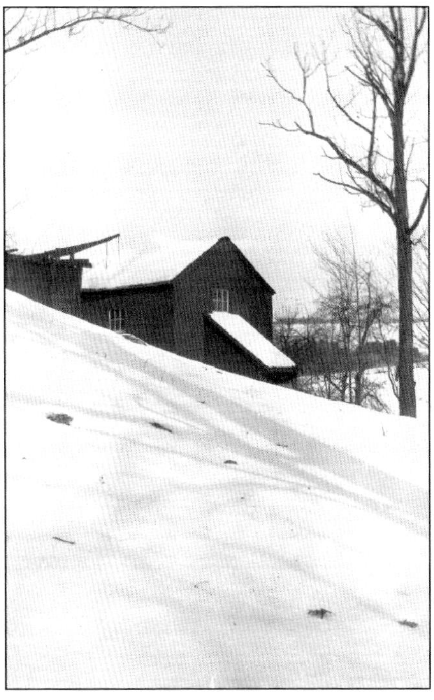

The Charles Shelton sawmill was on Nelson Brook near the Monroe town line. It is shown here *c.* 1910 under a fresh blanket of snow. The mill was torn down in 1934, and some of the lumber was recycled into a house on Barn Hill Road. (Photograph by Helen Jones; courtesy of Philip Jones.)

Two

The River

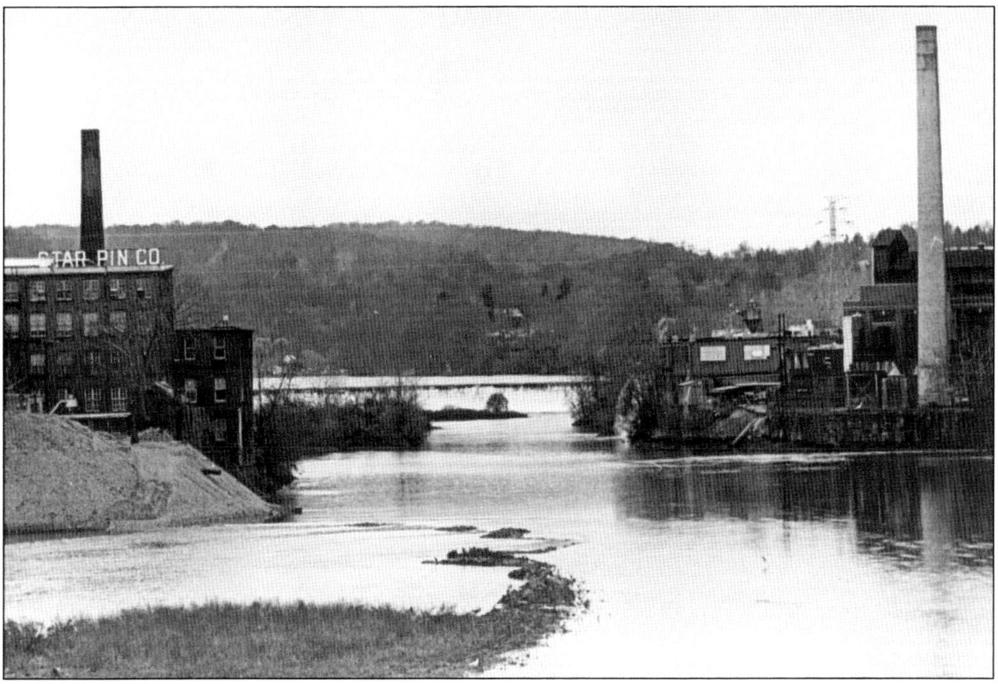

The Star Pin Company and the dam across the Housatonic River are prominent in this photograph taken on November 21, 1967. From the time of the Leavenworth shipyard through the Industrial Revolution to the present, the river has played a key role in the development of the city of Shelton. (Courtesy of the Shelton Economic Development Corporation.)

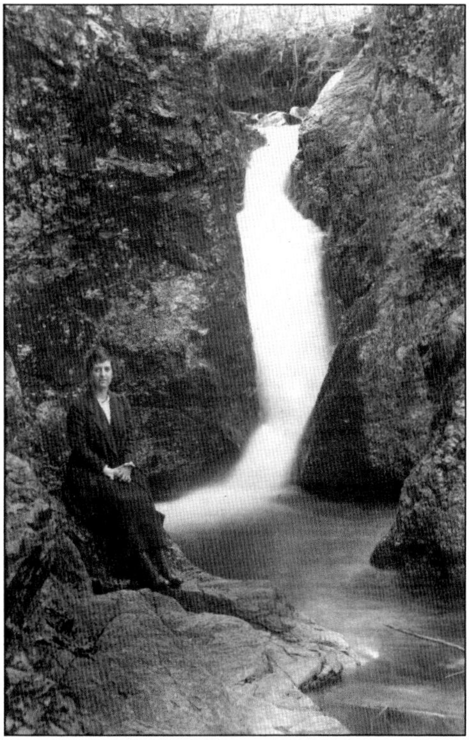

Indian Well served as a tourist attraction long before it became a state park in 1928. Here, Mrs. Didsbury enjoys the waterfall in 1919. (Courtesy of Dorothy Didsbury Mills.)

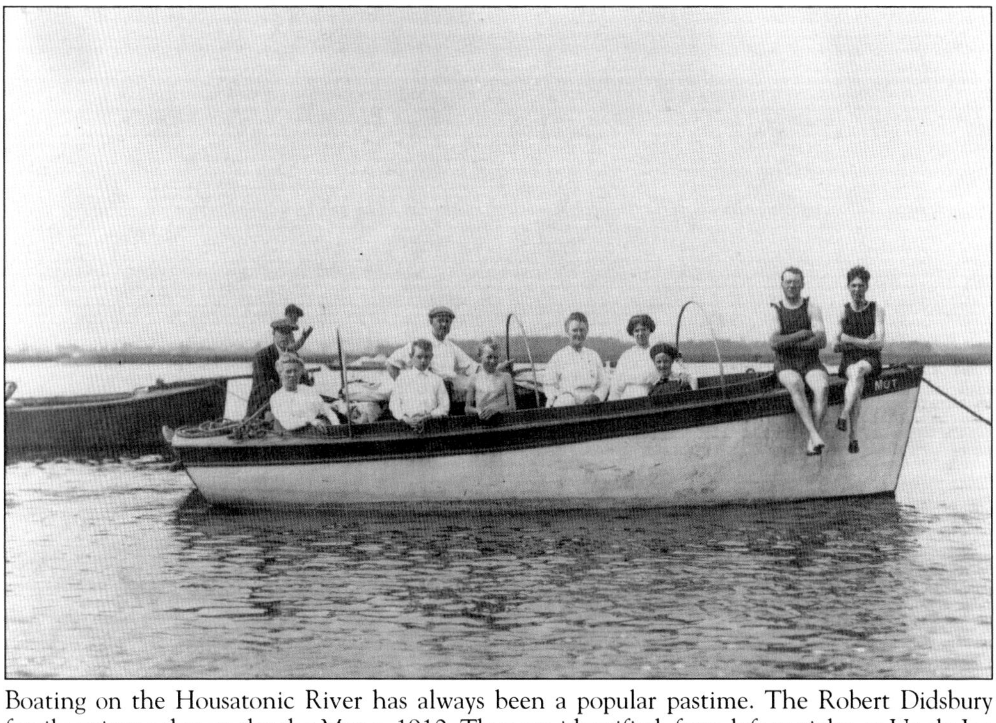

Boating on the Housatonic River has always been a popular pastime. The Robert Didsbury family enjoys a day on the the *Mut* c. 1910. They are identified, from left to right, as Uncle Joe Maskery, Grandmother Didsbury, Arthur, Grandpa Didsbury, Frank, Aunt Clara, Mrs. Harris, Aunt Mary, Uncle Rob Didsbury, and Mr. Harris. (Courtesy of Dorothy Didsbury Mills.)

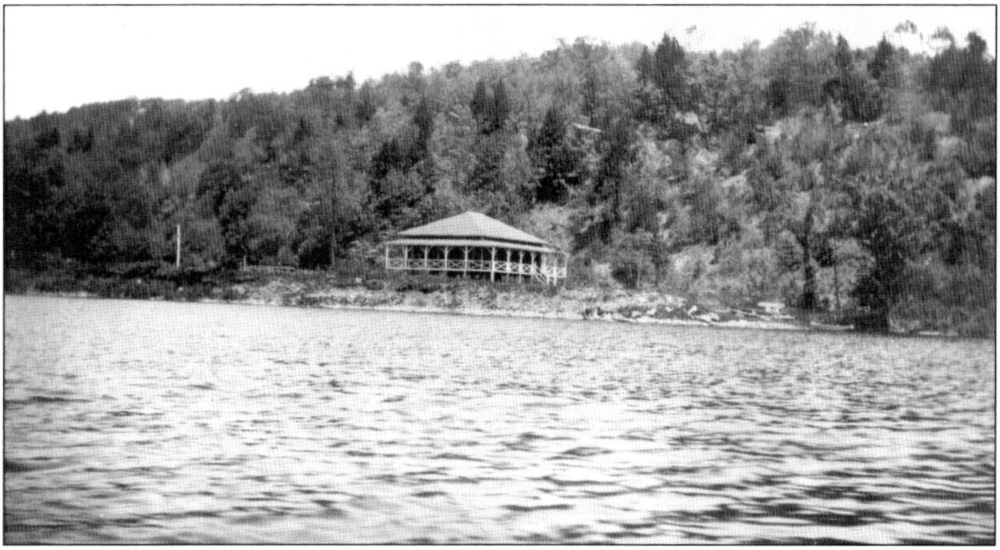

Amusement parks along trolley lines were commonly used by trolley companies to boost ridership and profits. Pine Rock Park was on the Shelton line. The pavilion that housed dances and musical programs is shown from the river. The park closed during the first decade of the 20th century.

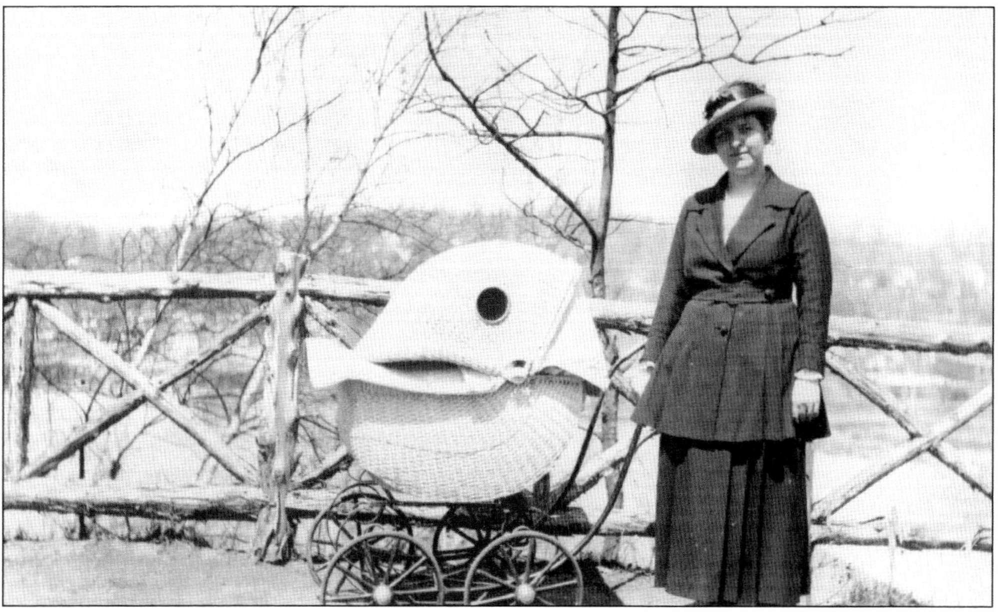

Gladys Didsbury and baby Bernard enjoy a stroll in Riverview Park in 1920. The land for the park was donated to the city of Shelton by the Ousatonic Water Company in 1887. David W. Plumb helped secure the gift, planned the park, and oversaw laying out the grounds. The park also contained a small pavilion and had walkways and bridges down to the dam. (Courtesy of Dorothy Didsbury Mills.)

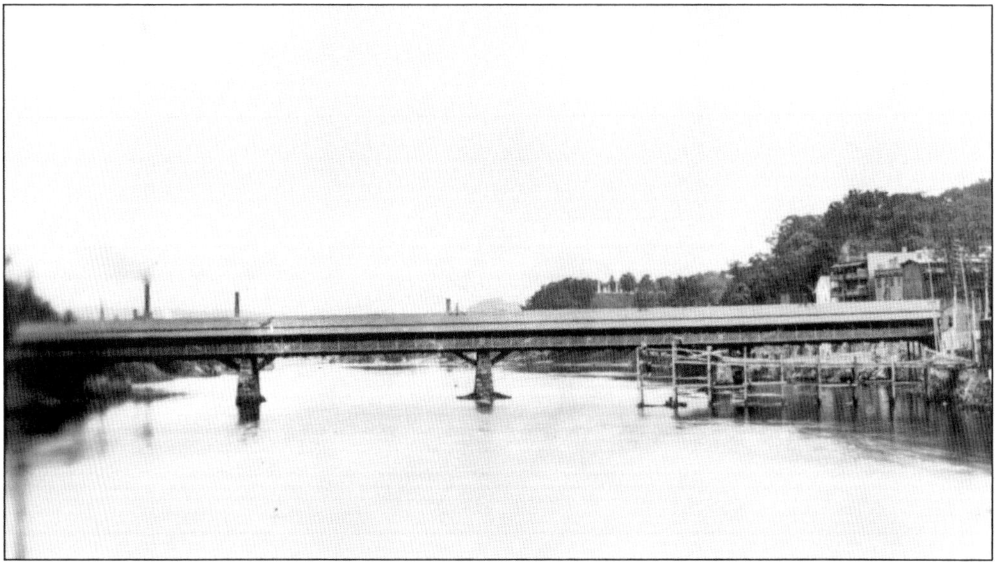

Bridges have crossed the Housatonic River between Shelton and Derby since the 1790s. For many years, the river was spanned by the covered bridge seen here in a view looking north, before its removal in 1891. (Courtesy of Philip Jones.)

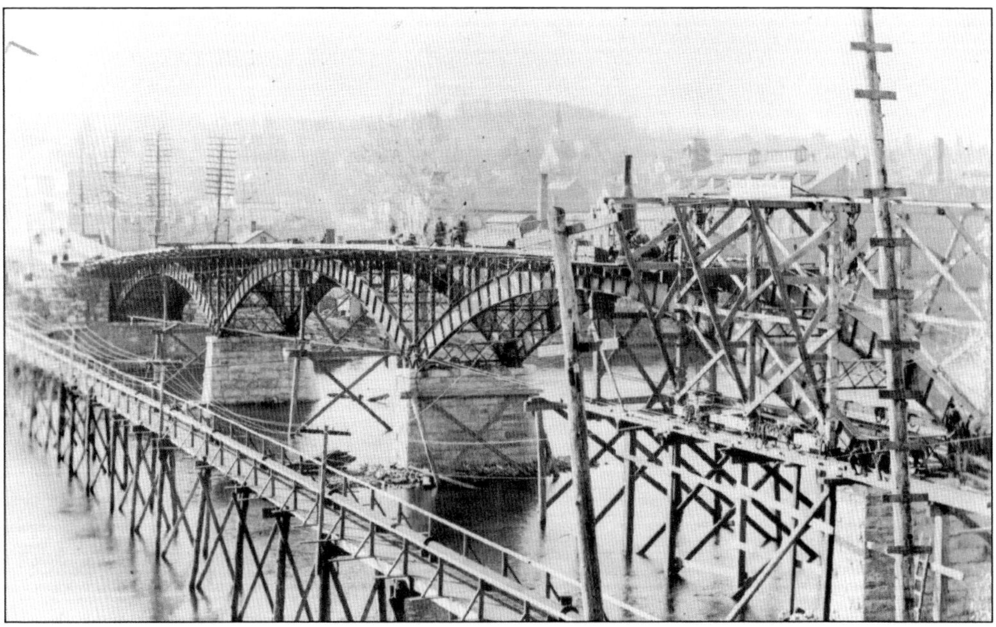

By 1891, it became necessary to replace the covered bridge with a modern iron structure. With the damming of the river and the increased traffic caused by the Shelton factories, a high-capacity bridge was a necessity. The bridge stood until 1918, when it was replaced with a concrete structure.

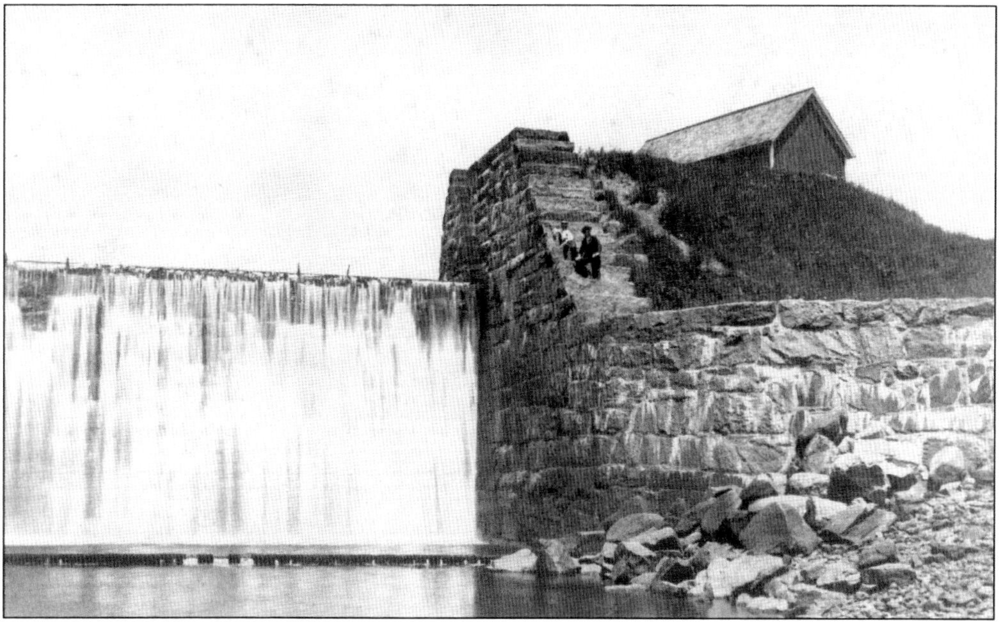

The Ousatonic Water Company was formed in 1863 for the purpose of building a dam across the Housatonic River and leasing its power to industries. While plans were put on hold by the Civil War, the company persisted, and on October 5, 1870, the final capstone was laid. The dam was a solid masonry structure 800 feet long and 22 feet high.

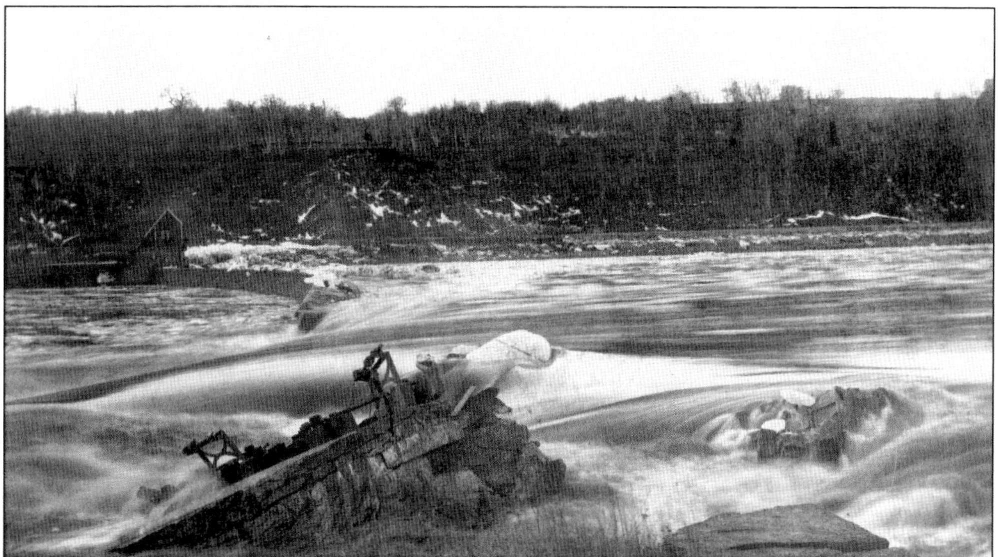

On January 21, 1891, the dam washed out due to a combination of an ice jam, an early thaw, heavy rain, and an undermined foundation from the straight drop configuration. The factories along the river were able to evacuate in time, and no one was reported to have been killed.

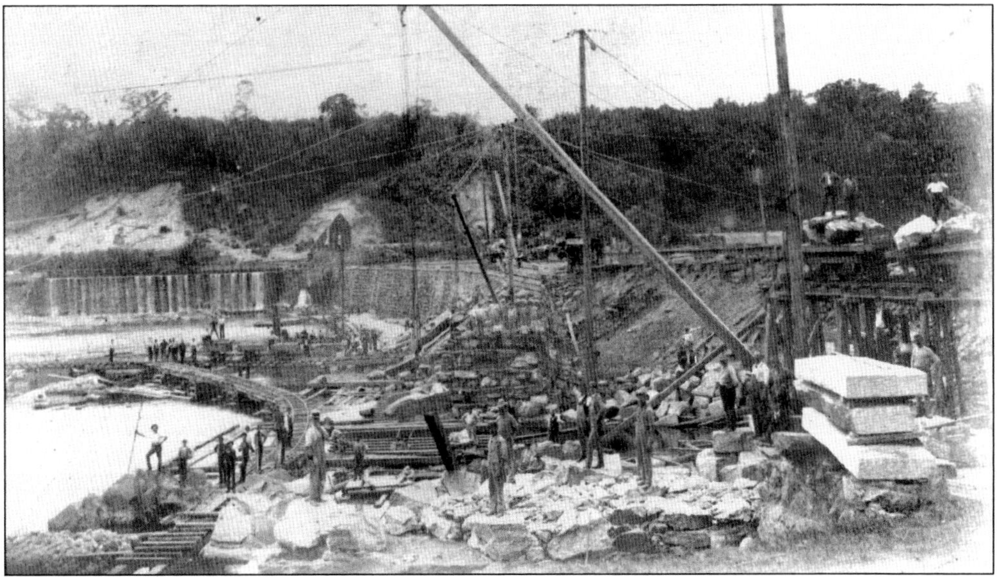

Reconstruction on the dam began in the spring and was well under way by July 21, 1891, when this photograph was taken.

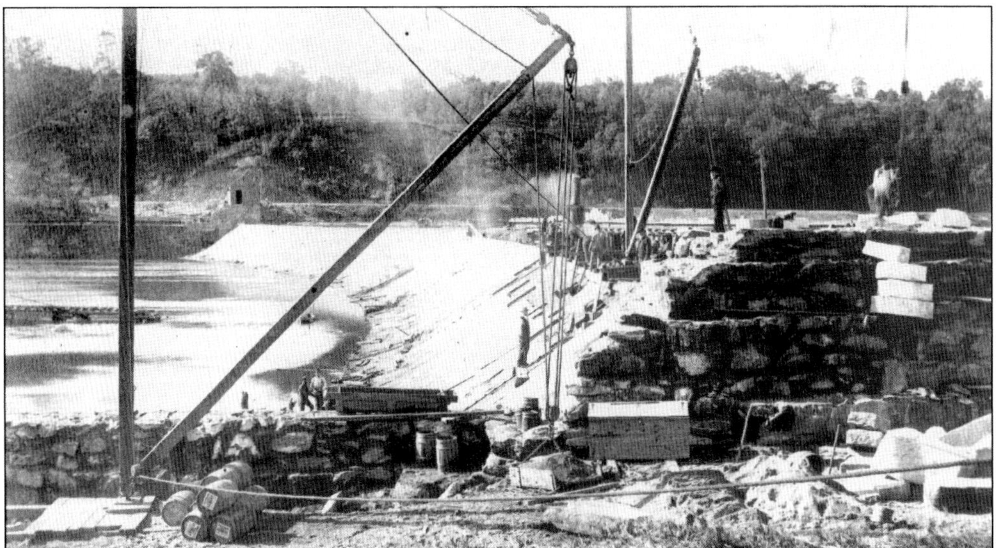

The new dam was completed in October 1891, two weeks after this photograph was taken. The new dam utilized a sloped apron design in order to avoid undermining the foundation. You can still see this dam holding back the Housatonic River today.

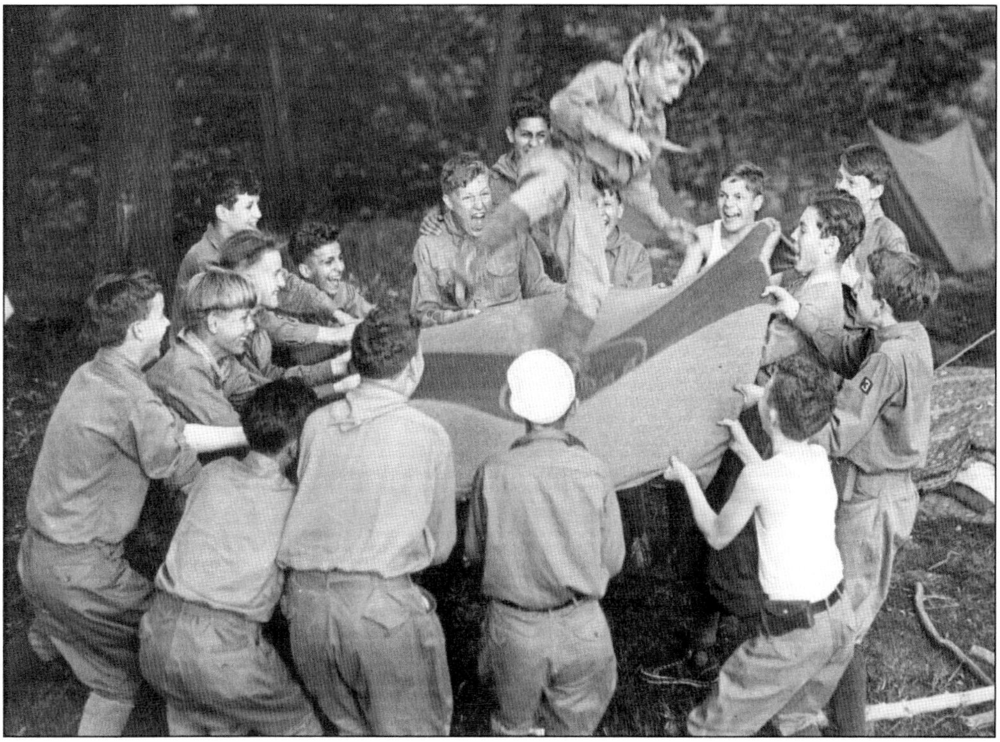

Camp Irving was founded in 1919 for use by the Boy Scouts of America (BSA). The camp was located along the Housatonic River north of Indian Well State Park, just off Birchbank Road. Here, scouts enjoy a blanket toss in 1937. The young man to the right with the number three on his arm is Rodman Kneen. (Courtesy of BSA Troop 3 Derby.)

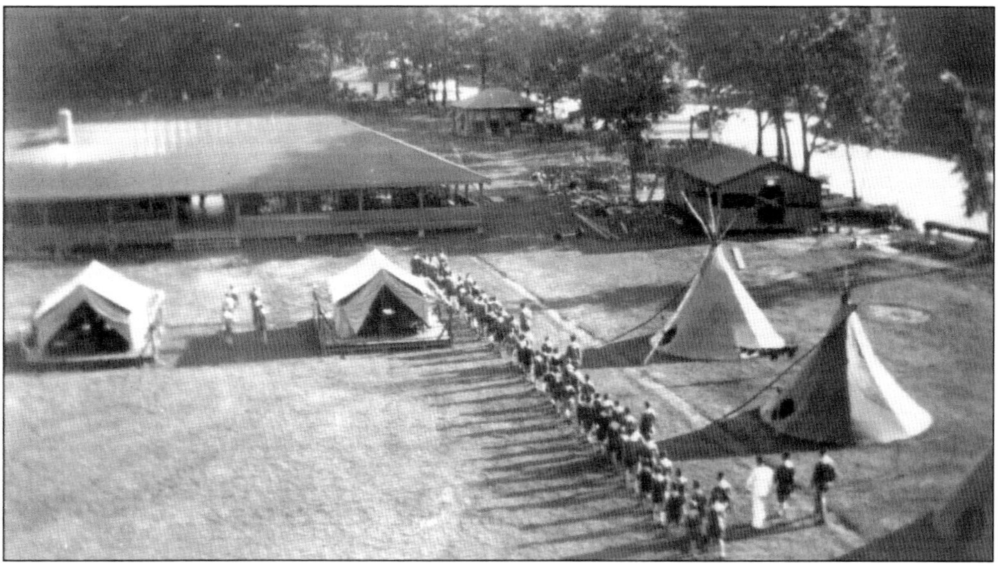

One of the most prominent structures at Camp Irving was the crow's nest. Rising high into the air, the view from the top was quite spectacular, as is seen in this 1937 view of the camp. The camp operated until the late 1940s, when it was taken over by the Bridgeport Hydraulic Company for use as a well field. (Courtesy of BSA Troop 3 Derby.)

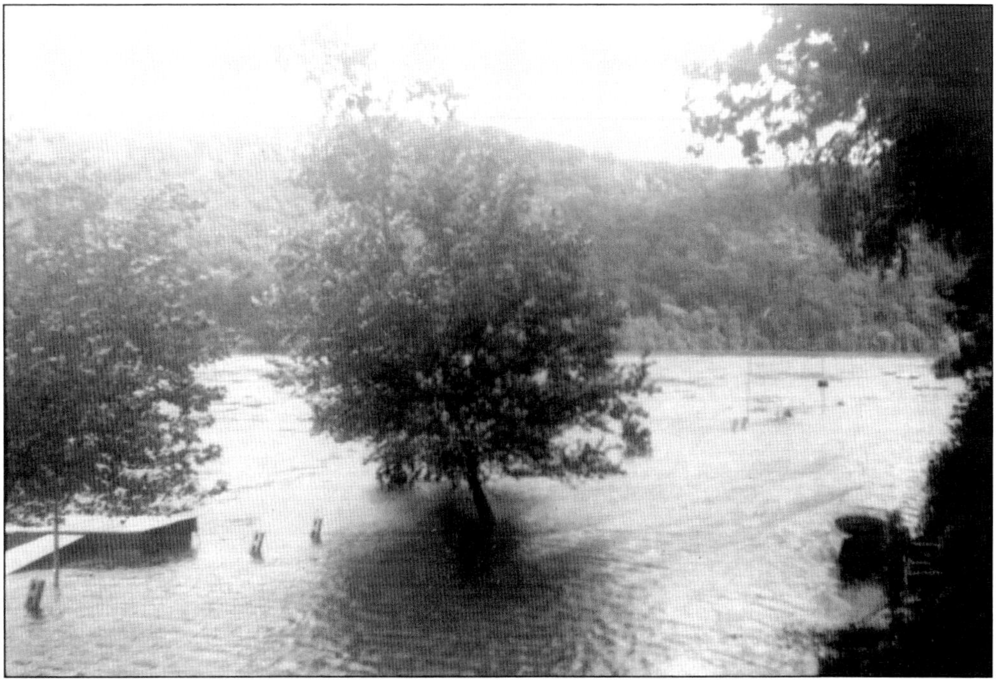

This is the Housatonic River from the backyard of 58 Birchbank Road during the Flood of 1955, which was caused by Hurricane Diane on August 19. While the Naugatuck River Valley was much more heavily impacted, the Housatonic Valley suffered damage and casualties as well. The river rose as high as the tracks on the railroad bridge and flooded several of the factories. (Courtesy of the Kisluk family.)

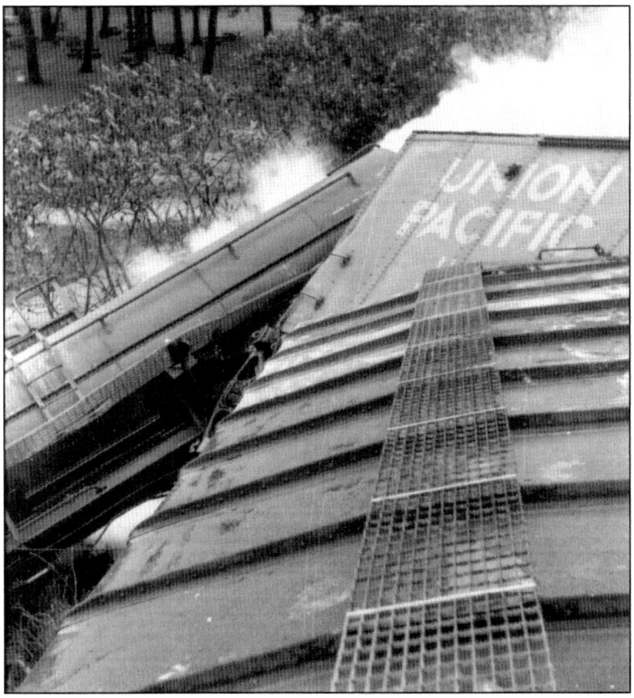

On October 19, 1964, a freight train with a tanker carrying 16,000 gallons of ammonia derailed at Indian Well State Park. Several people were affected by the fumes, and the rail line was shut down for over 24 hours. (Photograph by Paul Kassheimer.)

Three

INDUSTRY

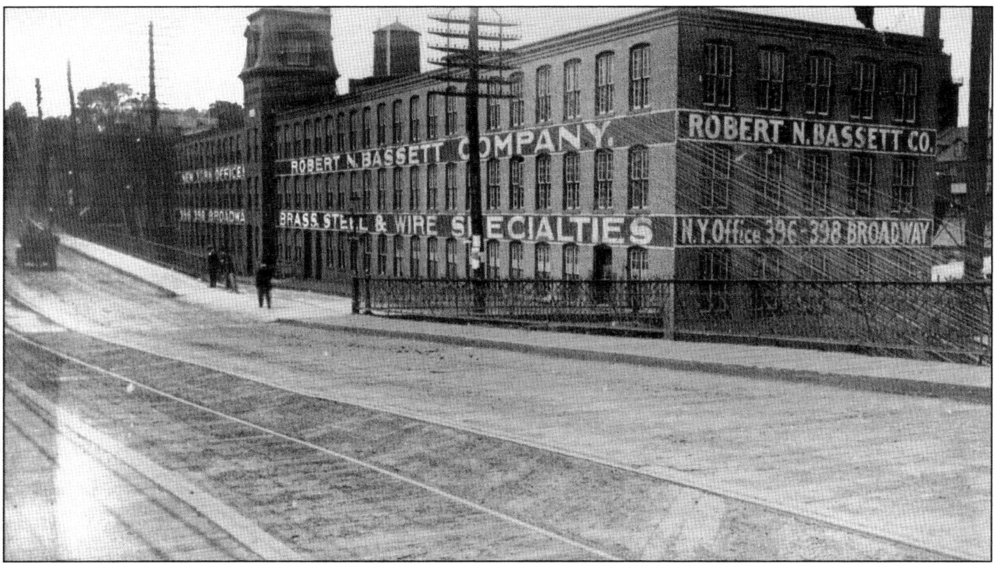

This view shows the end of the iron bridge and the beginning of the Viaduct Bridge. The building at 9 Bridge Street, which once housed the R.N. Bassett Company c. 1910, is still at the entrance to Shelton. Note the unpaved road with the trolley tracks and the utility lines running on the poles. (Courtesy of Philip Jones.)

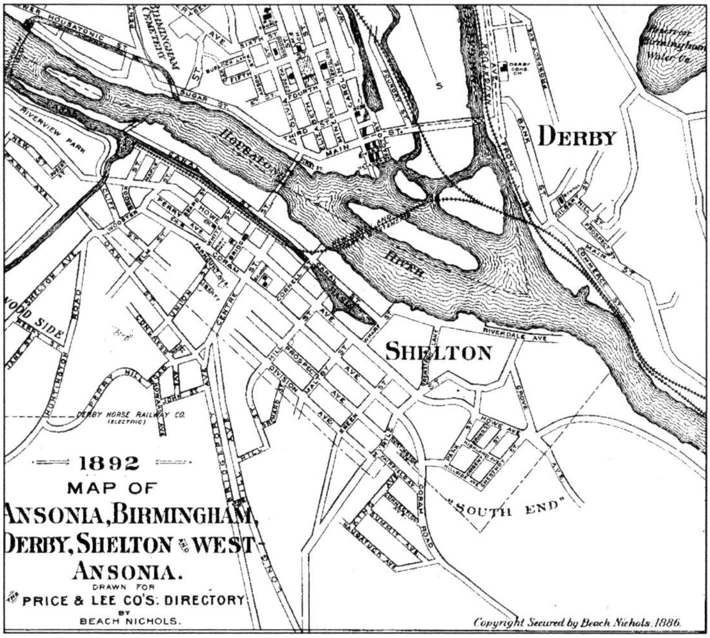

After the completion of the dam in 1870, downtown boomed. Suddenly, there were factories, a profusion of workers (many of them immigrants), and stores to provide services to them. Compare this 1892 map of the area to the 1867 one on page 2.

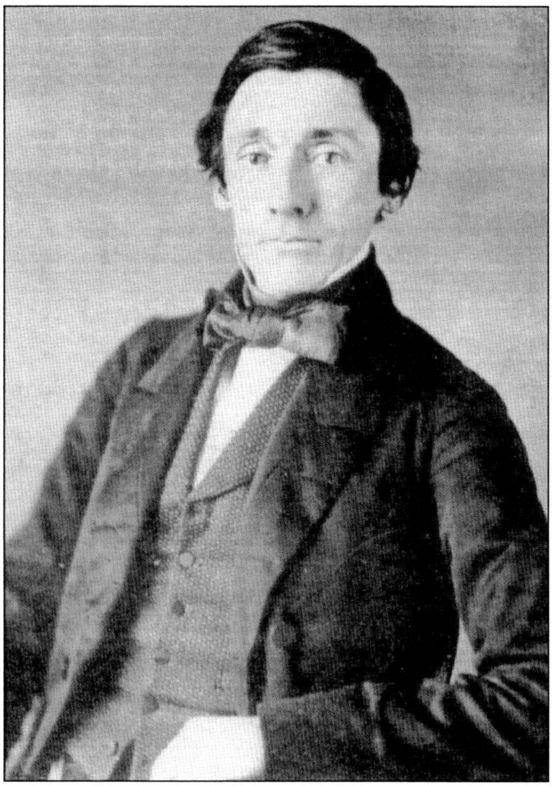

When Edward Nelson Shelton (1812–1894) sat for this portrait in 1859, he was well on his way to becoming a man of influence and power. One of the founders of the Ousatonic Water Company and the Shelton Tack Company, he was very active in the promotion of the valley as a site for manufacturing. The village along the banks of the Housatonic River was named in his honor.

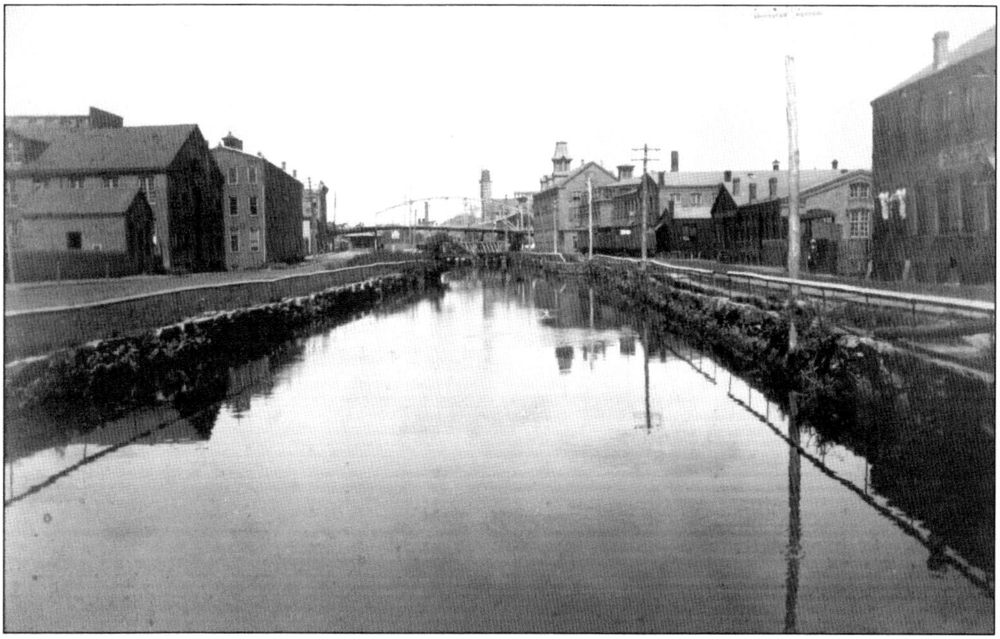

The canal was key to the industrial development of Shelton. It extended approximately two miles down from the dam to Wharf Street, providing power to the factories built alongside. This c. 1890 view looks from the south end toward Bridge Street. (Courtesy of the Frederick W. Ziegler family.)

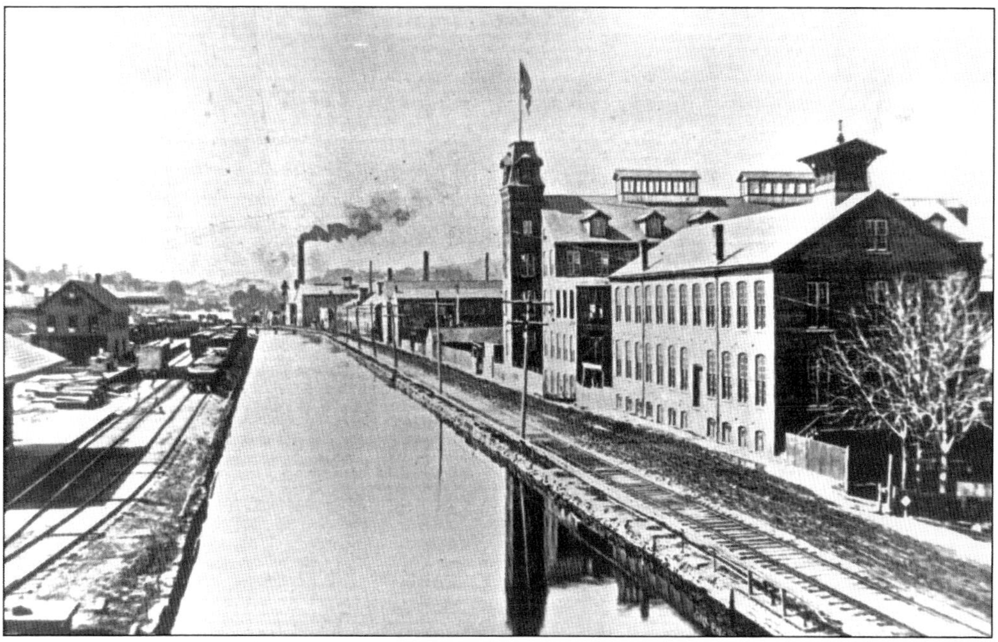

Water moved through the canal and entered the wheel pit of the factories through a tunnel under the road. The water-driven turbines turned and powered the machinery through a series of shafts, pulleys, and belts. The water exited the building through a tailrace and reentered the river. This c. 1910 view is from Bridge Street, facing north.

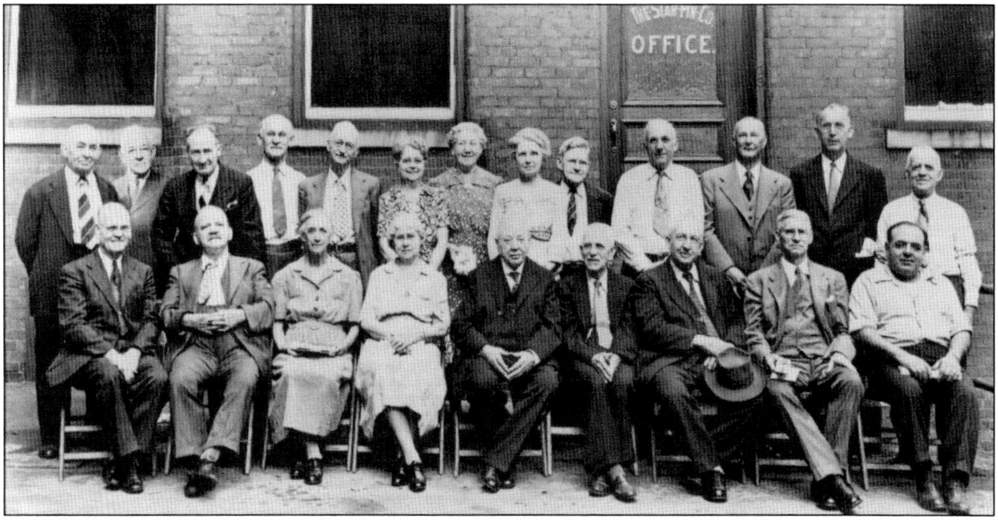

The Star Pin Company was located on the canal from 1875 until 1977. On September 25, 1946, veteran employees with 35 or more years of service gathered for a group portrait on the company's 80th birthday. The numbers following each name indicate years of service. The employees, from left to right, are as follows: (front row) William S. Harkins (37), John Peters (47), Grace Thompson (55), Mary E. Wright (55), John H. Cropper (63), Amos E. Piper (58), Albert L. Beach (56), Henry R. Regan (48), and Ernest Munsford (39); (back row) William G. Bauer (47), Pres. Irving H. Peck (53), Edward Bergin (39), Arthur Schummrick (36), Charles I. Sterling (38), Edna A. Vaughn (45), Elizabeth M. Flynn (50), Elsie D. Cropper (35), Colin C. Armour (38), Lester T. Bavier (41), August Baum (40), Frank W. Cramer (45), and William J. Piper (46).

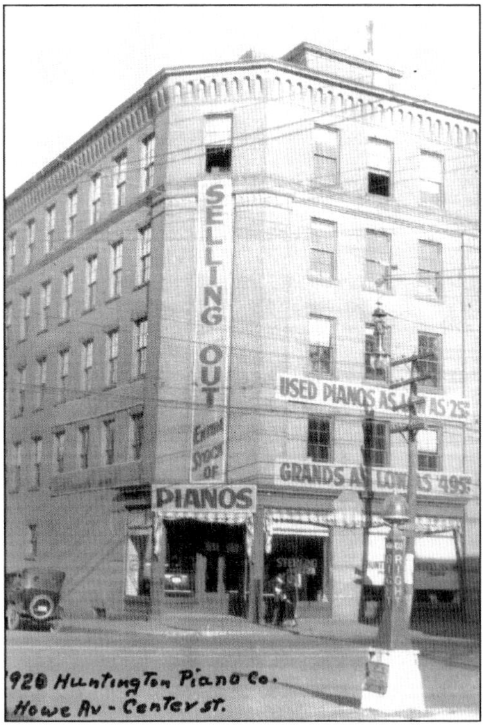

A Shelton saying was that along the canal everything was produced from "pins to pianos." The Huntington Piano Company, a subsidiary of the Derby-based Sterling Piano Company, was founded in 1894 to produce a more affordable piano. The building burned in 1922, forcing the company to close.

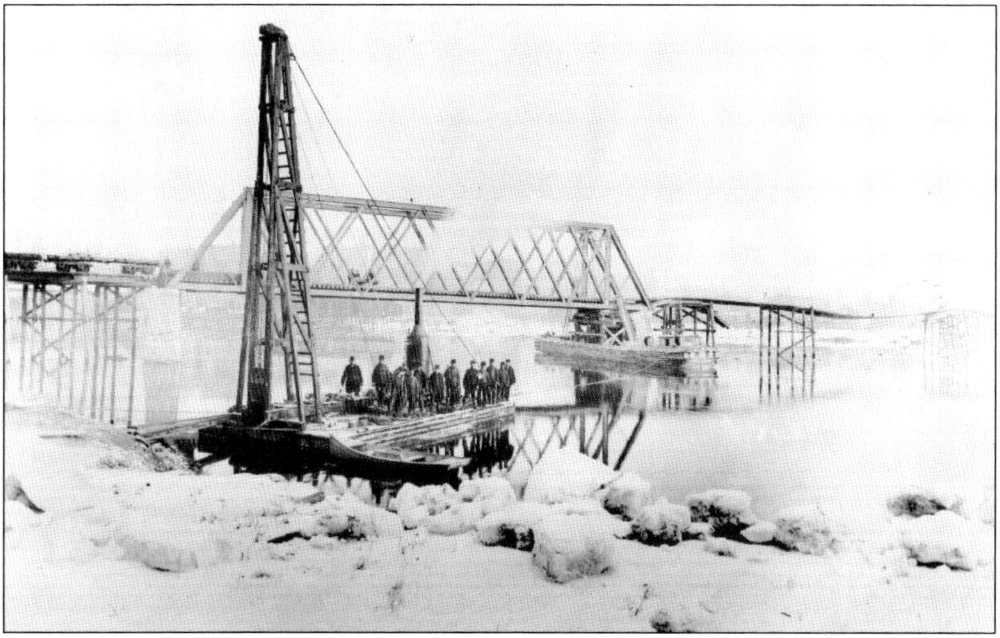

With the growth of industry, better transportation methods became a necessity. The railroad crossed the river from Derby and entered Canal Street across from Center Street. Here is the bridge under construction in 1888. The heavy volume of rail traffic required laying a second track in 1911.

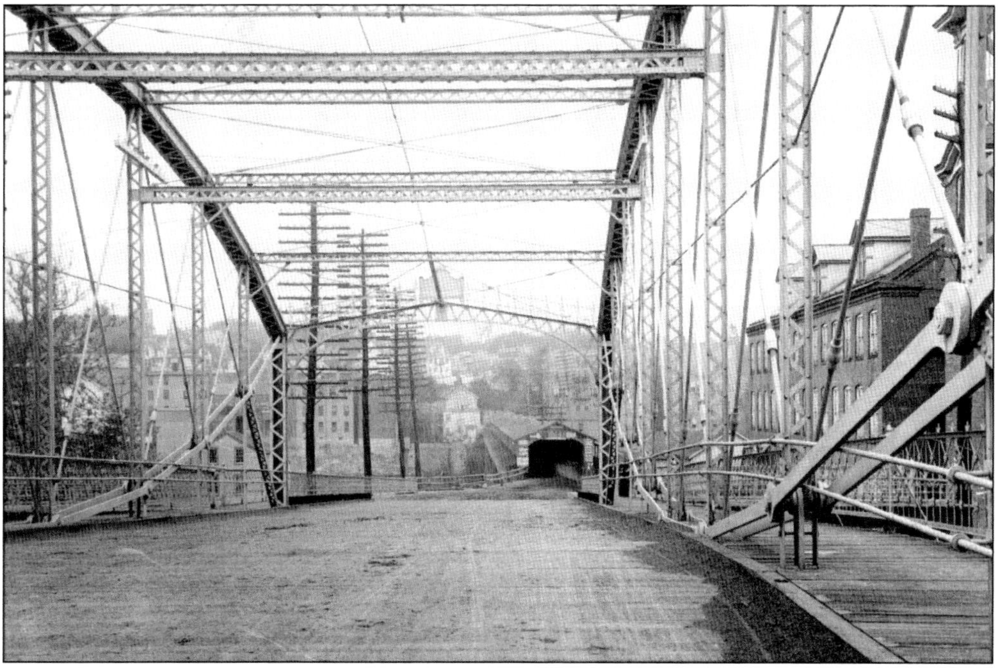

With the arrival of the railroad, Bridge Street was elevated over the railroad, canal, and Canal Street. The iron Viaduct Bridge was constructed by the Berlin Iron Bridge Company in 1888. In this early 1890s view, the covered bridge that connected Shelton and Derby can be seen in the background.

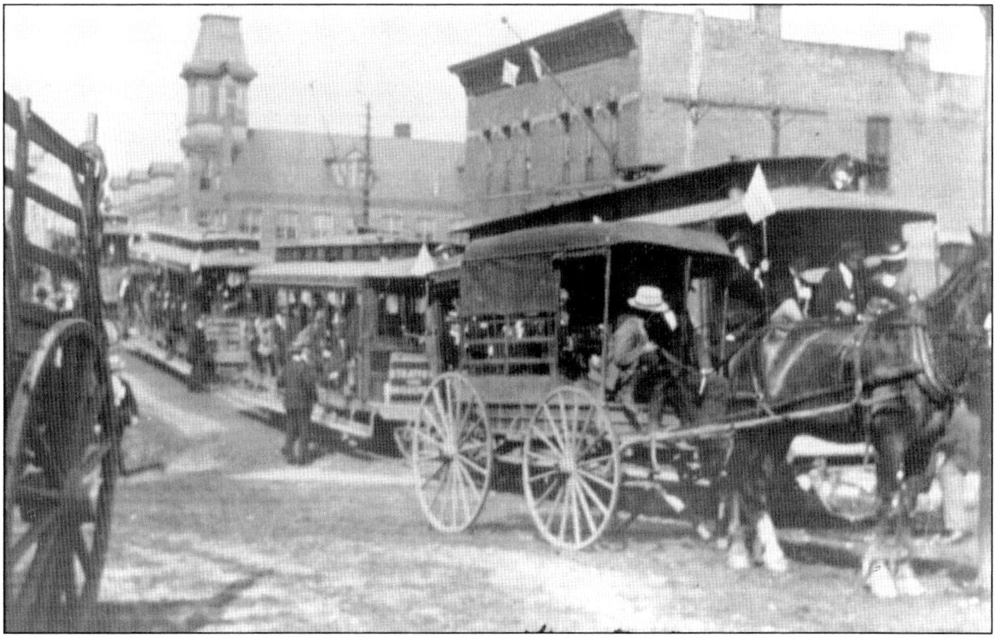

The trolley came to Shelton in 1899. Here, we see the first trolleys to come over the bridges and into Viaduct Square. Throngs of people warmly greeted this new mode of transportation.

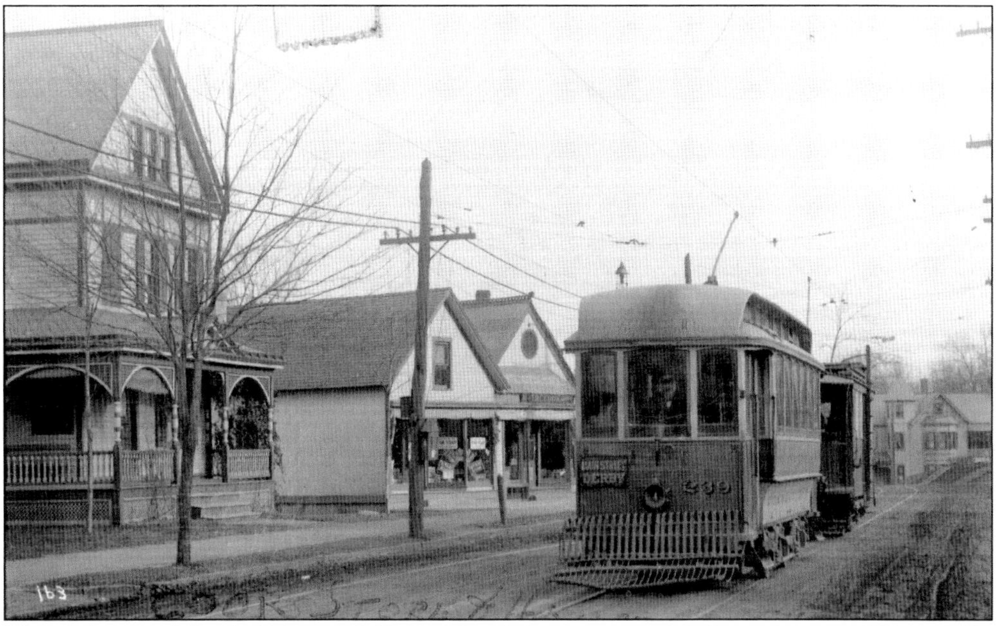

The trolley ran through downtown Shelton but did not extend into Huntington or White Hills. Here, the trolley is running past 69 Howe Avenue and the R.C. Cook grocery.

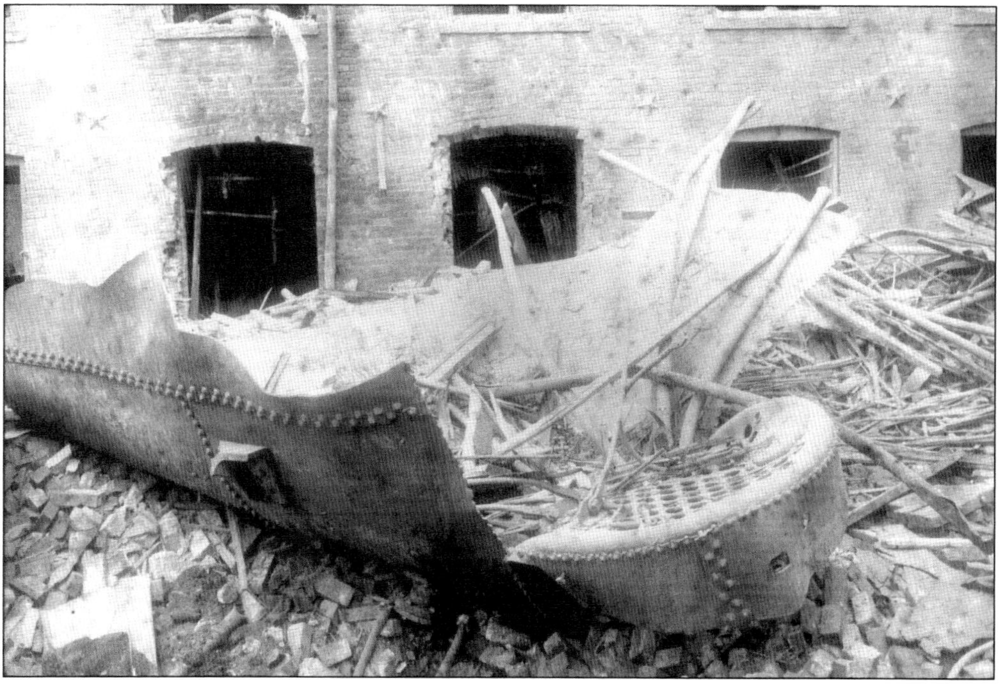

The Radcliffe Brothers boiler explosion on December 1, 1909, was one of the more spectacular industrial accidents in Shelton. The damage was estimated at $250,000. One onlooker, a veteran of the Civil War, is quoted in the *Evening Sentinel* as saying, "I saw buildings in Atlanta that resembled this for ruin."

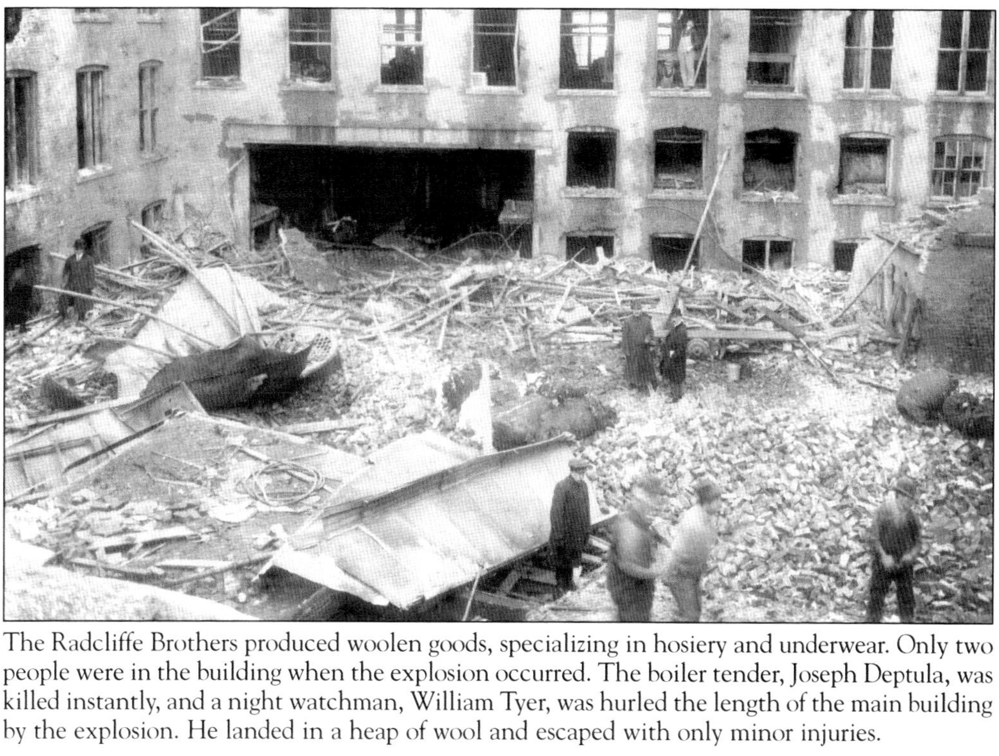

The Radcliffe Brothers produced woolen goods, specializing in hosiery and underwear. Only two people were in the building when the explosion occurred. The boiler tender, Joseph Deptula, was killed instantly, and a night watchman, William Tyer, was hurled the length of the main building by the explosion. He landed in a heap of wool and escaped with only minor injuries.

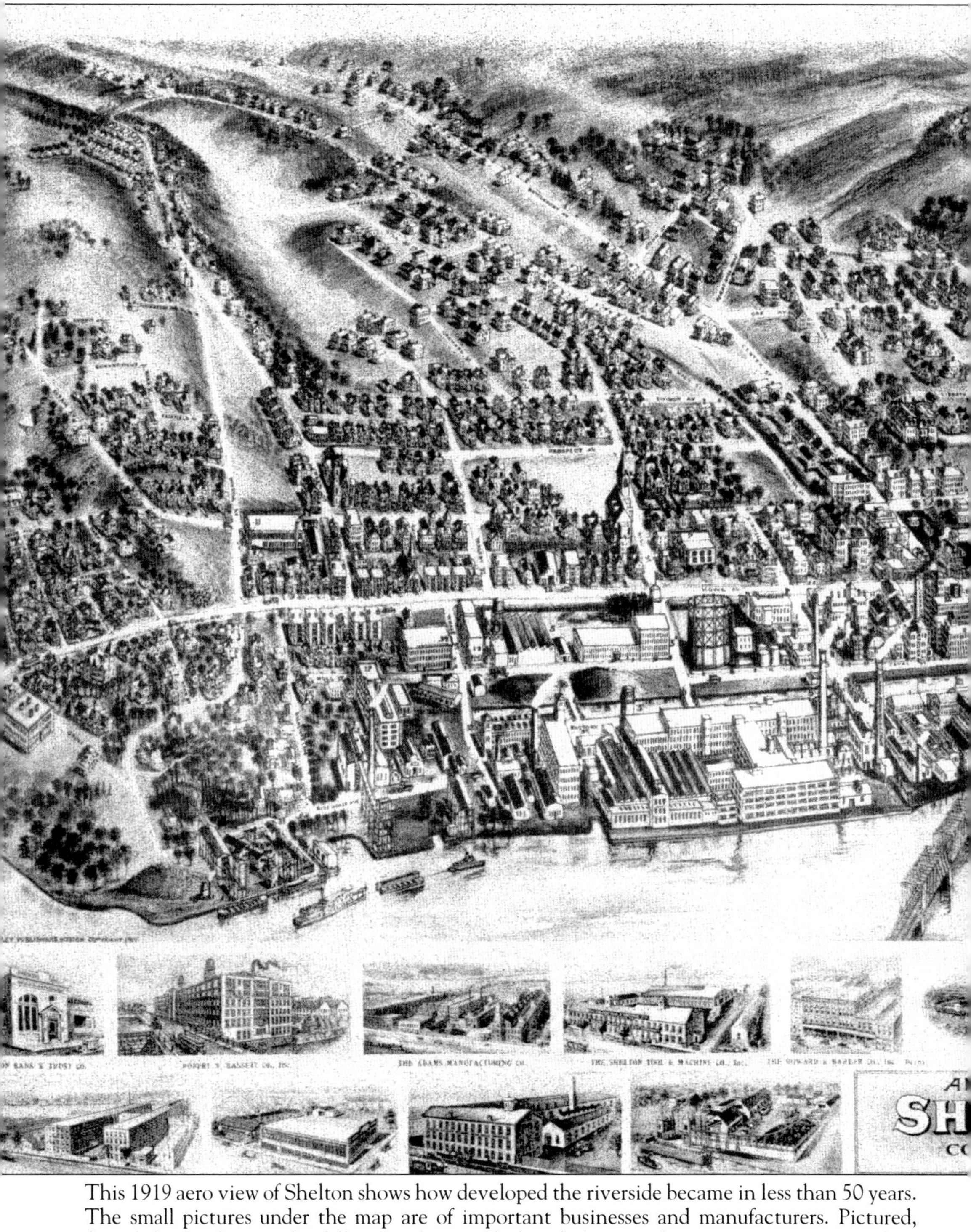

This 1919 aero view of Shelton shows how developed the riverside became in less than 50 years. The small pictures under the map are of important businesses and manufacturers. Pictured, from left to right, are the following: (top row) the Shelton Bank & Trust Company, Robert N. Bassett Company, Adams Manufacturing Company, Shelton Tool & Machine Company, Howard & Barber Company (Derby), Sidney Blumenthal & Company, Huntington Piano

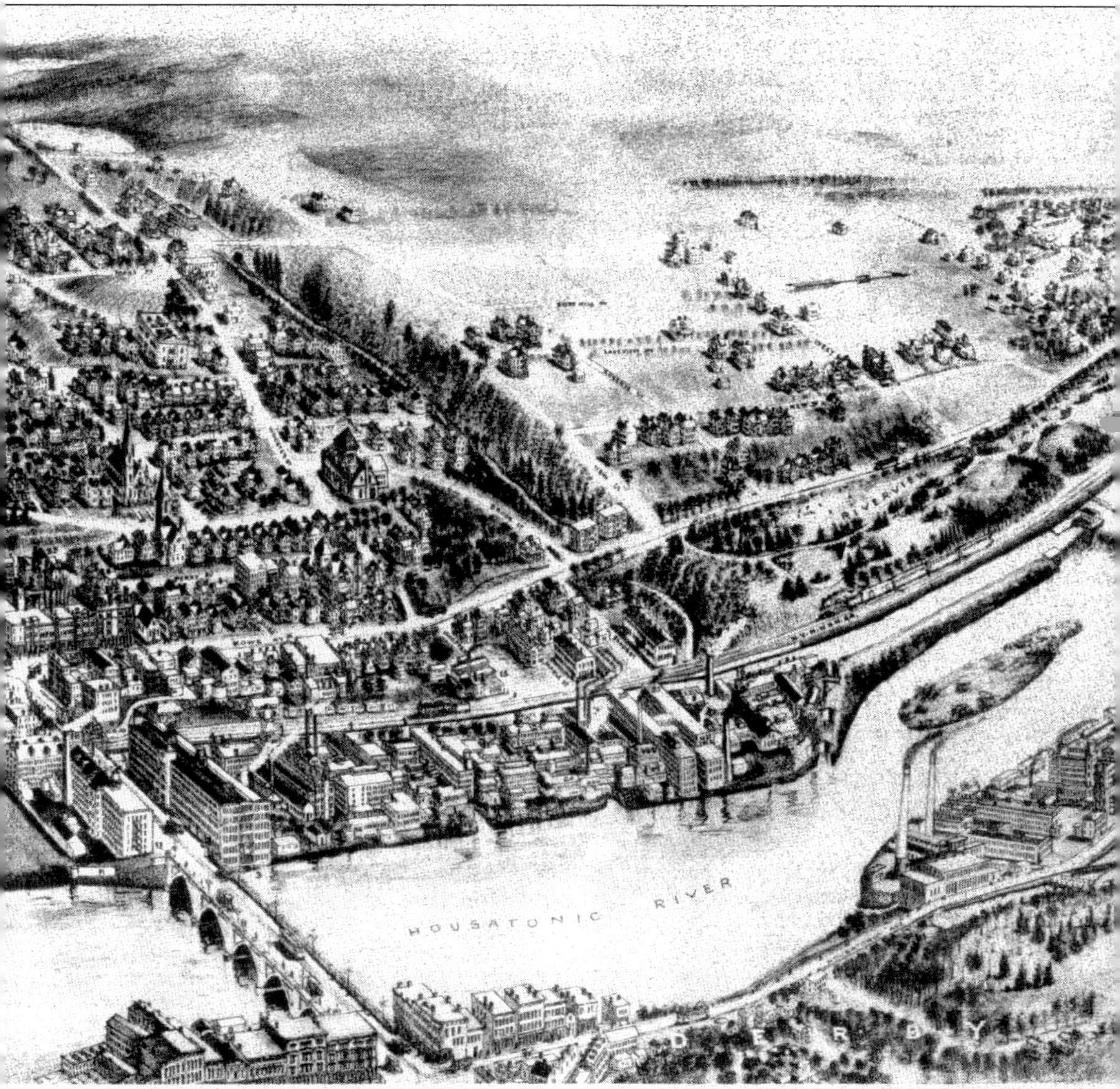

Company, Whitcomb Metallic Bedstead Company, the New Writerpress Company, Naugatuck Valley Crucible Company, and D.N. Clark Company; (bottom row) Star Pin Company, Holmes Manufacturing Company, D.N. Bassett Bolt Works, Wheeler-Schneider Coal Company, O.K. Tool Company, Shelton Laundry, Sheehy Trucking Company, and University Race Course.

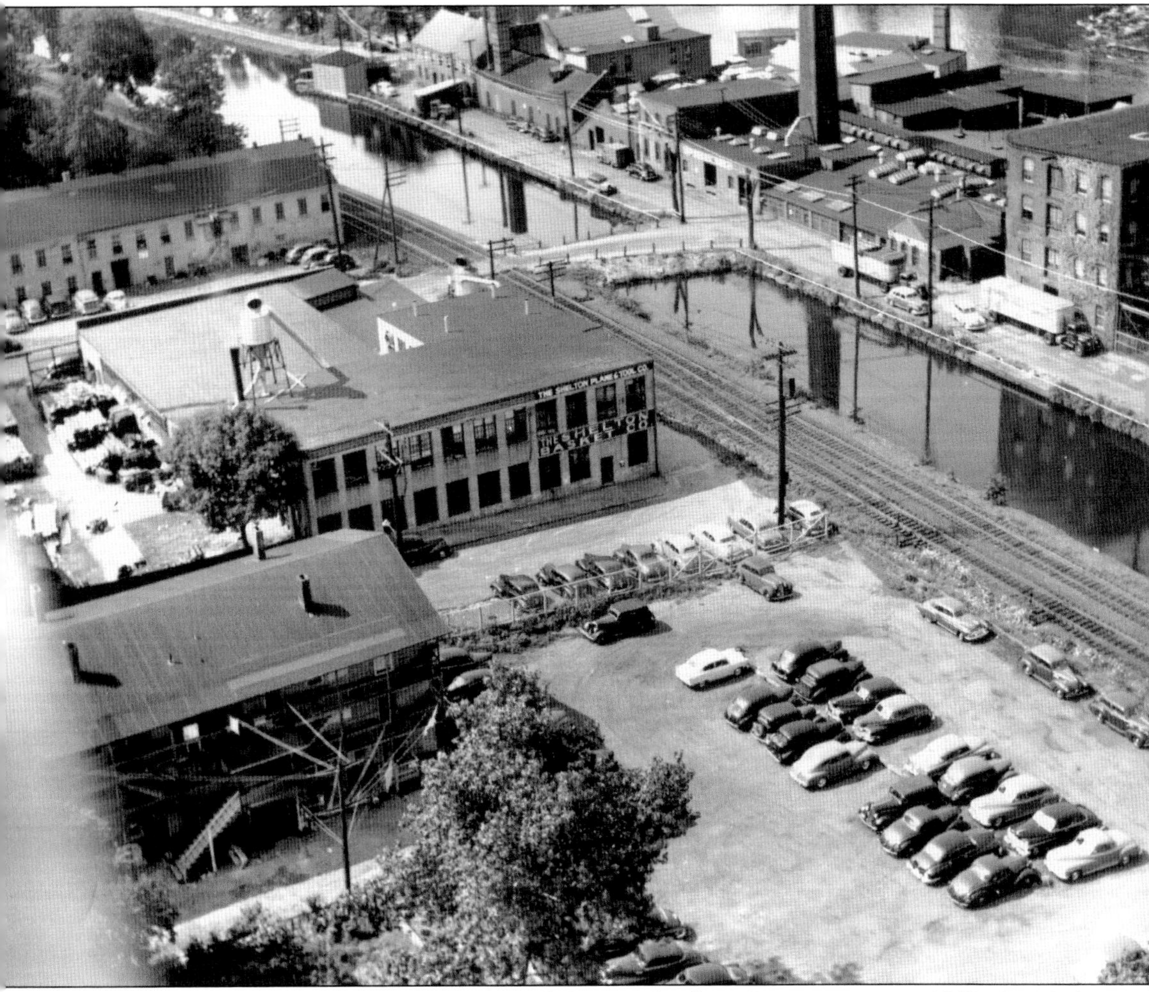

The Shelton Basket Company was founded in Columbia, Connecticut, in 1862. In 1910, employee Abraham H. Lavietes bought the company. He expanded the business and moved to Shelton for its better transportation system. In 1911, the company moved to 1 Maple Street. Its hand-drawn oak and ash splint baskets were hand crafted by skilled workers. The majority of the baskets were destined for industrial use by manufacturers, farmers, and oystermen of Long Island Sound. The company diversified into a related field and opened the Shelton Plane and Tool Company. Both names can be seen on the building in this July 21, 1951 aerial view. A portion of the canal is also visible. The building on the right with "Shelton" painted on its roof was part of the Star Pin Company.

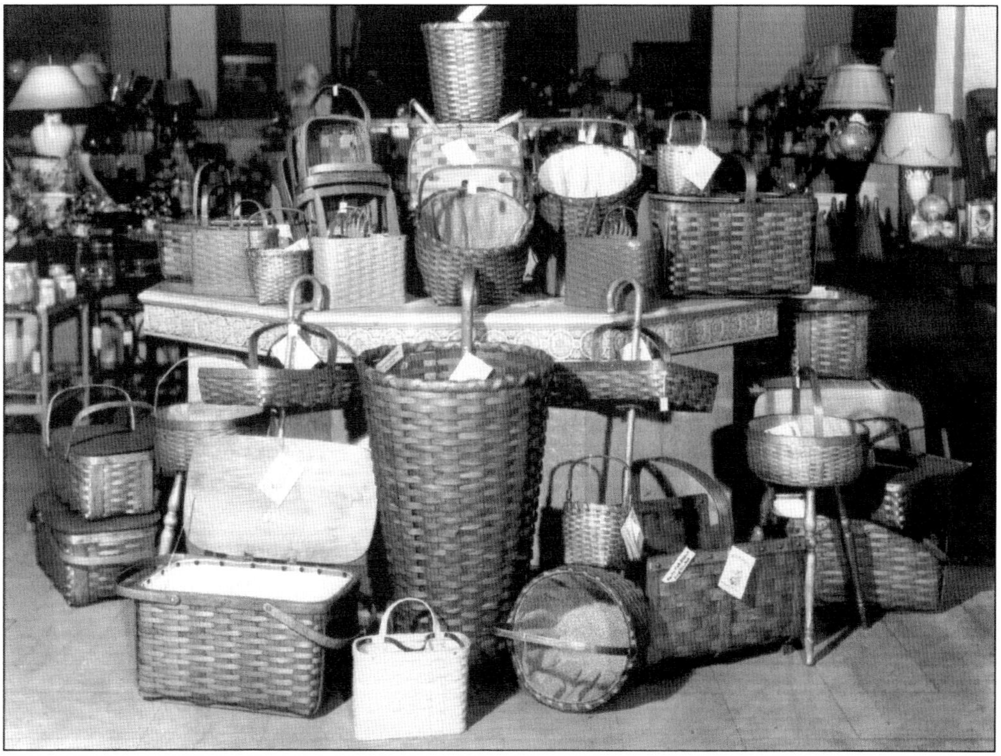

The Shelton Basket Company also produced baskets for the retail market. Pictured is an in-store display at the G. Fox Department Store in Hartford c. 1938.

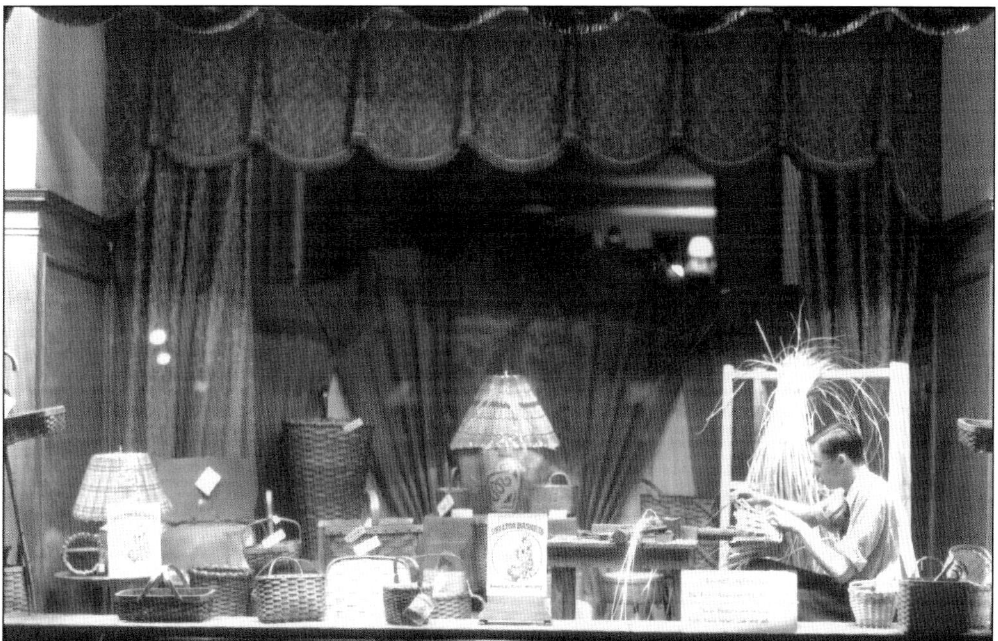

Norman Elwell of the Shelton Basket Company demonstrated how baskets were made in G. Fox's store window in Hartford c. 1938.

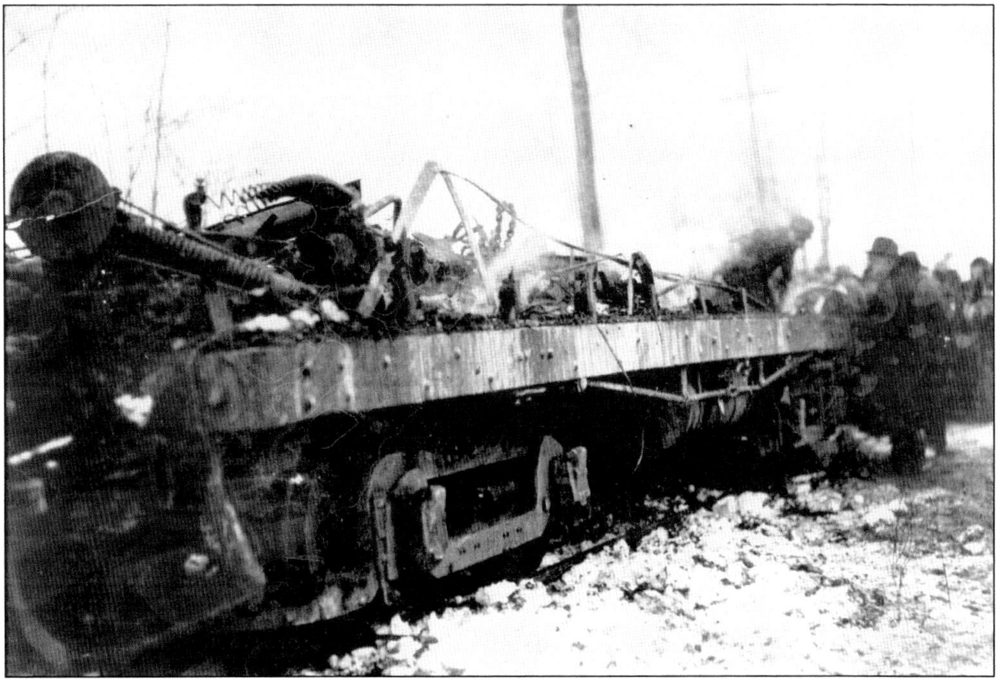

On February 22, 1921, a signaling error caused two trolleys to collide head-on near River Road. The trolleys exploded upon impact, and flames quickly engulfed the cars.

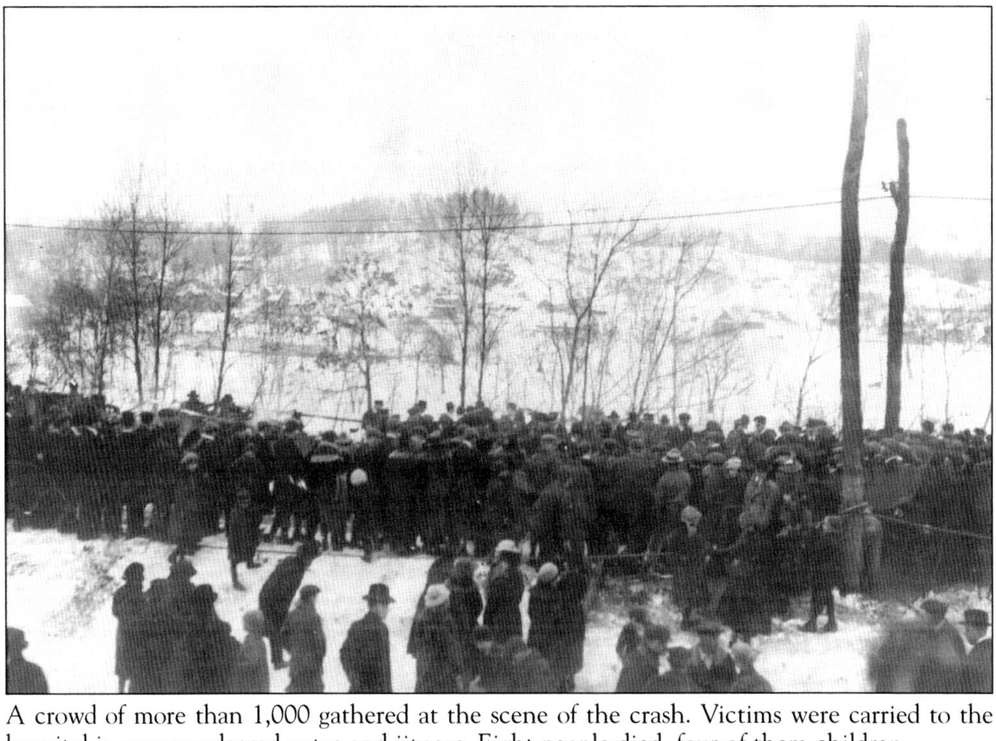

A crowd of more than 1,000 gathered at the scene of the crash. Victims were carried to the hospital in commandeered autos and jitneys. Eight people died, four of them children.

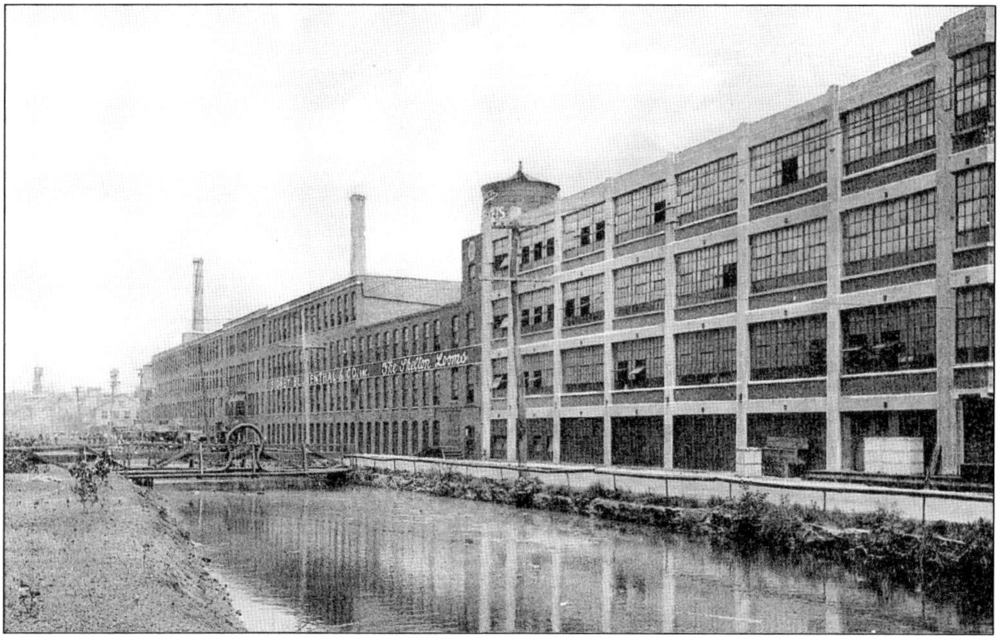

The Sidney Blumenthal Company, also known as the Shelton Looms, was the largest manufacturer in Shelton. Founded in New York City as a ribbon manufacturer in the late 1880s, the company moved to Shelton in 1897 and shifted over to the production of pile fabrics such as velvet, upholstery, fake furs, rugs, and bath mats. (Courtesy of Bryan Lizotte.)

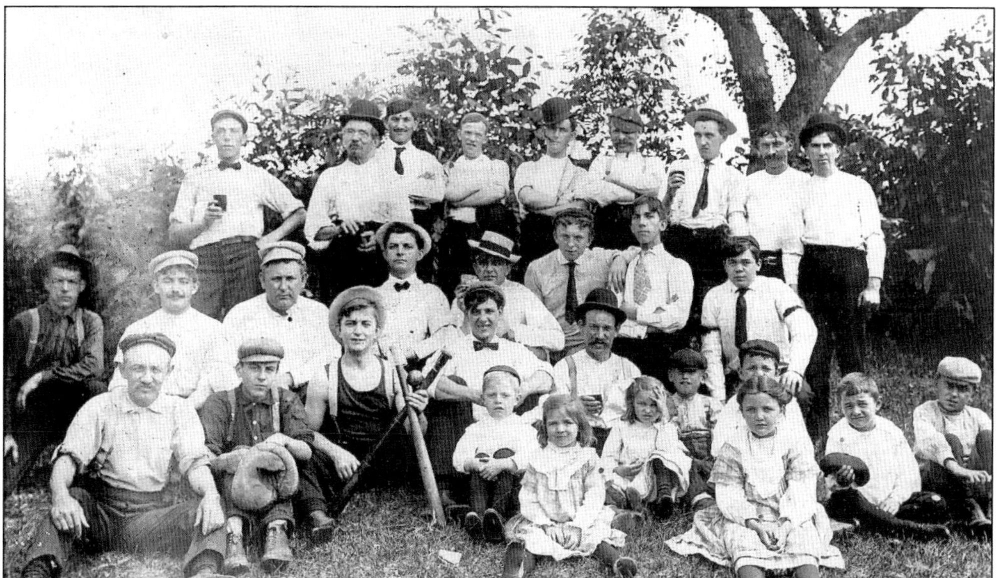

This 1905 baseball team was either associated with the Shelton Looms or the Shelton German Club. Sidney Blumenthal was very involved in the lives of his workers and the community. Large numbers of workers were German immigrants. The man in the front on the left with the moustache is Frank X. Kassheimer, who worked as a spinner at the Sydney Blumenthal Company. His daughter Frances is the older girl in the front row, and her brother Joseph is to her left. (Courtesy of Randy Ritter.)

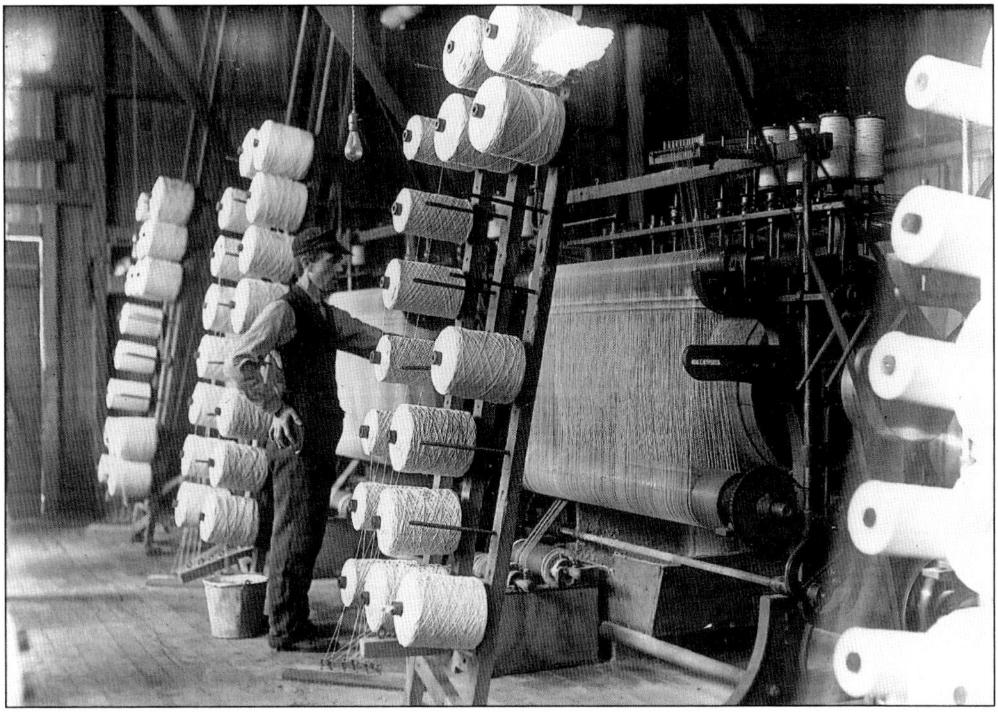

The Shelton Looms did all of its own weaving, dying, and finishing. It also did block, screen, and roll printing. Raw materials entered the factory and exited as finished textiles like the trademarked velvets Sealplush, Omeomi, and, in 1906, the first commercial rayon. (Photograph by Lewis W. Hine; courtesy of George Eastman House.)

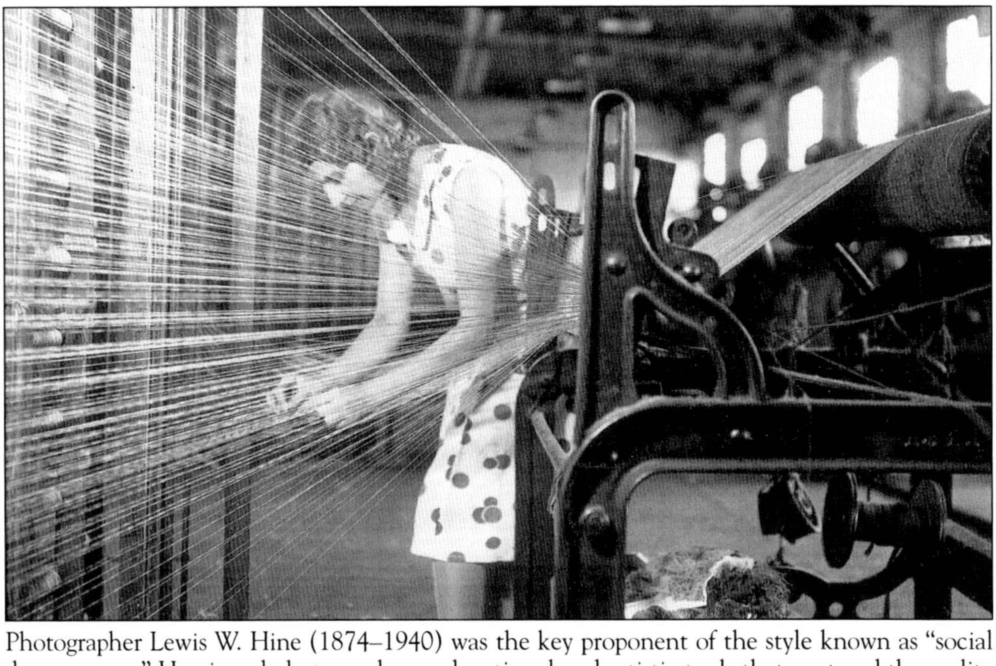

Photographer Lewis W. Hine (1874–1940) was the key proponent of the style known as "social documentary." He viewed photographs as educational and artistic tools that captured the reality of significant social issues. (Photograph by Lewis W. Hine; courtesy of George Eastman House.)

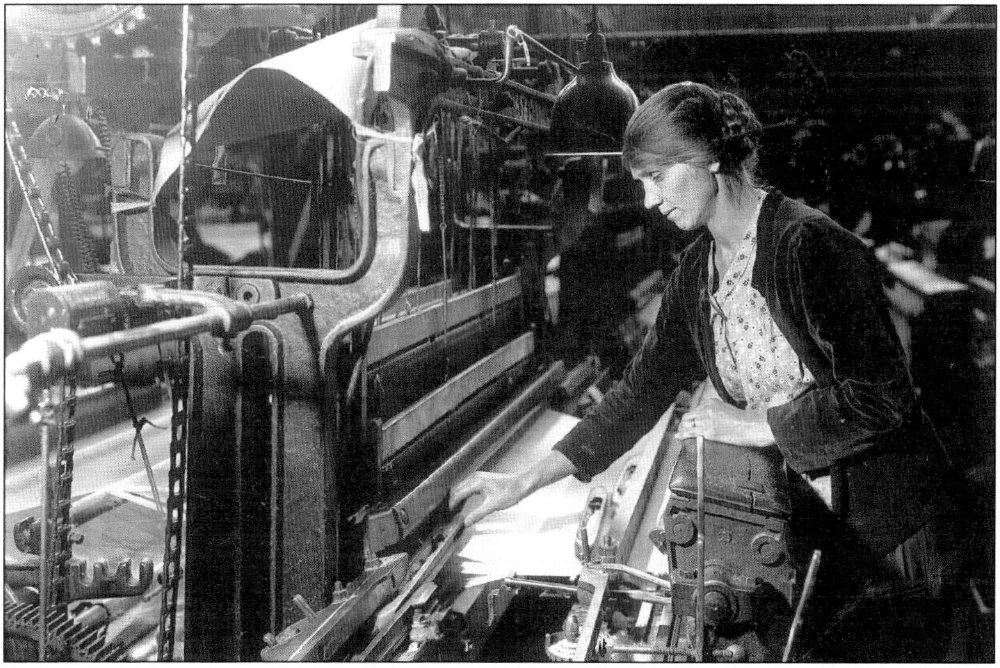

With his 1933 work at the Shelton Looms, Lewis W. Hine documented the factory of one of the most progressive industrial leaders in the country, Sidney Blumenthal. The photographs were published in the portfolio *Through the Threads of the Shelton Looms* and also displayed by the company at the 1933 Chicago World's Fair, A Century of Progress. (Photograph by Lewis W. Hine; courtesy of George Eastman House.)

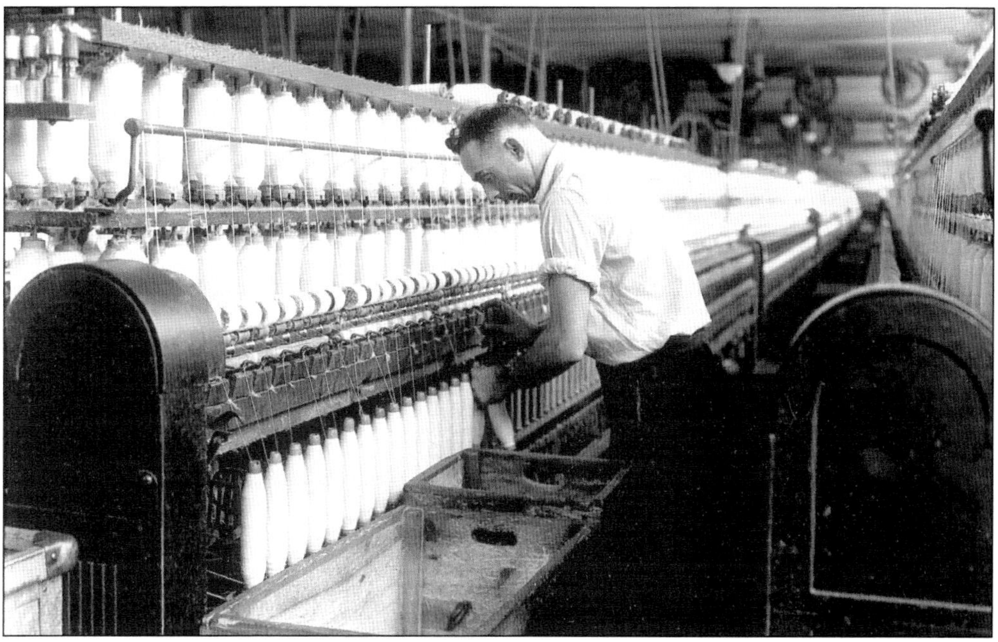

The Shelton Looms was the largest factory in Shelton. The spinning machine this man is operating seems to continue on into infinity, giving an impression of the size of the factory. (Photograph by Lewis W. Hine; courtesy of George Eastman House.)

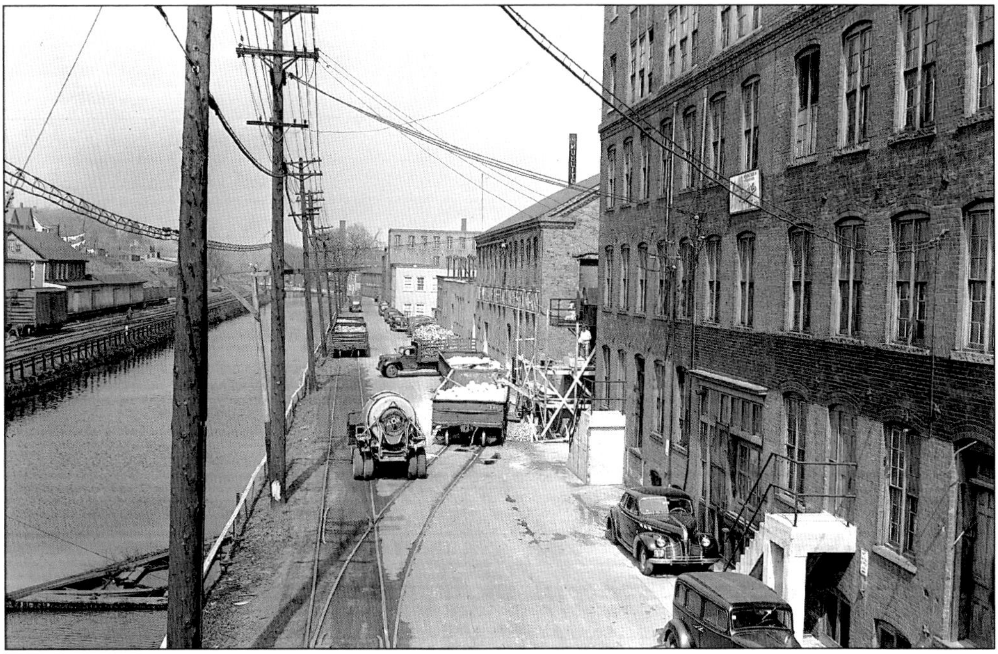

Manufacturing along the canal declined after World War I, when waterpower became less important. The Great Depression closed many factories, while others moved south. In this c. 1940 photograph, the smokestack for the Mullite Company is seen toward the right. The company produced refractory bricks and was a division of Shelton Cement Products. (Photograph by Anthony Zisek.)

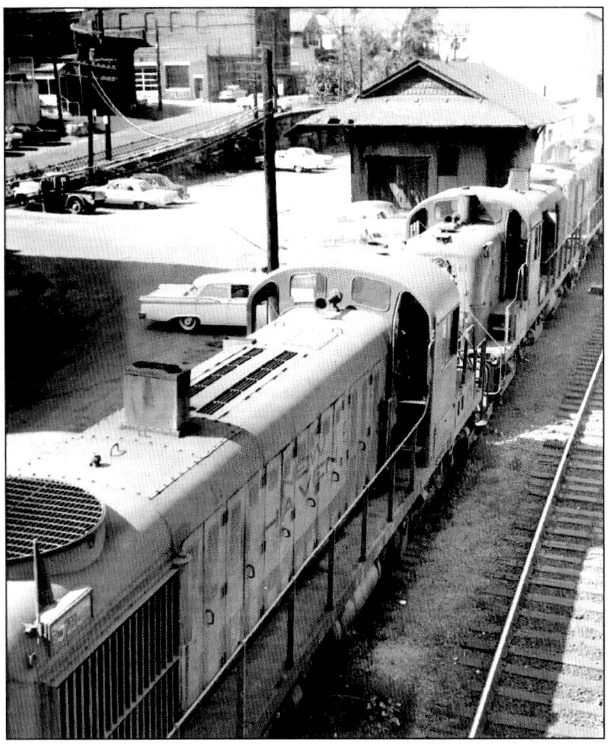

The Shelton train station still served freight traffic when this photograph was taken in October 1964. The building was torn down in the 1970s. (Photograph by Paul Kassheimer.)

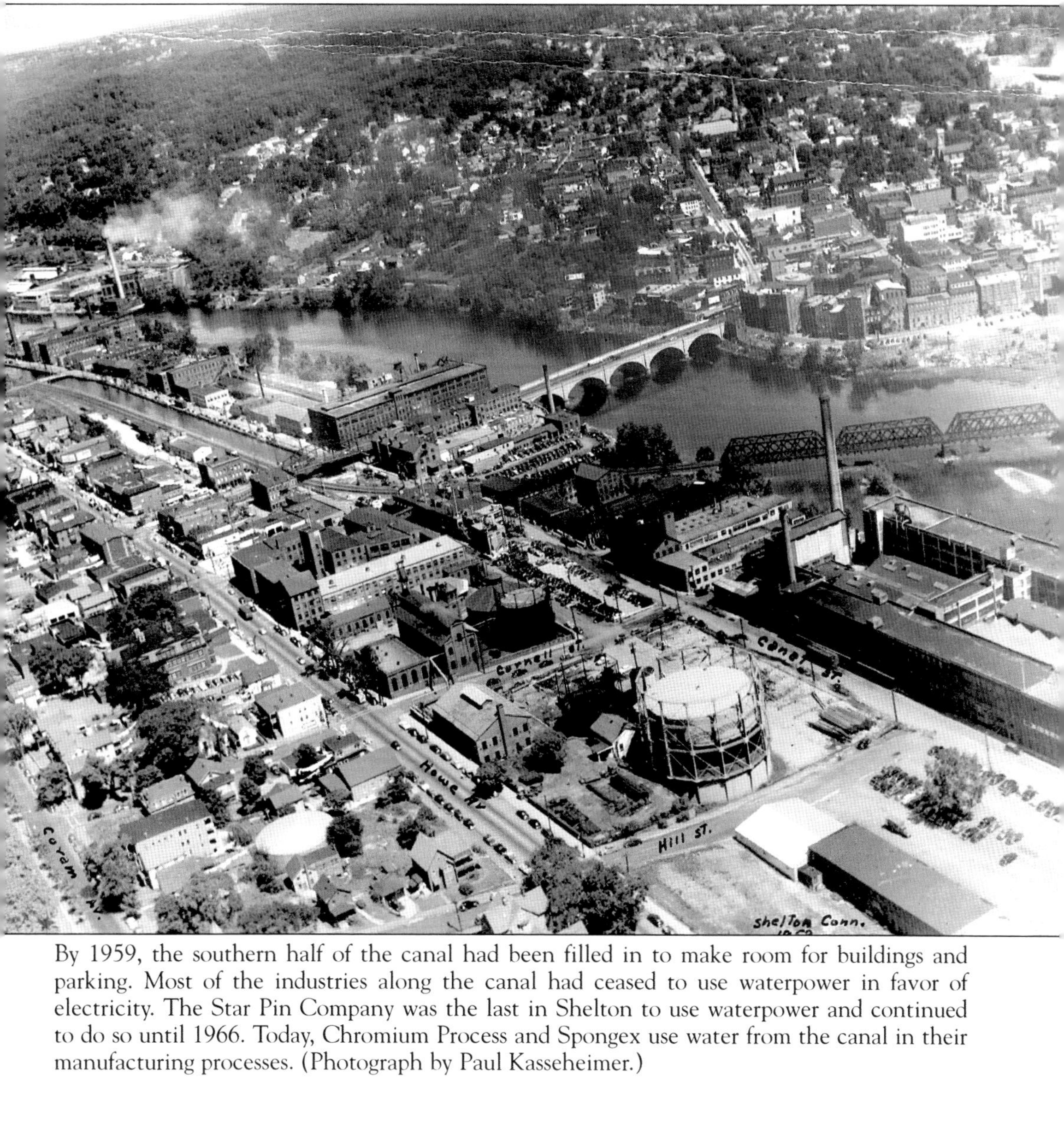

By 1959, the southern half of the canal had been filled in to make room for buildings and parking. Most of the industries along the canal had ceased to use waterpower in favor of electricity. The Star Pin Company was the last in Shelton to use waterpower and continued to do so until 1966. Today, Chromium Process and Spongex use water from the canal in their manufacturing processes. (Photograph by Paul Kasseheimer.)

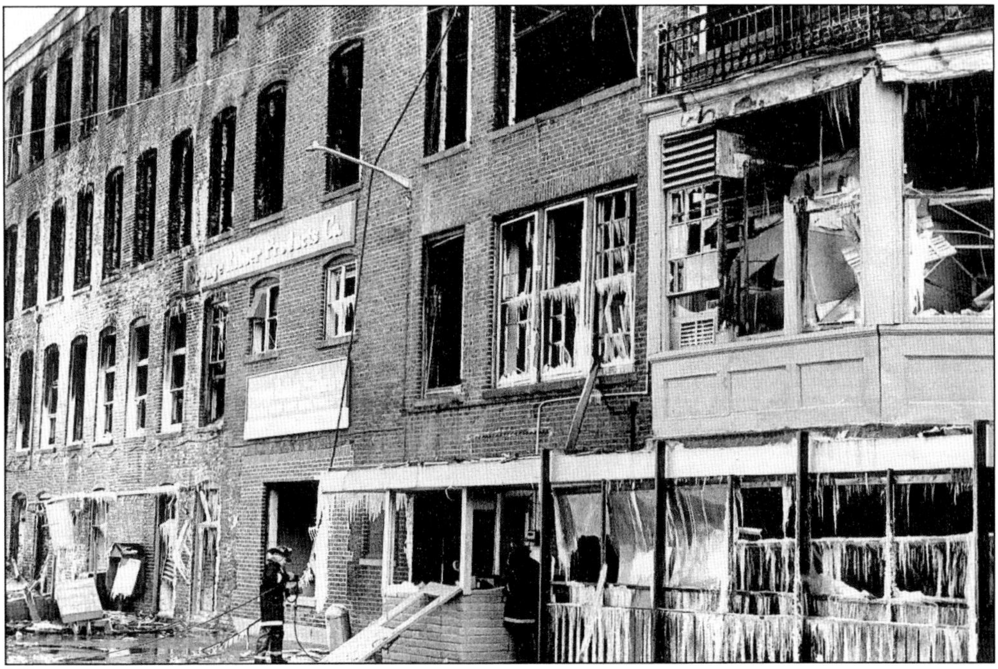

After the Sidney Blumenthal Company moved south in the 1950s, the site became the home for several manufacturers. The last to occupy the building was the Sponge Rubber Company. It was burned for the insurance money on March 1, 1975. At the time, it was the largest arson fire in the United States. (Photograph by Paul Kassheimer.)

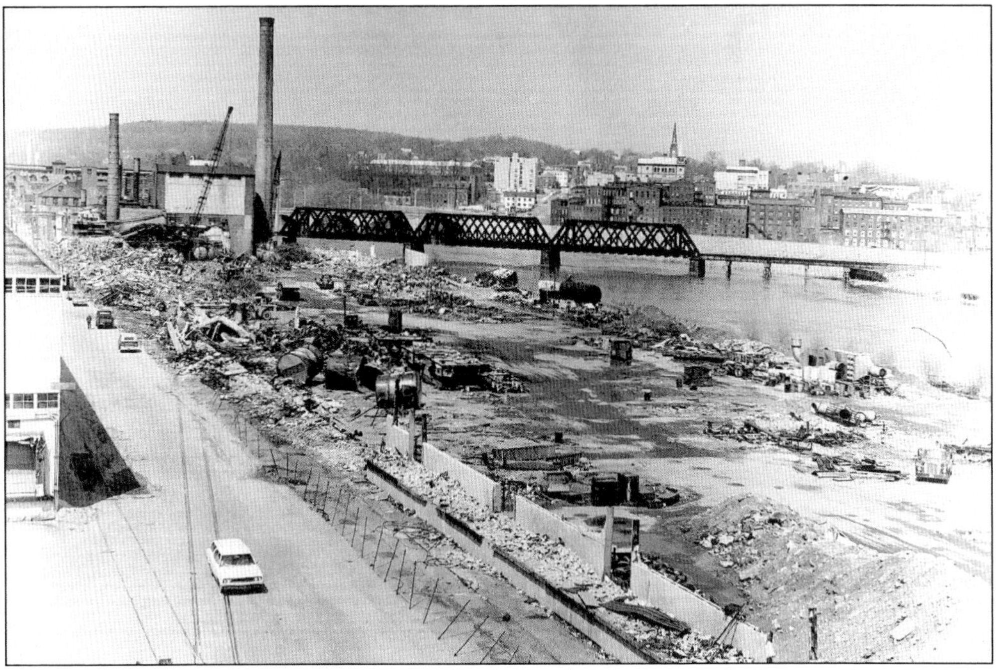

More than 350 firefighters from 15 towns fought the fire for over eight hours to bring it under control. The factory site, known as "the Slab" for many years, has now become the Shelton Industry and Commerce Park. (Photograph by Curt A. Scheibner.)

Four

WORSHIP

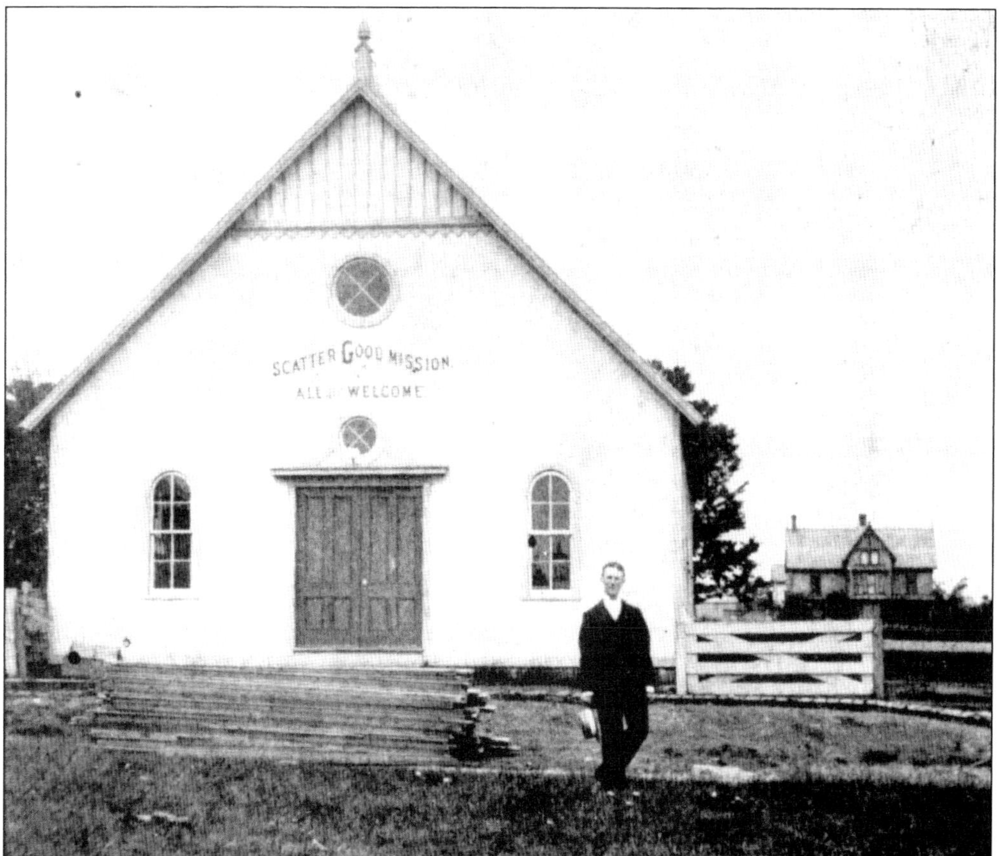

The Scattergood Mission is mentioned in Samuel Orcutt's 1880 *History of the Old Town of Derby* as "the beginning of a church, supported by all denominations, which is prosperous under the energy and perseverance of Rev. Friend Hoyt." This dapper young man may be Reverend Hoyt.

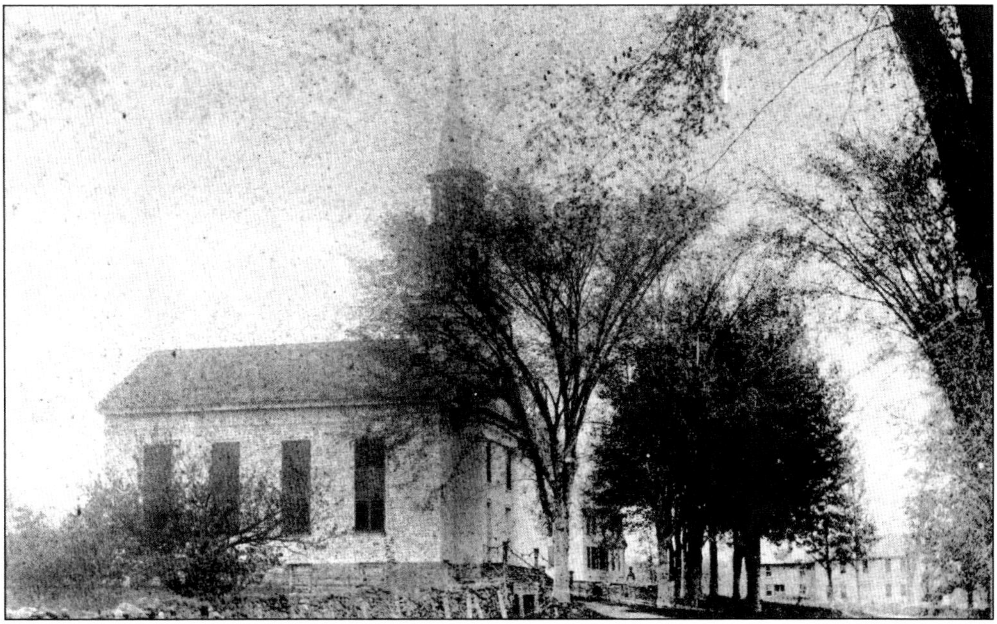

The Huntington Congregational Church has had four houses of worship over the years. This building, on the same site as the present church, was the third. Built between 1831 and 1833, it burned in 1892 due to a chimney fire.

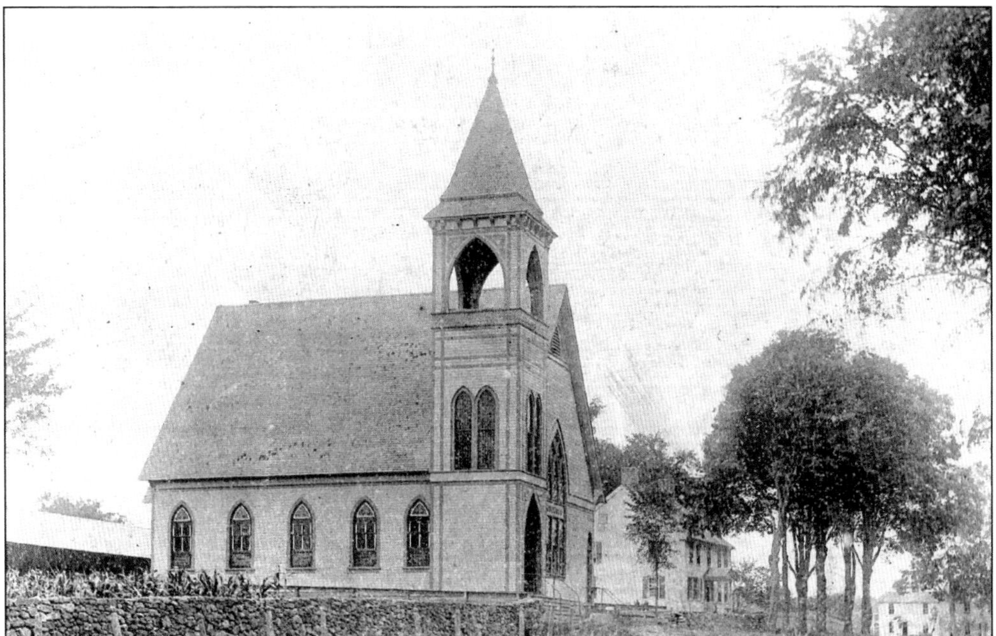

The fourth church, built in 1893, is still standing today. The cornfield to the left of the church gives a hint of the rural character of the area around the Huntington Green. (Courtesy of Philip Jones.)

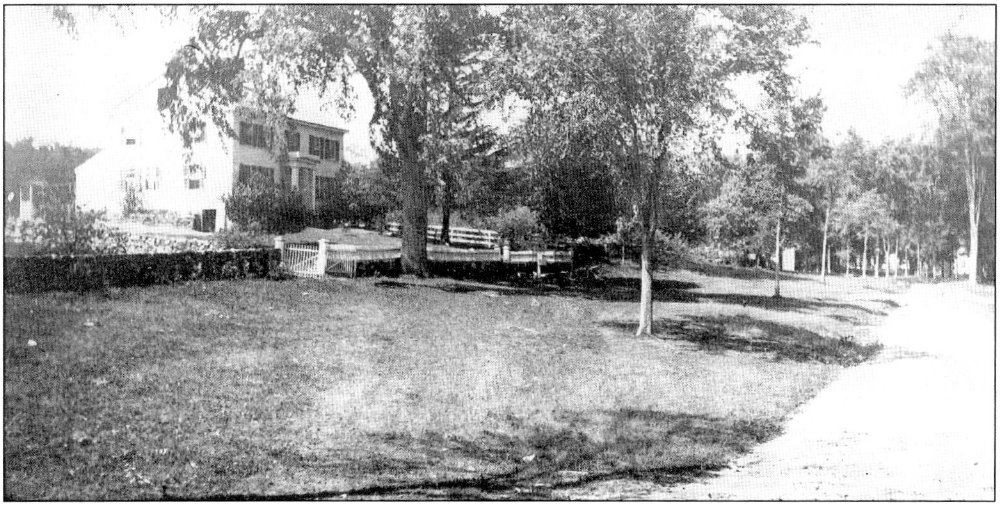

This view shows Church Street along the edge of the Huntington Green *c.* 1910. The building at 47 Church Street was purchased in 1844 by the Huntington Congregational Church for use as a parsonage. (Courtesy of Philip Jones.)

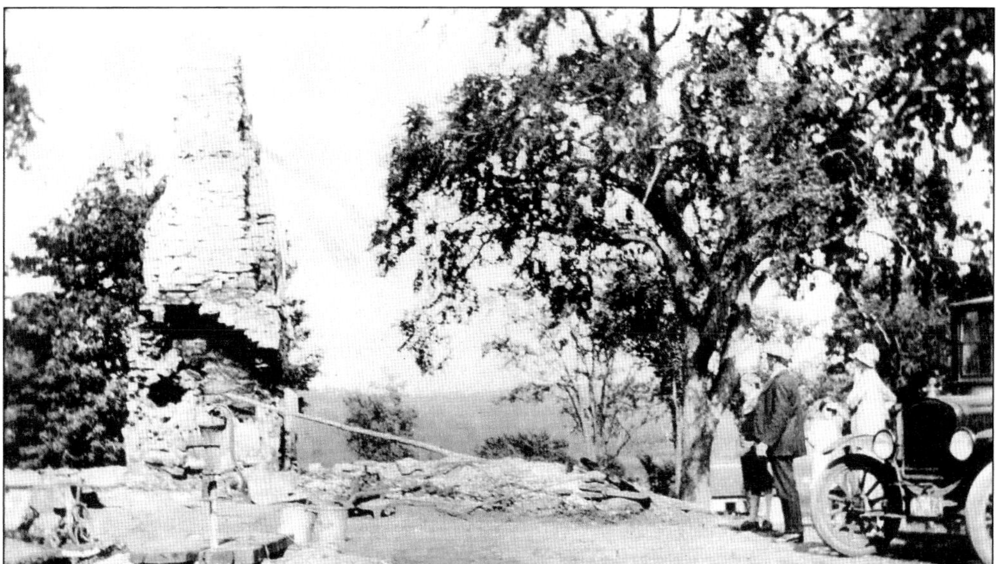

The parsonage burned to the ground in 1925. Here, some spectators view the ruins. The cause of the fire remained unknown because Rev. Walter Denny was in the process of moving to Boston and was not home at the time. He lost all of his furniture. (Courtesy of the Wells family.)

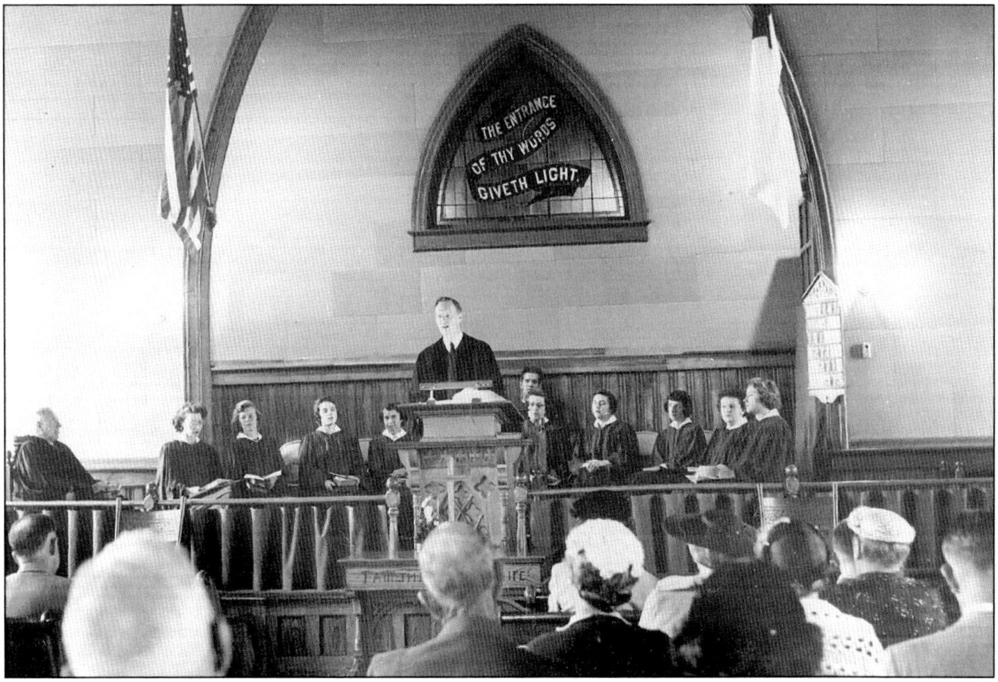

Rev. Charles Smith served the Huntington Congregational Church from 1957 through 1977. This *c.* 1958 view shows the interior before the choir loft was moved upstairs and the pulpit to the right. In the choir, from left to right, are Rev. Otto Reuman, Betty Carpenter, Jean Edwards, Carol Cockerill, Helen Webb, Reverend Smith, Howie Heavens, Louise Smith, Sue Taylor, Jean Nicholas, Arlene Fair, and Nancy Ibsen. (Courtesy of the Wells family.)

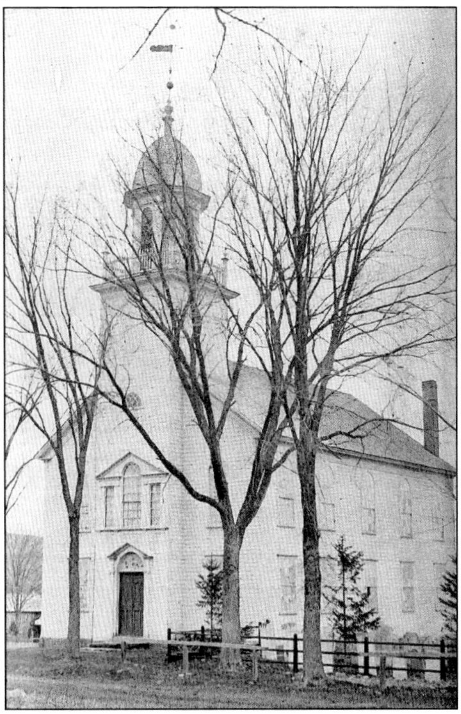

The original St. Paul's Episcopal Church was destroyed in 1811 by a fire started by Sidney DeForest, who was shooting at pigeons in the belfry. Construction on the second church began in 1812 and was completed in 1823. This image dates from *c.* 1870.

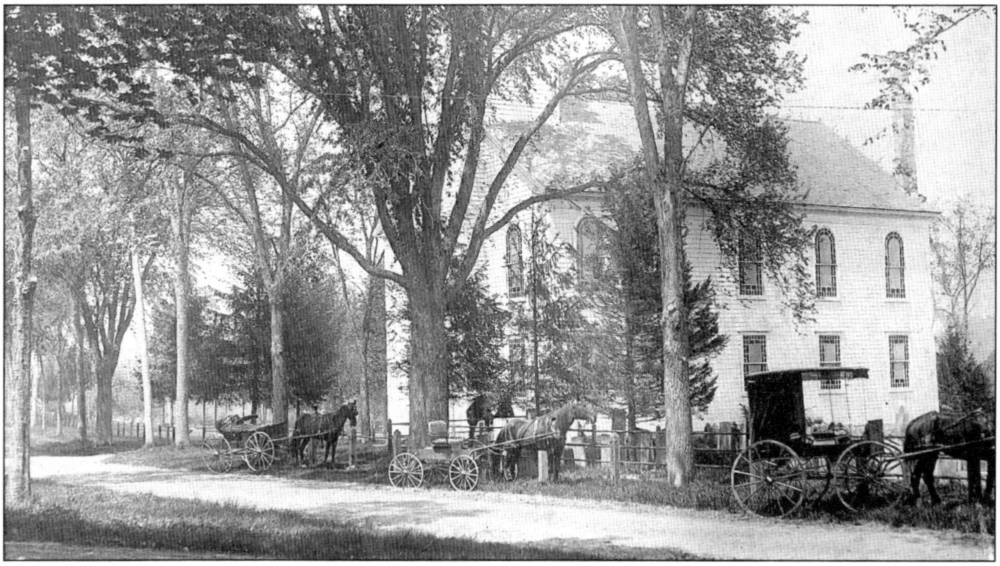

This photograph of the church was taken *c.* 1890. The Norway spruce trees along the cemetery fence were planted during the Civil War and appear to be about 30 years old.

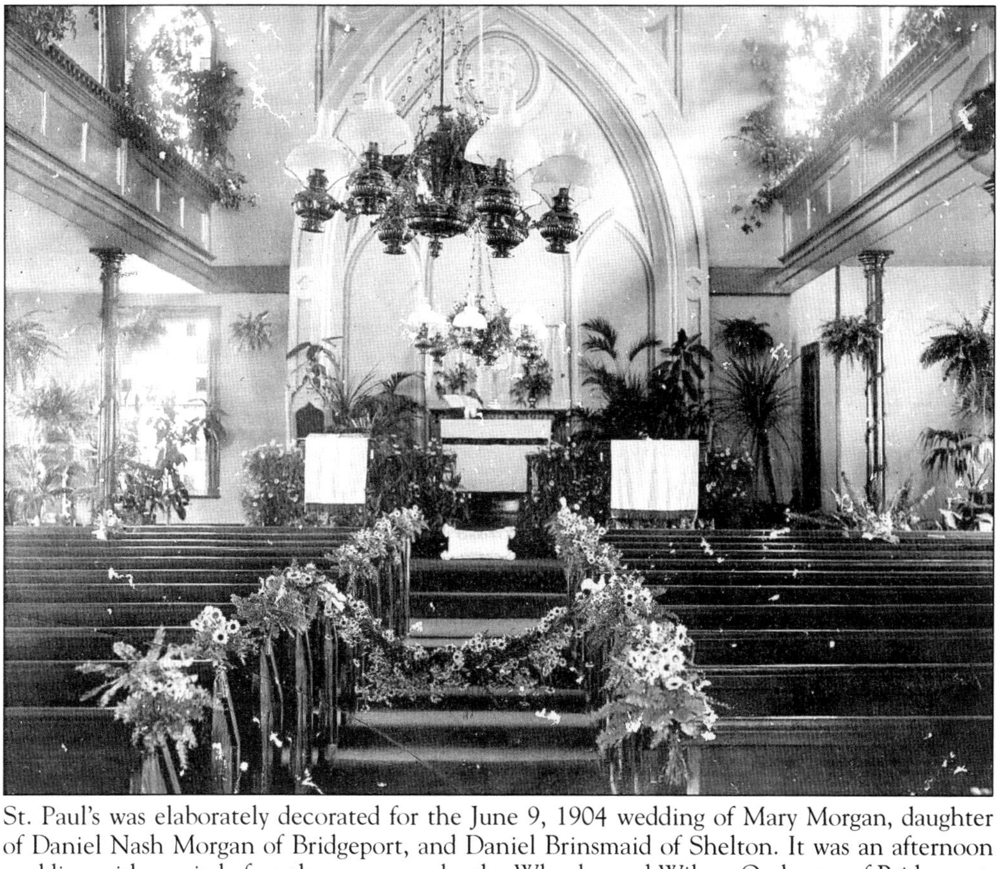

St. Paul's was elaborately decorated for the June 9, 1904 wedding of Mary Morgan, daughter of Daniel Nash Morgan of Bridgeport, and Daniel Brinsmaid of Shelton. It was an afternoon wedding with music before the ceremony by the Wheeler and Wilson Orchestra of Bridgeport. The bishop of Connecticut, Chauncey Brewster, performed the ceremony.

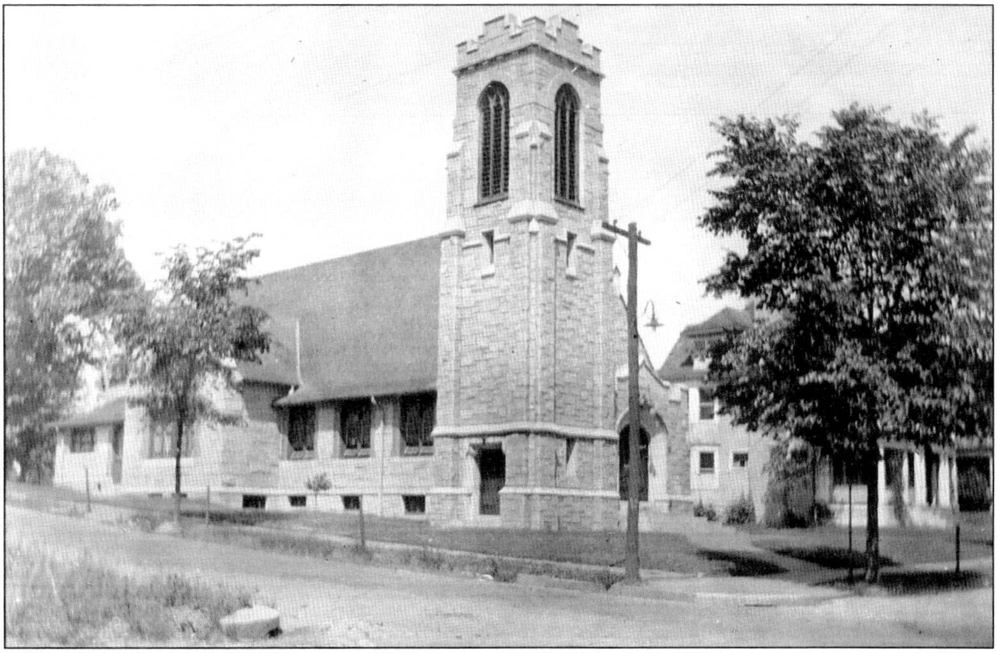

The Church of the Good Shepherd at the corner of Coram Avenue and Kneen Street was formally consecrated on June 22, 1907. In this early photograph of the church, the road is unpaved even though there are modern conveniences such as sidewalks, streetlights, and storm drains. (Courtesy of Dorothy Didsbury Mills.)

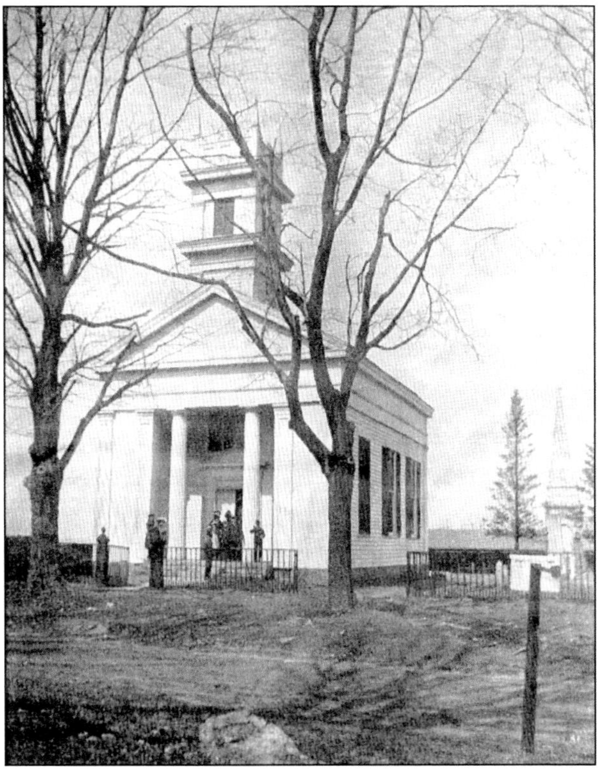

The White Hills Baptist Church, on School Street, was built in 1839. It closed for regular Sunday services in 1916 and now is maintained by the Upper White Hills Cemetery Association and used for community events.

Rev. A.A. Bickford was the last minister at the White Hills Baptist Church. Here, he is shown with his wife, Clara, in 1915. (Photograph by Helen Jones; courtesy of Philip Jones.)

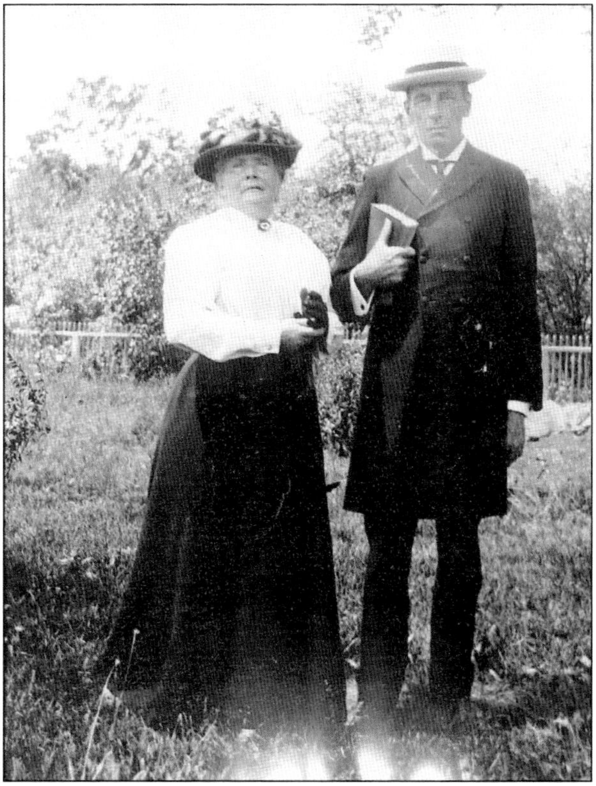

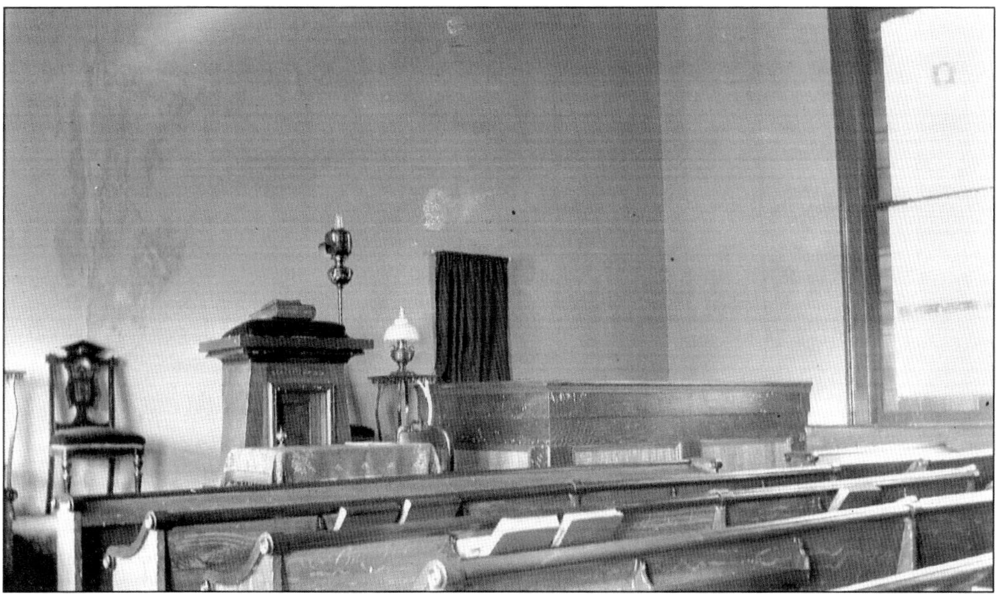

The full-immersion baptismal tank to the right of the altar in the White Hills Baptist Church was installed in 1894 and removed in 1930. (Photograph by Helen Jones; courtesy of Philip Jones.)

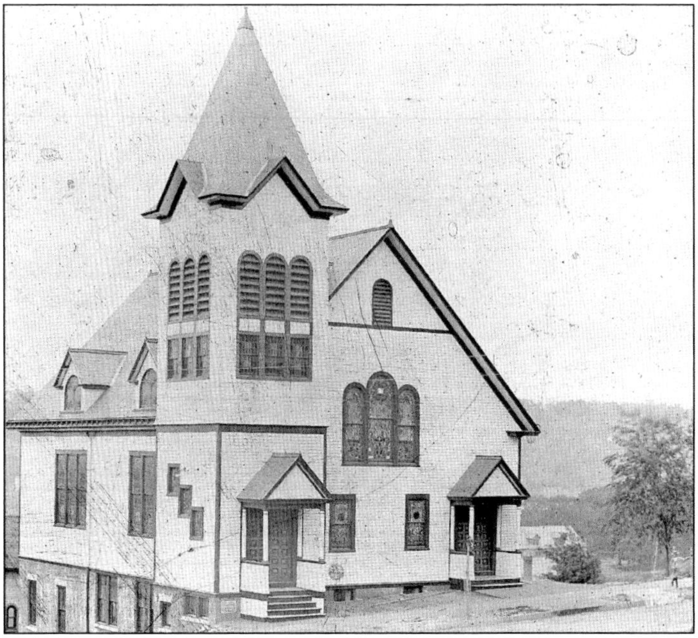

The Shelton Congregational Church, at the corner of Coram Avenue and Hill Street, was dedicated on June 20, 1895. The two separate entrances seen in this late-1890s view were merged into a wider central entrance between 1916 and 1923.

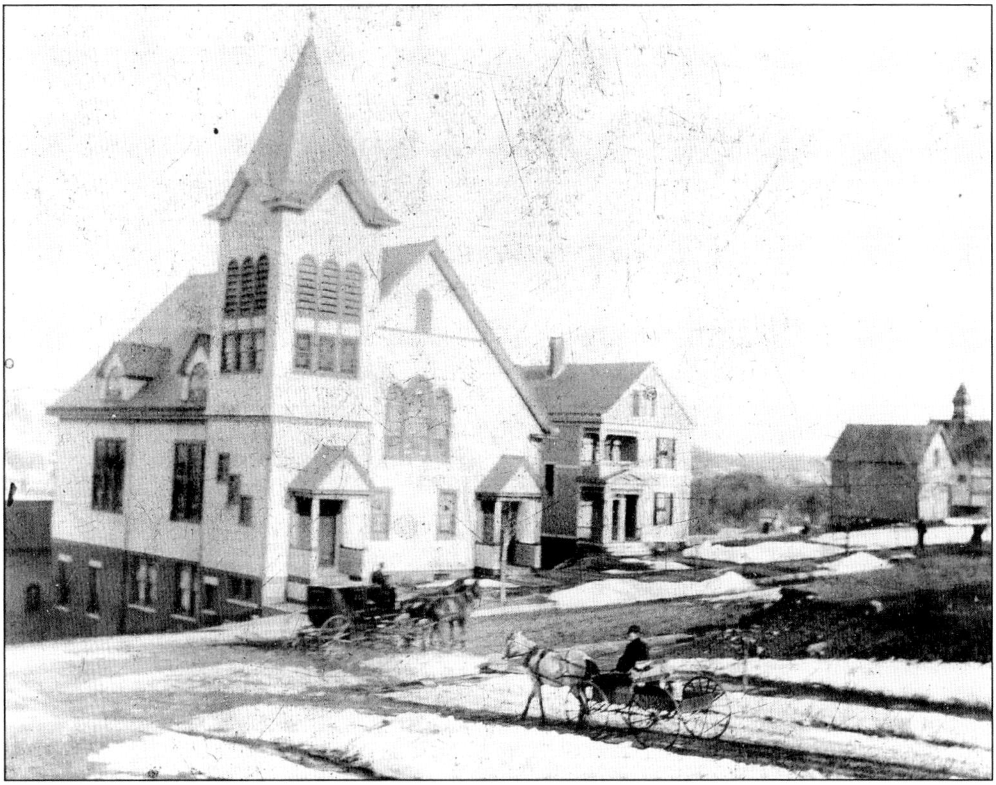

This image of the Shelton Congregational Church is dated April 11, 1899. The tree to the right of the church in the previous photograph has been replaced with a house. The small tree in front of the church has gained a year or two of growth between the pictures. Note the snow still on the ground in April. (Courtesy of the Frederick W. Ziegler family.)

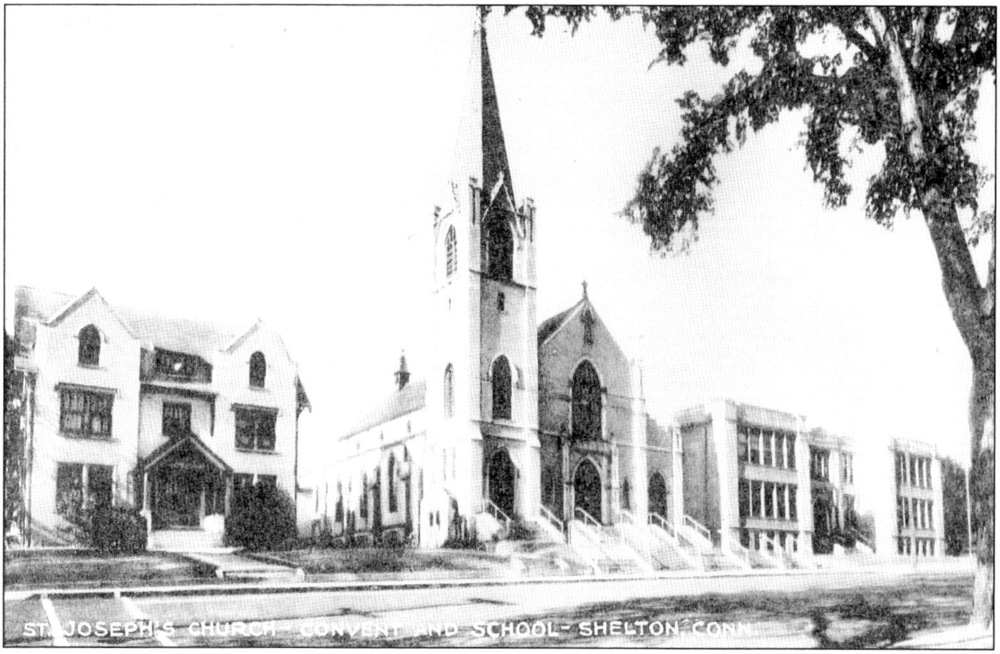

The first Catholic mass celebrated in Shelton took place on April 22, 1906. Prior to that, Catholics had to cross the river to Derby and worship at St. Mary's. St. Joseph's Church was under construction from 1907 to 1913. The rectory, which later became the convent, was built in 1916 and 1917, and the school opened in 1928. (Courtesy of Philip Jones.)

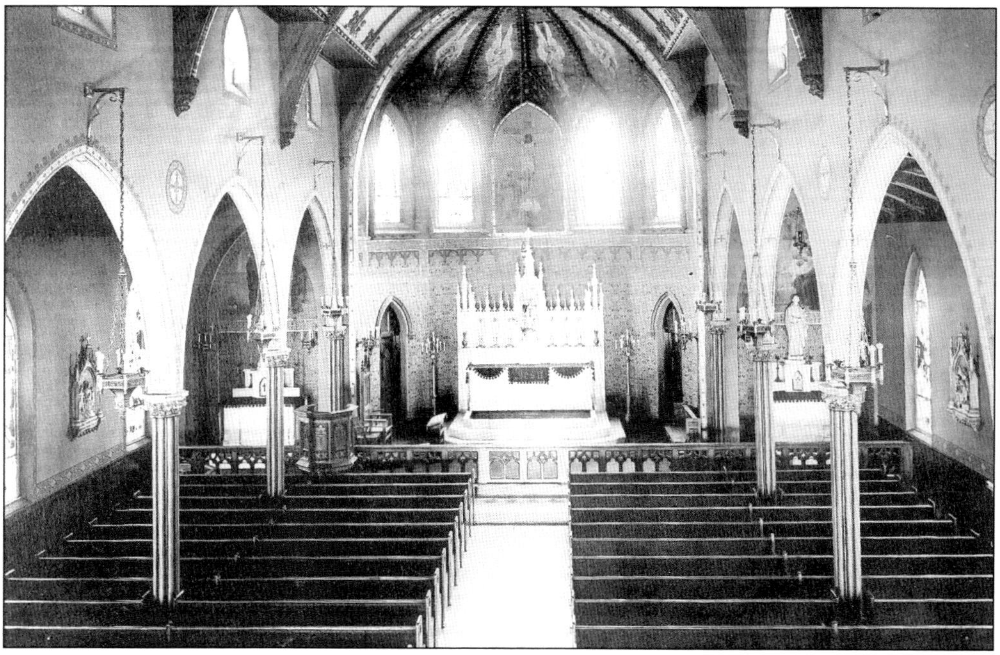

This interior photograph of St. Joseph's church was taken prior to 1965, when the altar was moved to the right as proposed by Vatican II. In the 1990s, the altar was returned to its original position and the interior repainted to reflect the original grand appearance. (Courtesy of Frank and Ann Rossi.)

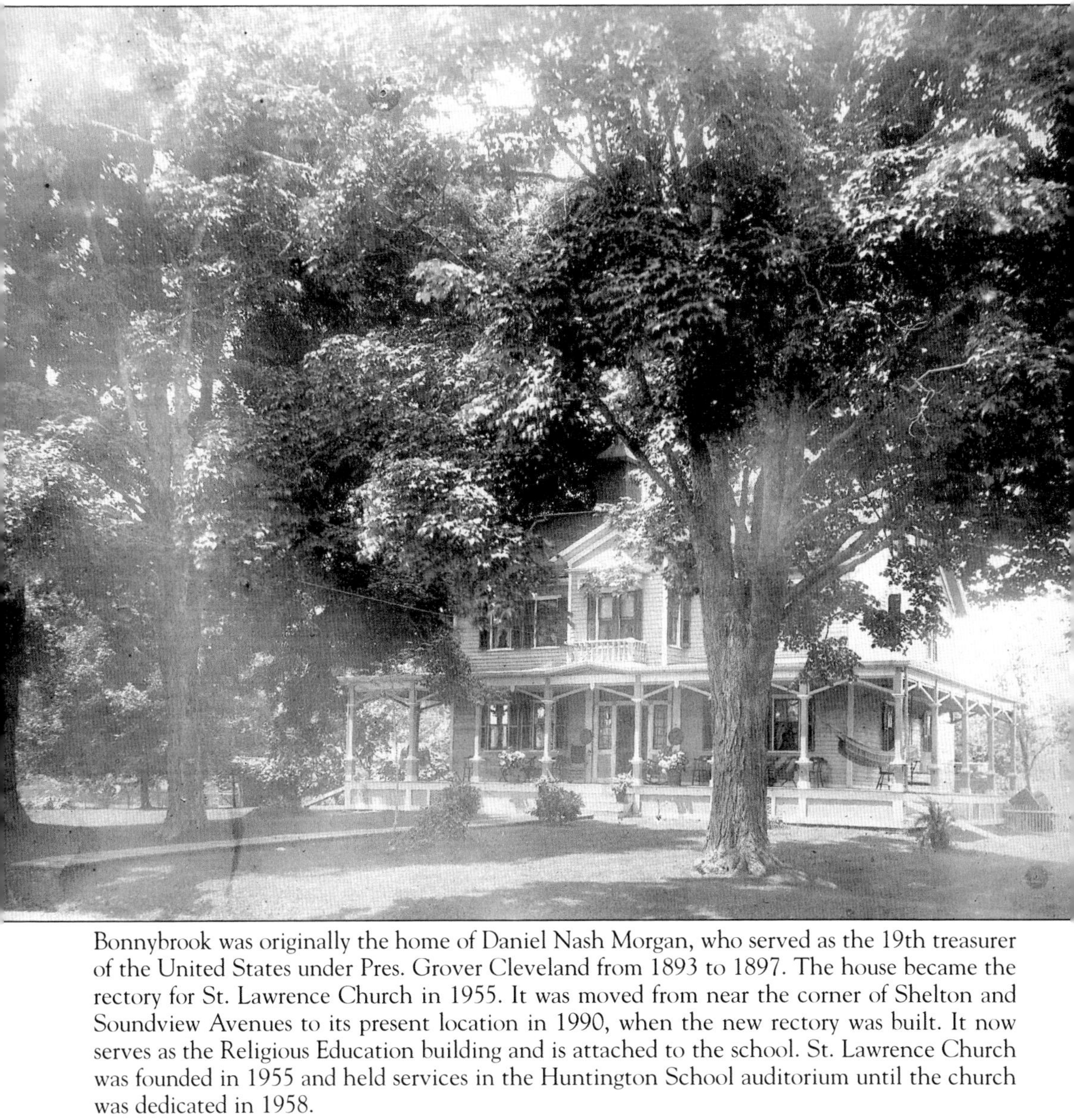

Bonnybrook was originally the home of Daniel Nash Morgan, who served as the 19th treasurer of the United States under Pres. Grover Cleveland from 1893 to 1897. The house became the rectory for St. Lawrence Church in 1955. It was moved from near the corner of Shelton and Soundview Avenues to its present location in 1990, when the new rectory was built. It now serves as the Religious Education building and is attached to the school. St. Lawrence Church was founded in 1955 and held services in the Huntington School auditorium until the church was dedicated in 1958.

Five

SCHOOL DAYS

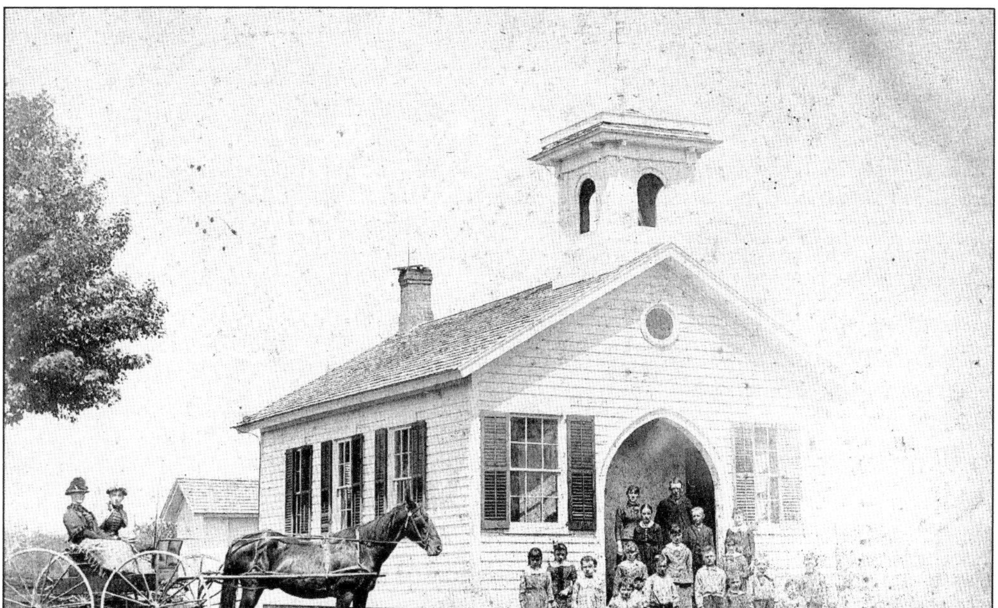

Students of the Walnut Tree Hill School gather for a photograph on the front steps c. 1900. The school was located at Walnut Tree Hill Road and Thompson Street. (Courtesy of Jim Fair.)

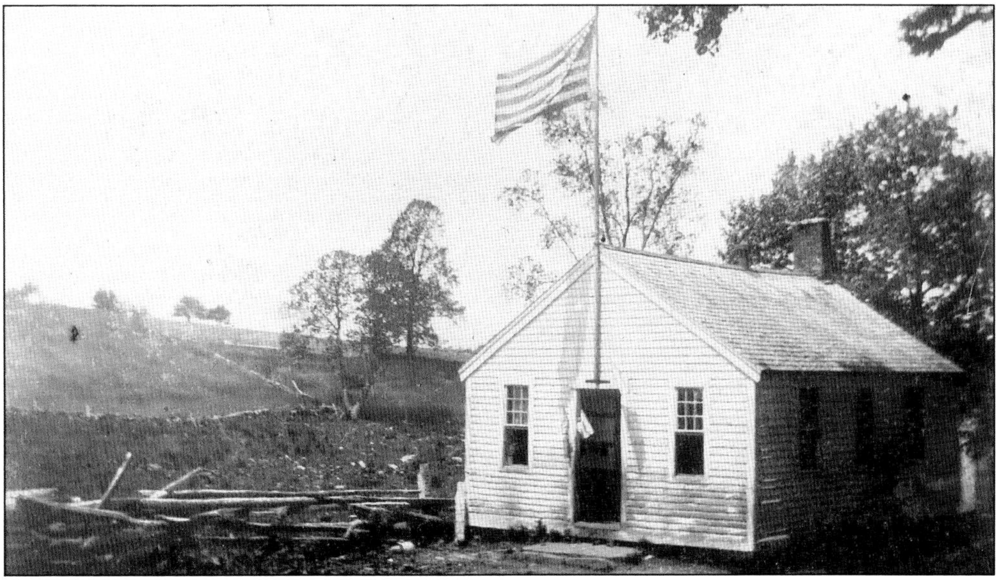

The first Upper White Hills School was built *c.* 1755 at Dimon and Beardsley Roads. As the population shifted, a new school, seen here, was erected at French's corner on East Village Road in 1839. (Courtesy of Philip Jones.)

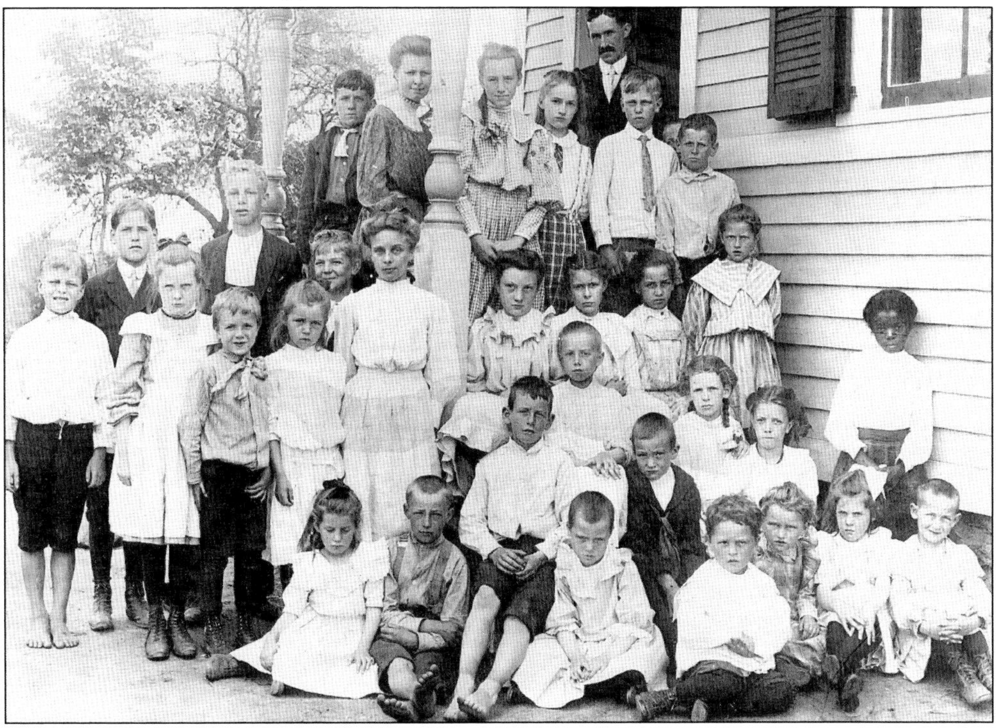

This 1906 class portrait of the Upper White Hills School was probably taken at someone's house because the school did not have a porch. The first girl sitting on the ground to the left is Sue Beardsley, the tall blond boy near the pillar is Fritz Von Werder, and the tall girl to the left of the pillar on the porch is Gladys Shelton. Note the girls in the front row with the shaven heads, who may have had a case of lice. (Courtesy of Helen and Fred Glover.)

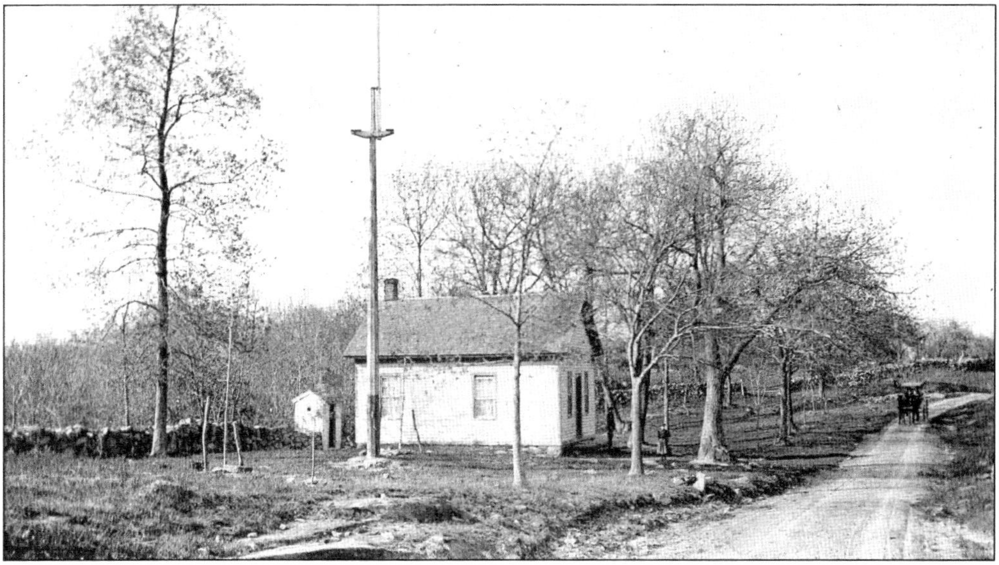

The Lower White Hills School was built before 1799 at the corner of Birdseye Road and Soundview Avenue. This view is from *c.* 1890. The building was sold in 1911 and converted to a private residence. (Courtesy of Ruth and Rod Kneen.)

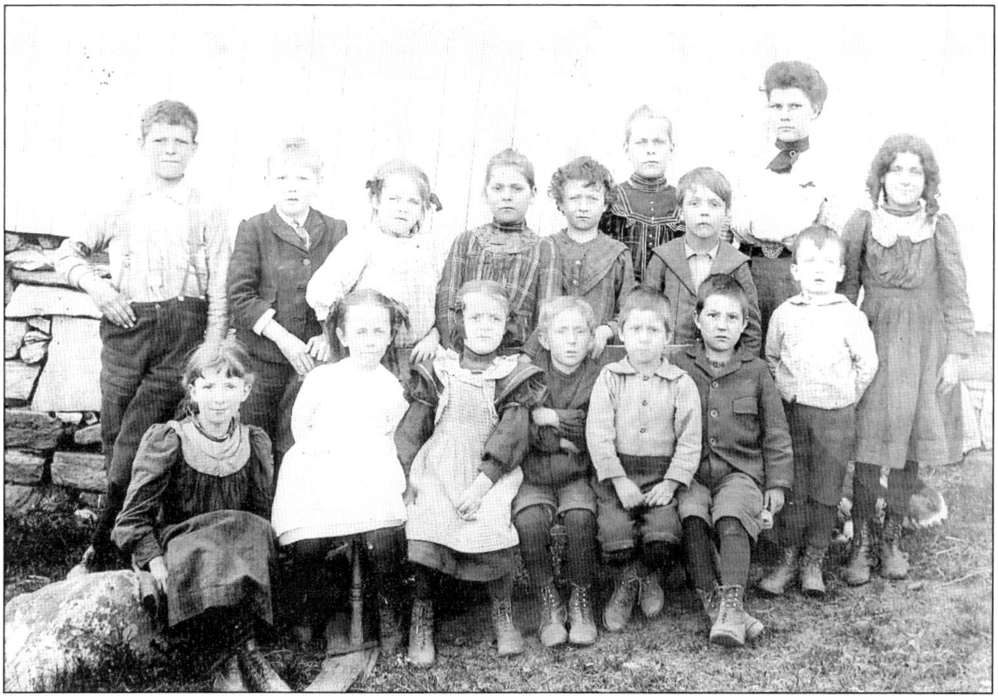

These are the students of the Wells Hollow School *c.* 1910. Benjamin Wells is the young man second on the right. (Courtesy of the Wells family.)

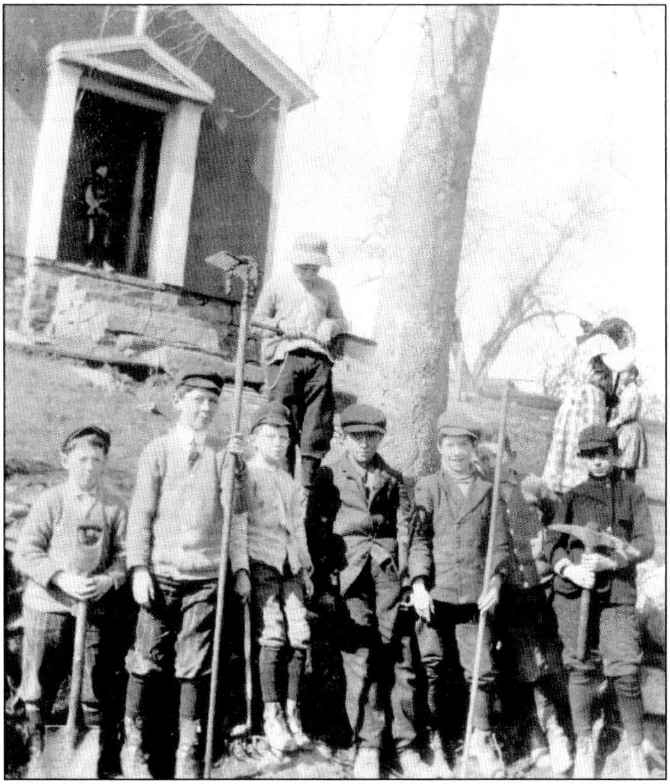

This photograph is titled "The Wall Builders 1910-11." The boys are at the Wells Hollow School on the corner of Mill Street and Bridgeport Avenue. They are, from left to right, Billy Cordon, John Cordon, Billy Wells, Frank Imbimbo, Edward Boutilier, and Raymond Cordon. Standing in back is Henry Wells. (Courtesy of the Wells family.)

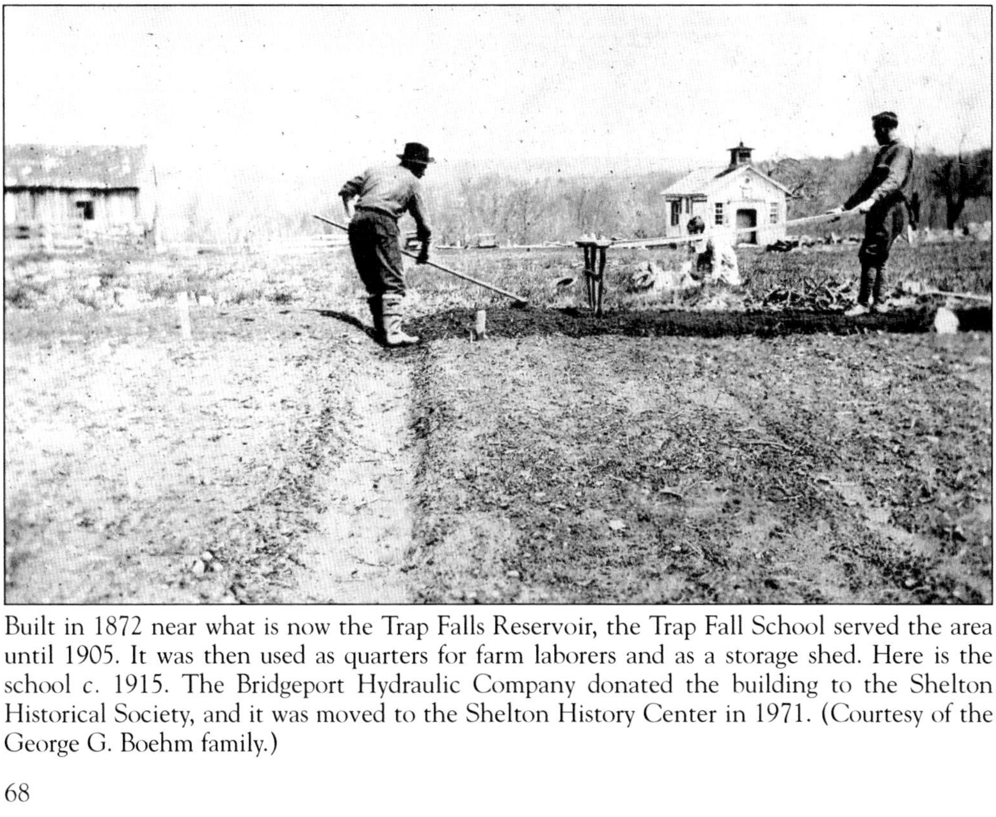

Built in 1872 near what is now the Trap Falls Reservoir, the Trap Fall School served the area until 1905. It was then used as quarters for farm laborers and as a storage shed. Here is the school *c.* 1915. The Bridgeport Hydraulic Company donated the building to the Shelton Historical Society, and it was moved to the Shelton History Center in 1971. (Courtesy of the George G. Boehm family.)

Ferry School, on Howe Avenue, was built in 1885 as a grammar school. The first high school classes in Shelton were housed there beginning in 1887. The first graduation was held in 1889. The building is now the Victorian Condominiums. (Courtesy of the Frederick W. Ziegler family.)

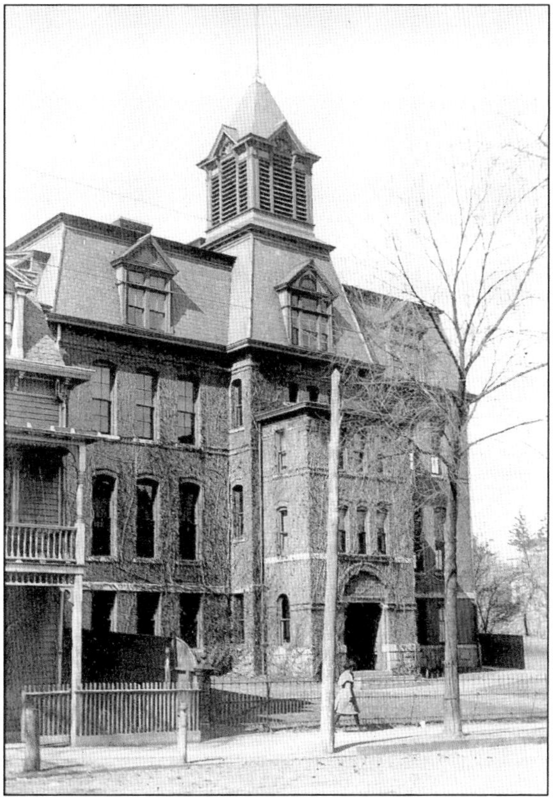

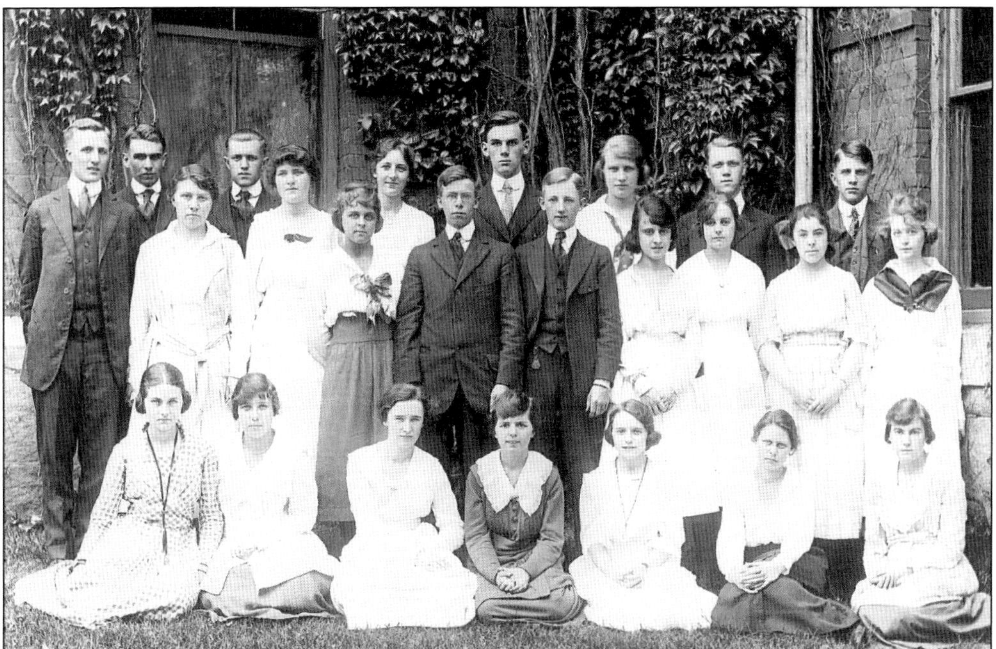

The Shelton High School class of 1919 gathers for their photograph outside the Ferry School. (Courtesy of the Wells family.)

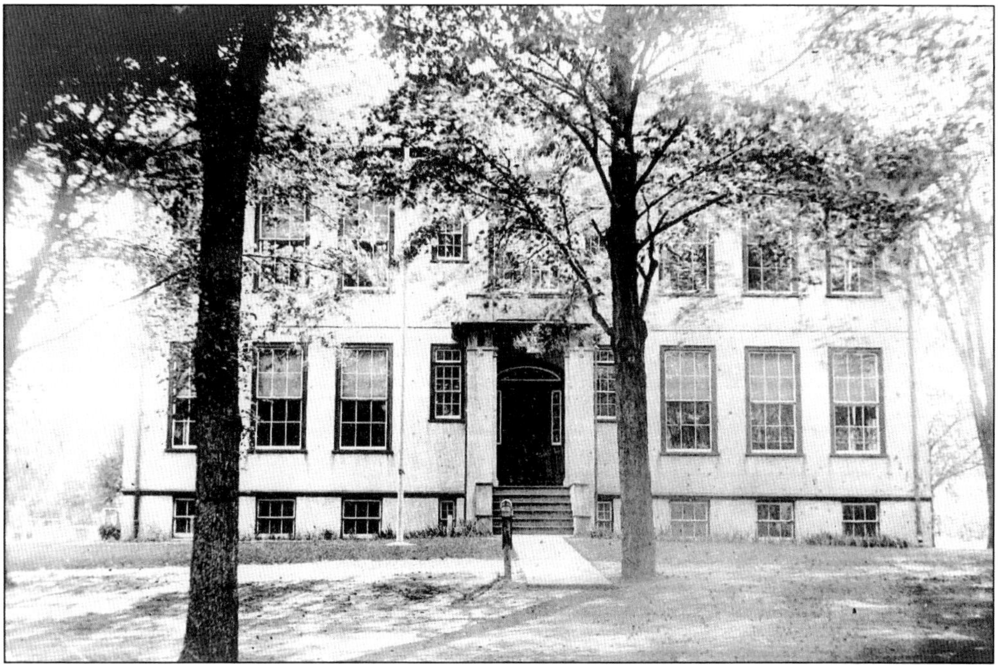

Lafayette School was built on Grove Street in 1911. The facade was originally stucco. In the 1980s, the school was extensively refurbished and expanded to accommodate the growing population.

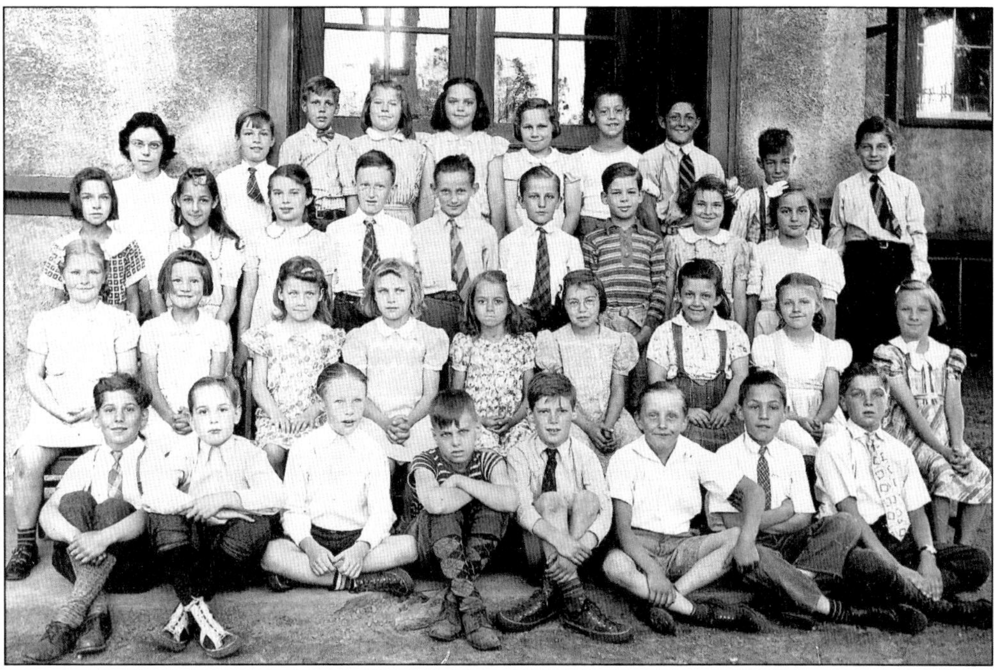

The Huntington School, on Church Street, was built as a grammar school in 1911. Here is the combined third- and fourth-grade class of 1939–1940, taught by Miss MacDonald. The building now serves the city as a community center. (Courtesy of the Willoughby family.)

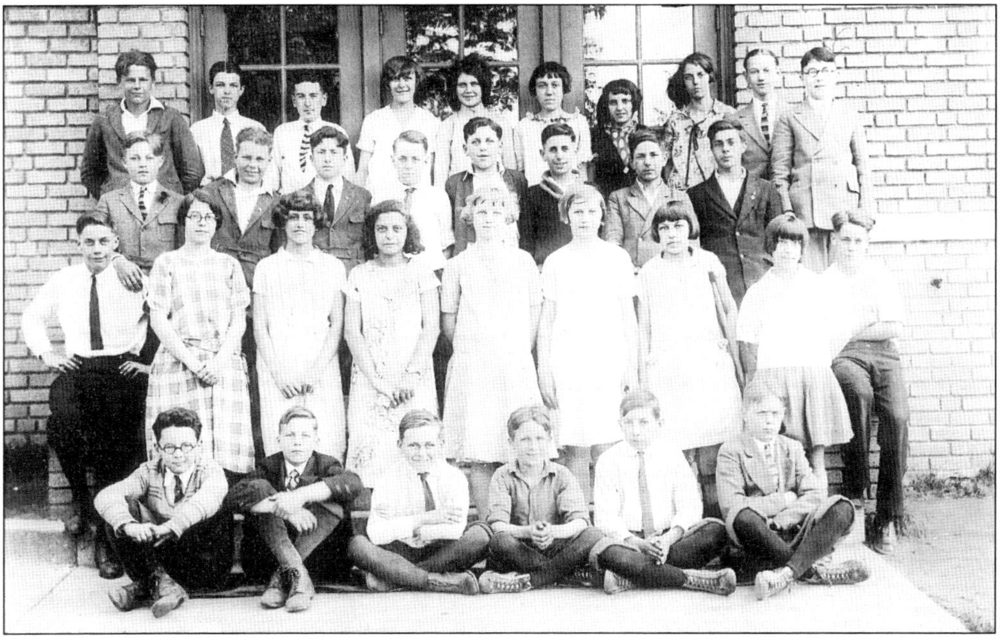

Members of the Fowler School eighth-grade class are gathered for their graduation photograph in 1926. At the top left is Martin Savitsky. (Courtesy of Rosalind and Linda Savitsky.)

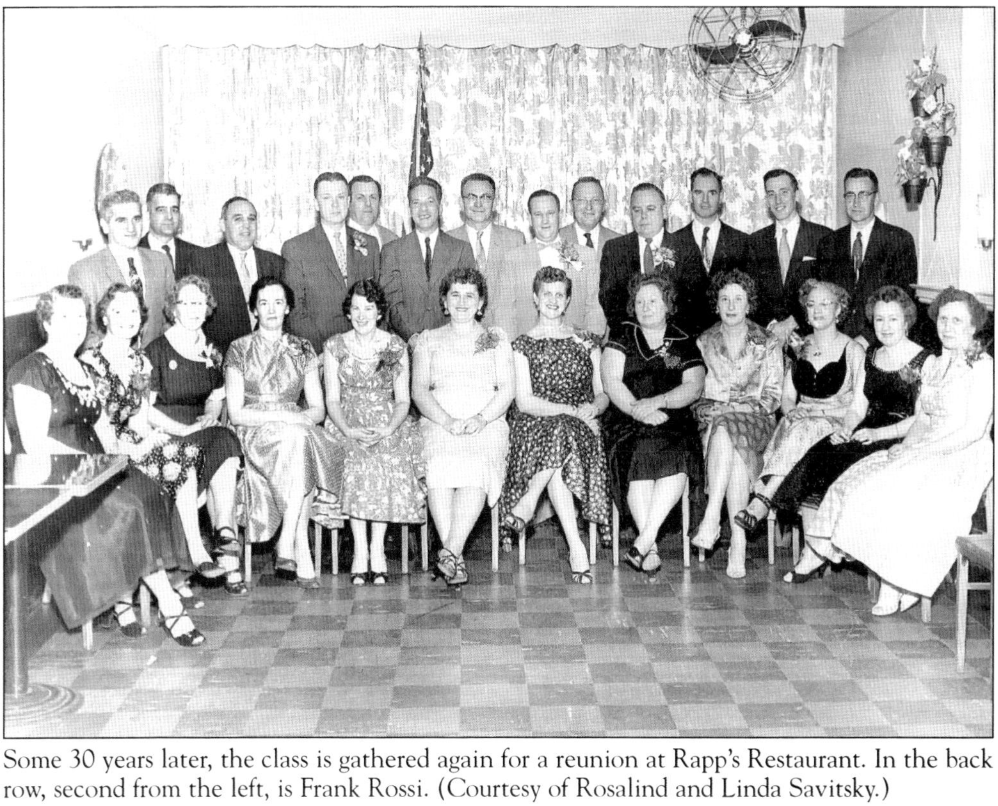

Some 30 years later, the class is gathered again for a reunion at Rapp's Restaurant. In the back row, second from the left, is Frank Rossi. (Courtesy of Rosalind and Linda Savitsky.)

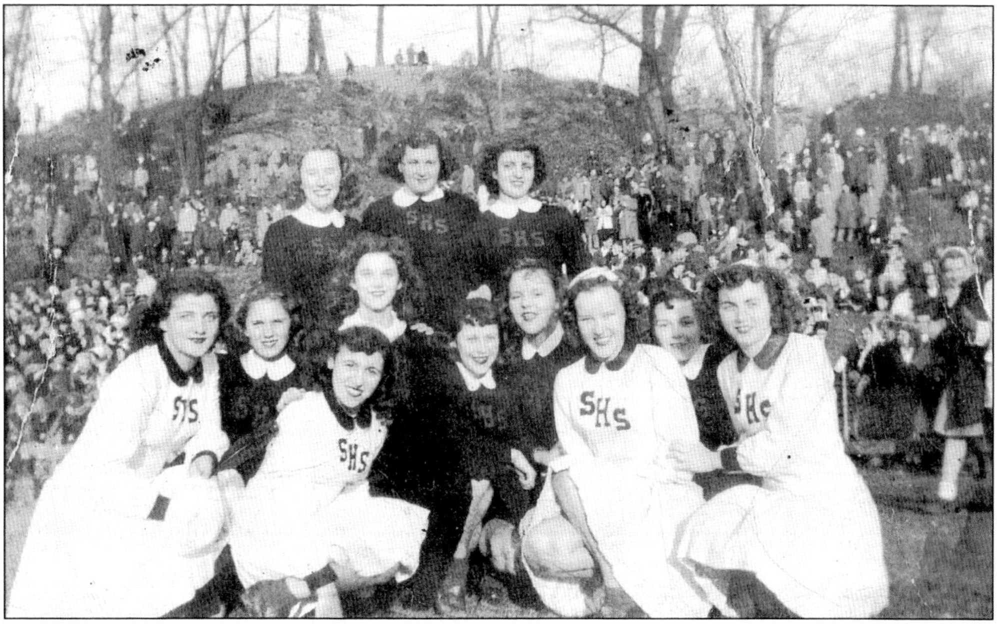

The Thanksgiving Day Shelton-Derby football game is a longstanding tradition. Here, the cheerleaders from Shelton High gather at Ryan Field in Derby c. 1950. (Courtesy of Ruth and Rod Kneen.)

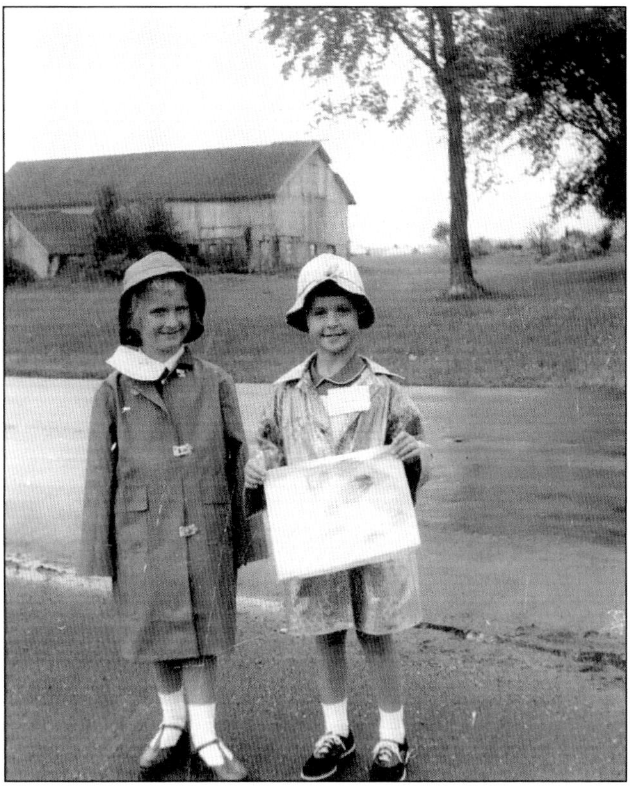

Luanne Westman and Elizabeth Santa are ready for their first day of kindergarten in September 1962. They are standing at 157 Ripton Road with one of the many barns that once dotted the landscape in the background. (Courtesy of Janet N. Santa.)

Six

THOSE WHO SERVED

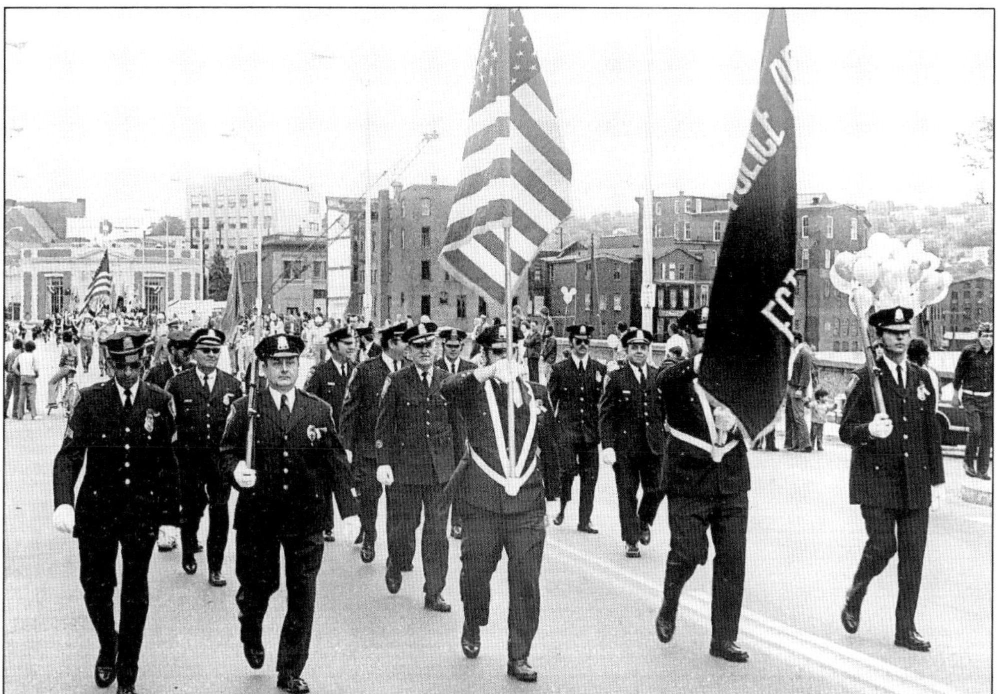

The annual Shelton-Derby Memorial Day Parade left from Derby in 1975. Here is the Shelton Police Department after the Memorial Wreath was lowered into the Housatonic River by Joseph Sojka, parade marshal. (Courtesy of Fred Anthony.)

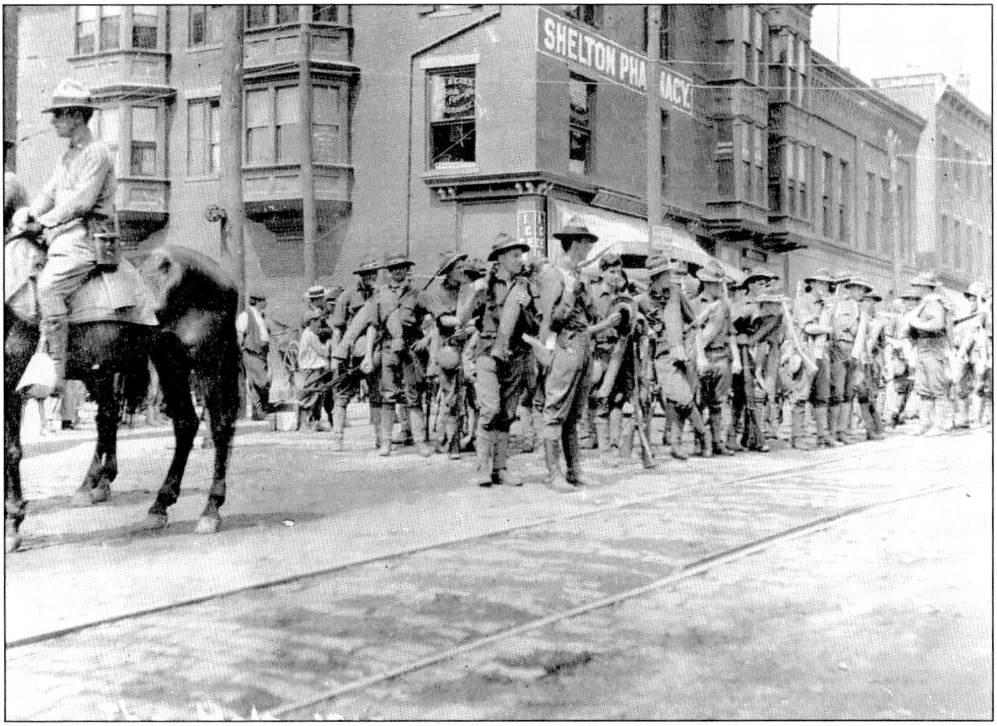

The War Games of August 1912 were probably the largest ever held on the East Coast. The Red Army was the foreign invader attempting to take over New York City and its water supply. The Blue Army marched into Shelton on August 10 to defend the bridges across the Housatonic River. (Photograph by Helen Jones; courtesy of Philip Jones.)

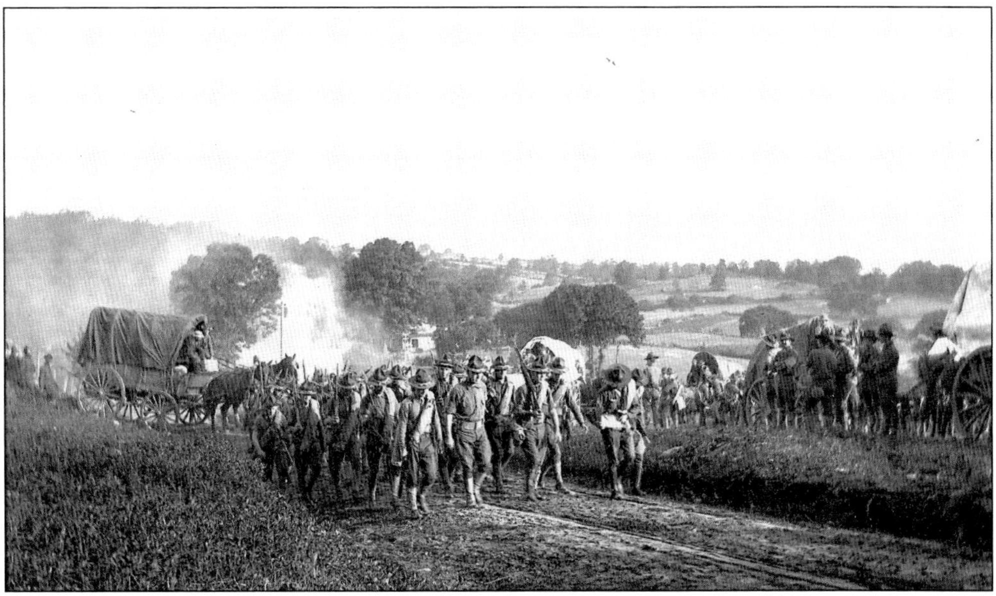

During the campaign, more than 20,000 men participated and discharged more than 500,000 pounds of blank ammunition. Here, one of the armies marches near the Jones farm in White Hills. (Photograph by Helen Jones; courtesy of Philip Jones.)

While the games were hard work for the participants, onlookers experienced a carnival-like atmosphere. People visited the army camps, watched the battles, and even saw their first airplanes, which were used by the armies as spotters. (Photograph by Helen Jones; courtesy of Philip Jones.)

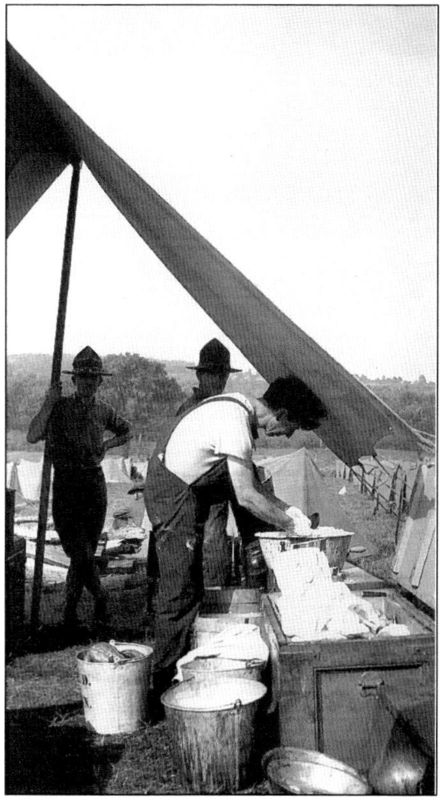

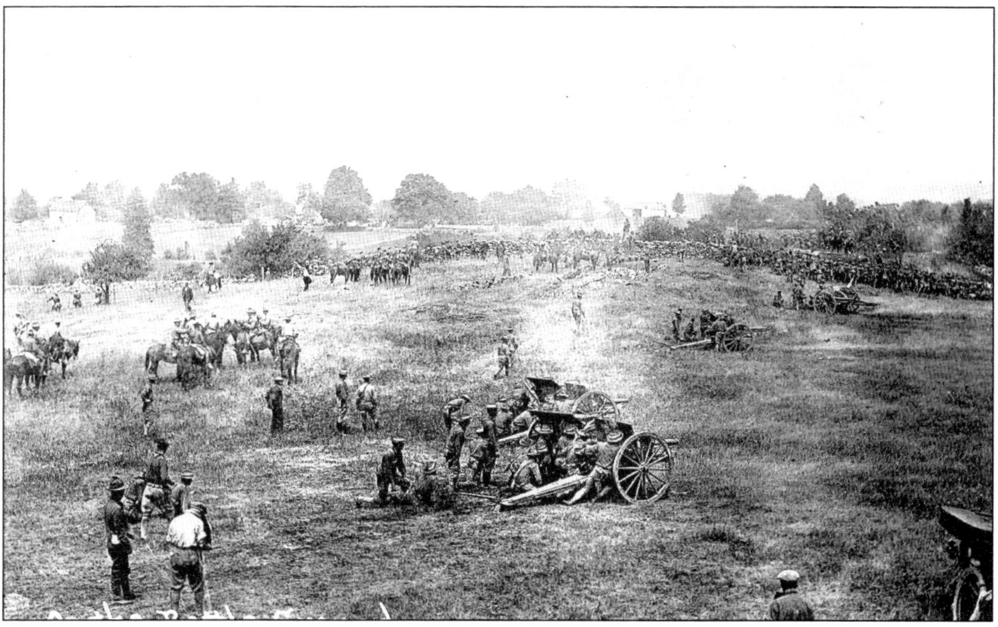

More than 8,000 men participated in the Battle of Huntington on August 14. It was held about one mile from the Huntington Green with the armies entrenched on Walnut Tree Hill. The Blue Army held their lines but later lost the war in a battle near Danbury. (Courtesy of Bryan Lizotte.)

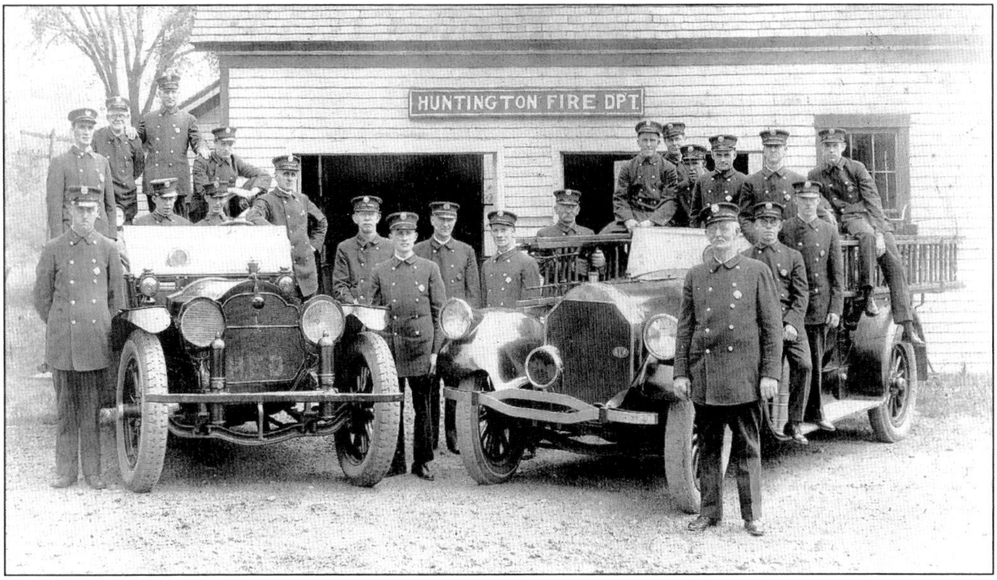

The Huntington Fire Department was established in 1919. Raising money entirely through members' dues, donations, and by hosting dances and carnivals, the department was able to purchase equipment and uniforms. The company is pictured *c.* 1920 with the department's mobile equipment.

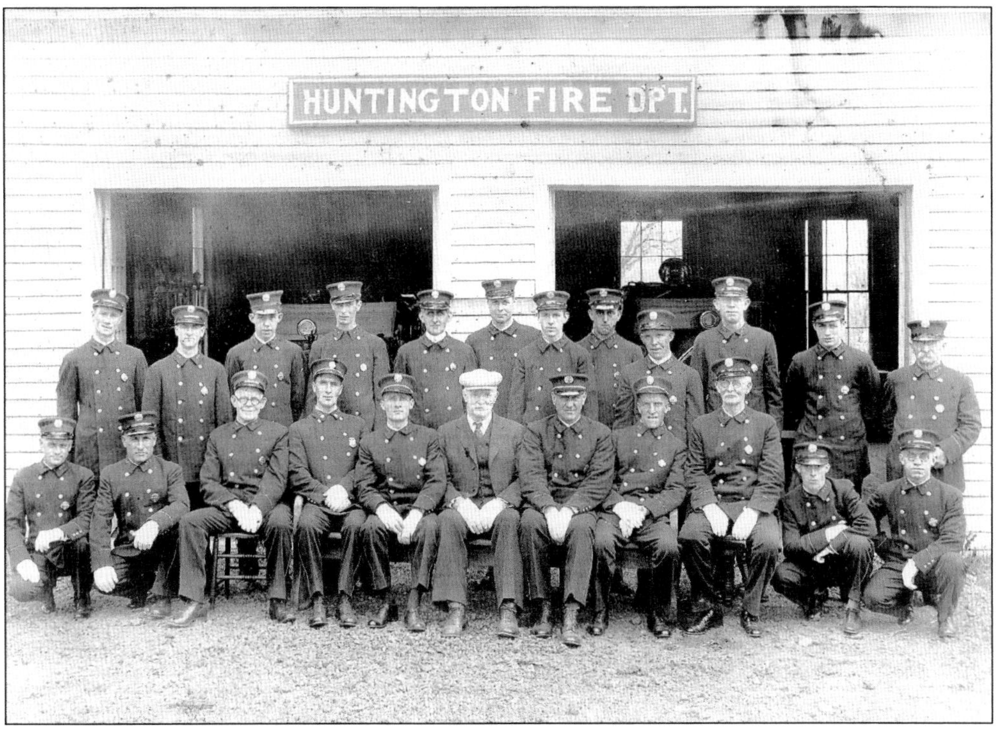

The members of the Huntington Fire Department are, from left to right, as follows: (front row) ? Ross, Tony Papale, ? Cawthra, George Arundell, Willard Nicholas, an unidentified member, Ed Vargoshi, Steve Tucker, ? Beatty, an unidentified member, and ? Chordas; (back row) John Peterson, Charlie Goldspink, Ed Millard, and nine unidentified members.

The sons of Joseph and Rosa Kassheimer were two of the many men Shelton sent into service during World War II. Charles served in the navy and Paul was a marine. They are standing in front of 51-53 Congress Avenue. (Courtesy of Randy Ritter.)

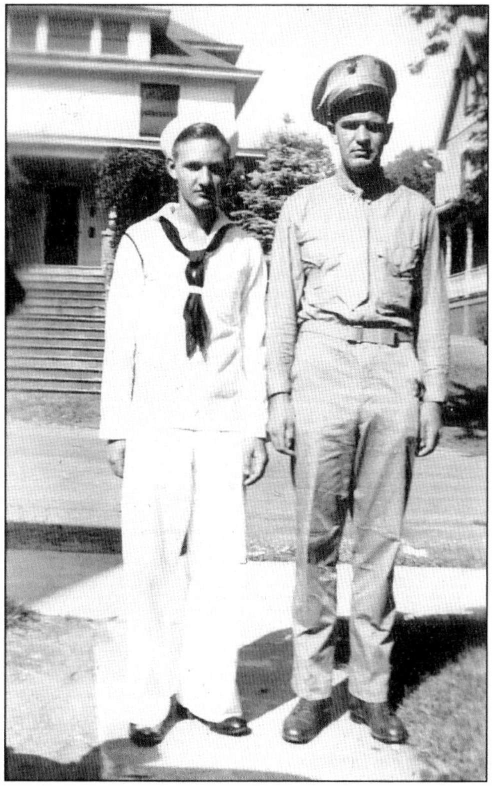

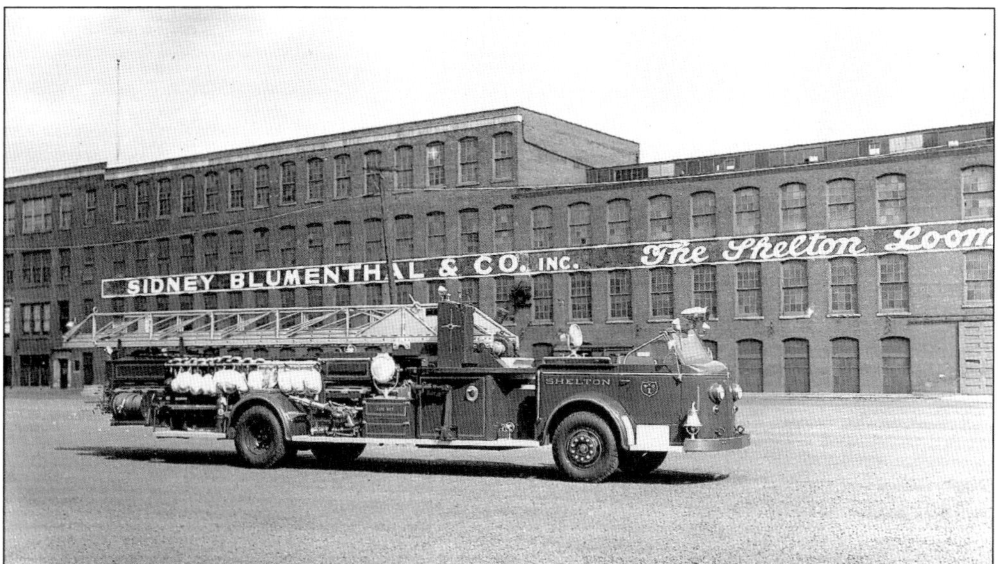

Echo Hose Hook and Ladder Company No. 1 has been protecting the residents of Shelton for more than 110 years. In 1950, the company acquired its first aerial ladder truck. (Photograph by Anthony Zisek.)

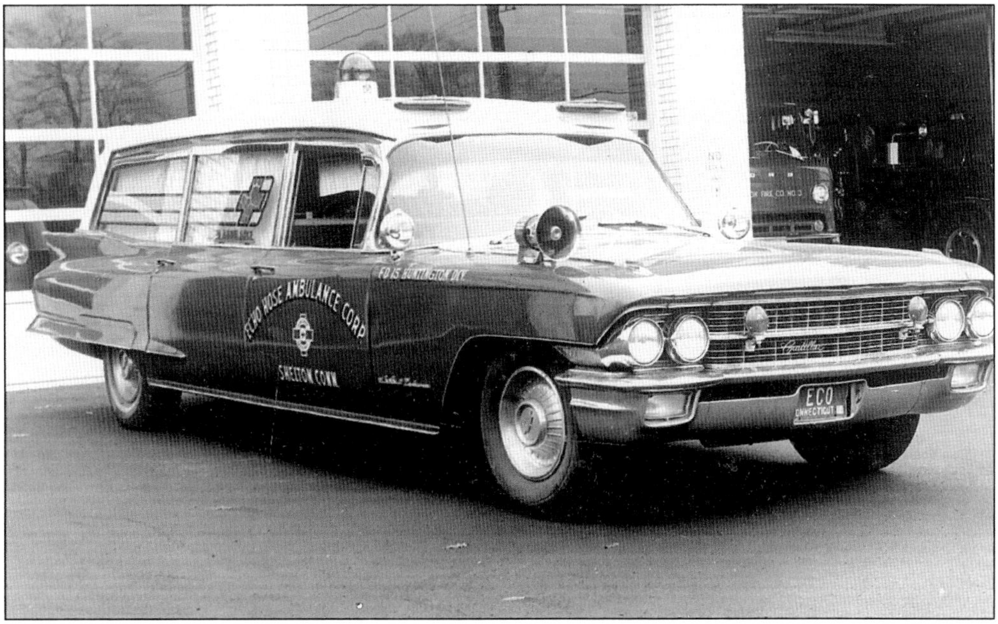

The volunteer Echo Hose Ambulance Corps was established in 1949. Here is the corps' Cadillac ambulance c. 1970.

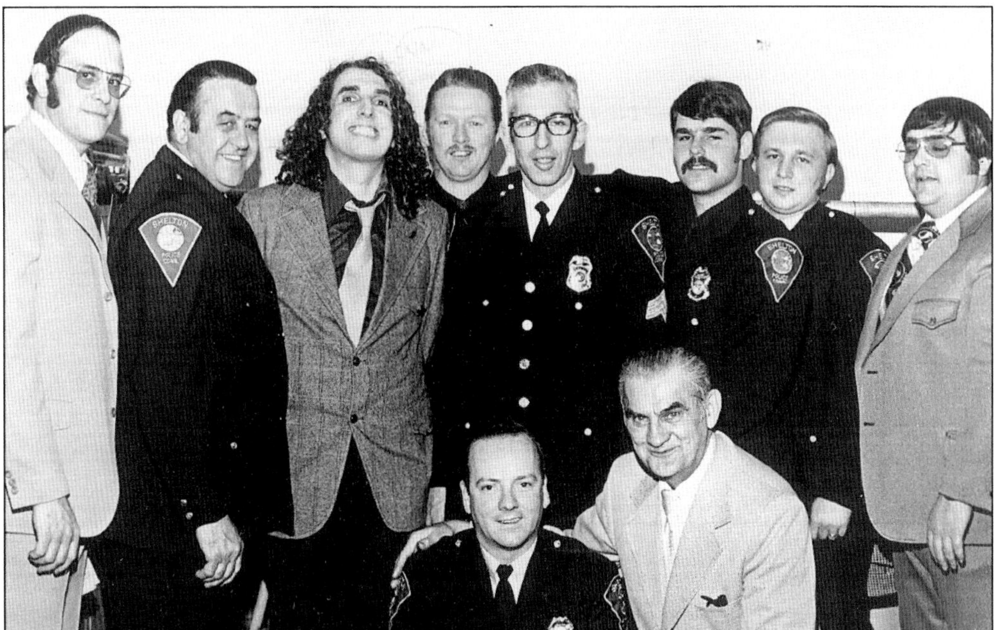

Entertainer Tiny Tim appeared at the 18th Annual Shelton Police Variety Show on February 8, 1973. The show was a vaudeville-style production and raised money for the Shelton Police Association to promote the advancement of police endeavors. The participants are, from left to right, as follows: (front row) Arthur Martin and Chester Karkut; (back row) Ken Nappi, James Santelli, Tiny Tim, Charles Sutton, George Anthony (chairperson), Joseph Bienkowski, Ned Rydzy, and Donald Ramia. (Courtesy of Fred Anthony.)

Seven

IF WALLS COULD TALK

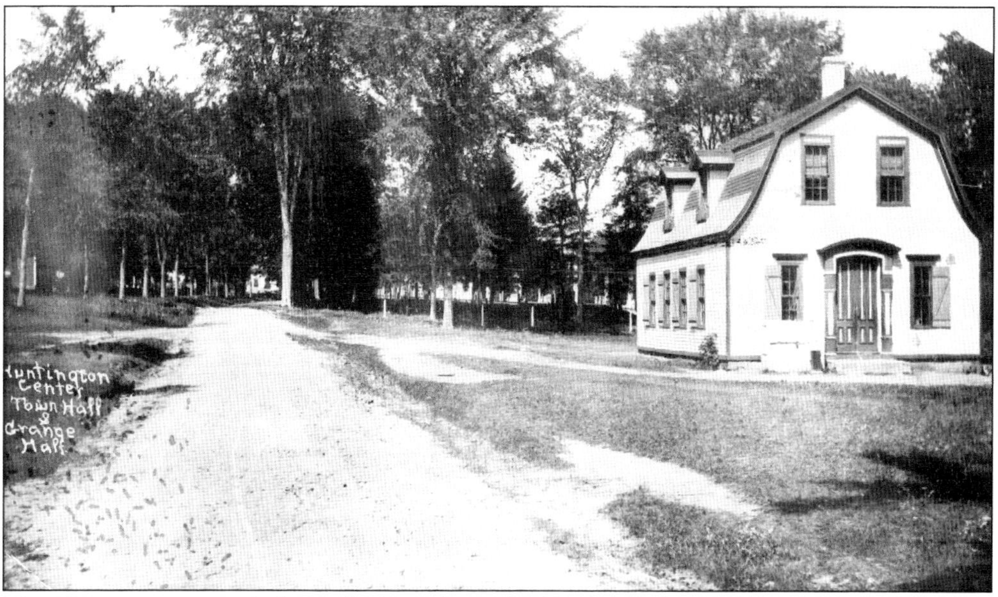

The Huntington town hall was built at the end of the green in 1869. Later, it was used as a Grange hall and a meeting place for the Philomathian Society, a literary group for young adults. The building was taken over by the Huntington Fire Department, and the current firehouse is located on the same property. (Courtesy of Philip Jones.)

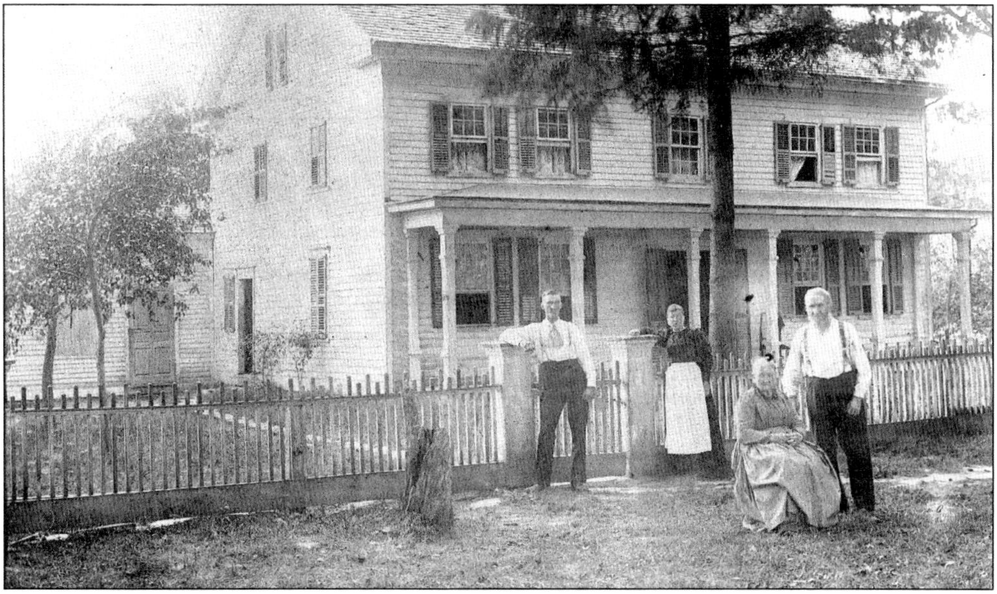

The Lattin-Parrott House was located at the corner of Bridgeport Avenue and Armstrong Road where the Staples store is now. On May 30, 1896, Charles Lattin, Rose Lattin, Lovisa Olmstead Lattin, and her husband, Lyman Lattin, gathered for their photograph. (Courtesy of the Wells family.)

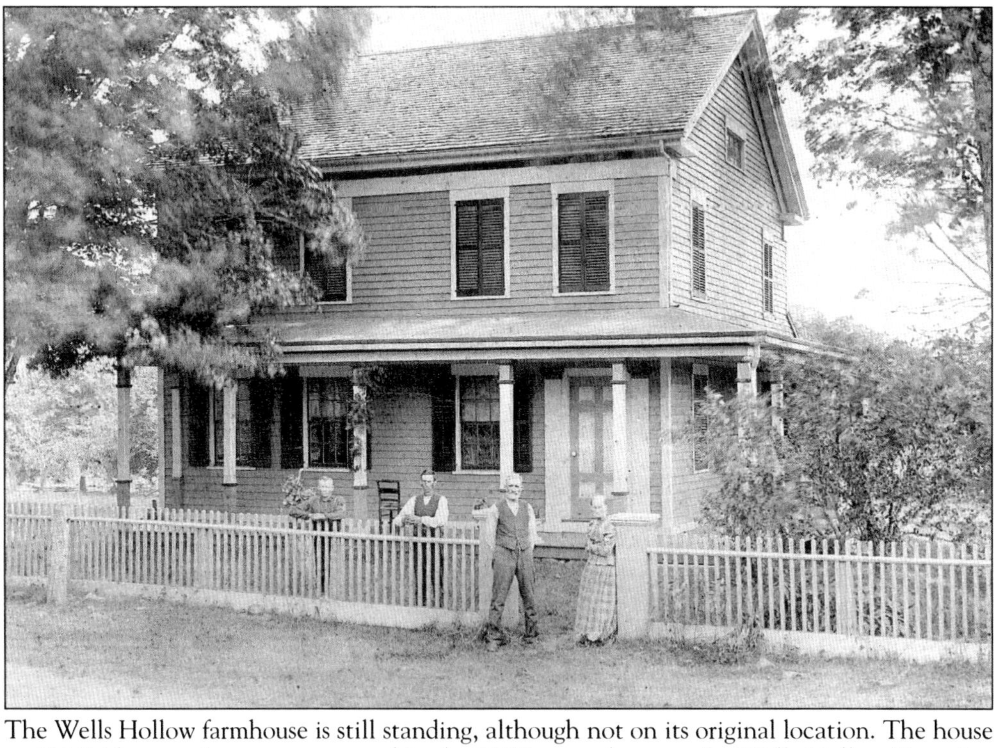

The Wells Hollow farmhouse is still standing, although not on its original location. The house at 656 Bridgeport Avenue was moved in the 1930s to make room for Wells Hollow Turnpike. On May 30, 1896, the hired man, Franklin Henry Wells, Henry Shelton Wells, and Laura Bennett Wells had their portrait taken. (Courtesy of the Wells family.)

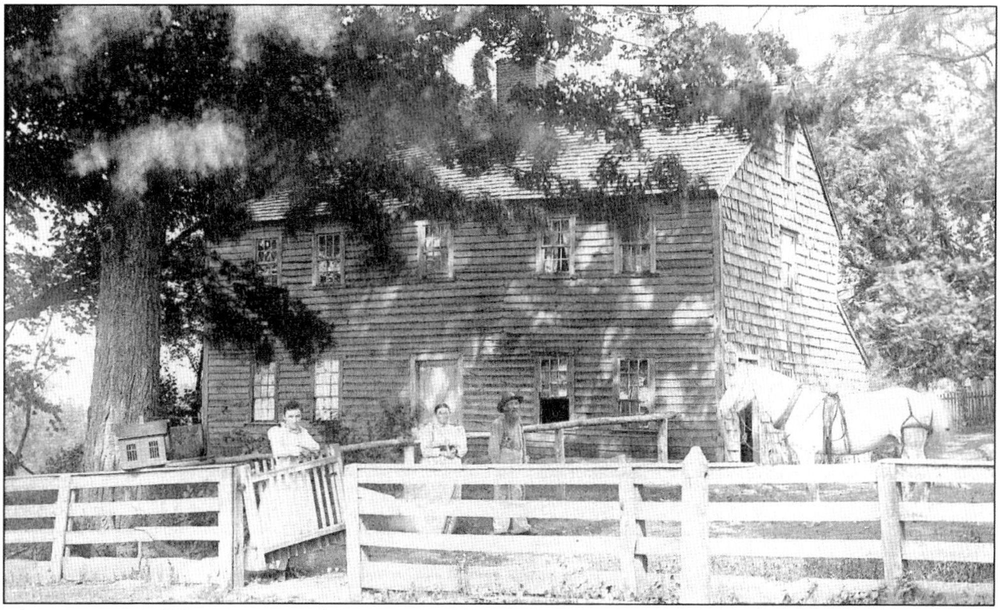

This picture and the two preceding it were all taken by the Northern Survey Company of Albany, New York. Company photographers would travel to rural areas and, for a modest fee, would photograph people. This image of the Laborie House on Walnut Tree Hill Road near the junction of Short Street is not dated; however, it seems likely that it was taken the same day as the previous two. Pictured are Aunt Fannie, Grandma Charlotte Hubbell Laborie, and Grandpa Laborie.

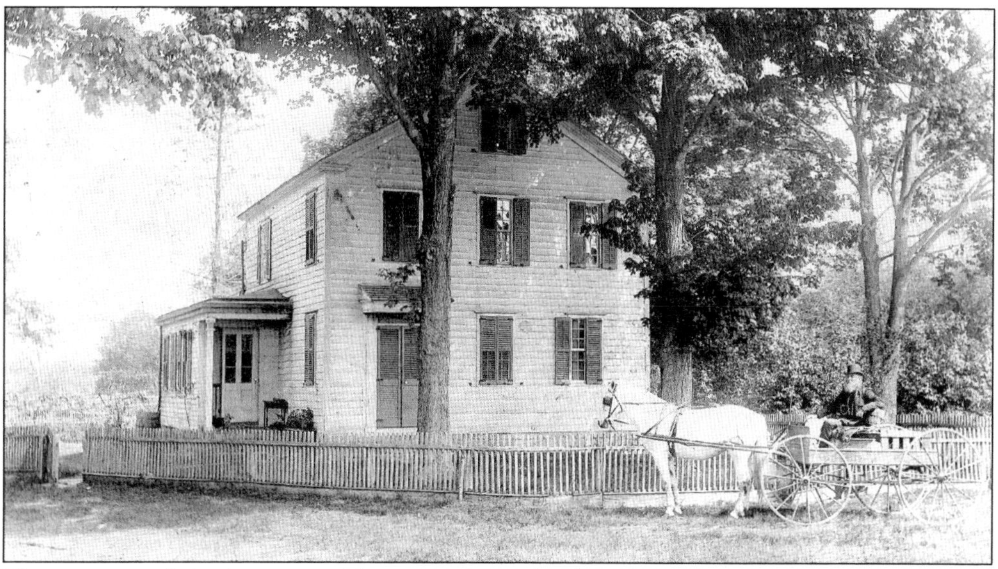

The area around this house at 1 Thompson Street has been known as "Bloody Point" for many years. The reason behind the grim name is unclear. Here is the house, which is extant, around the turn of the century.

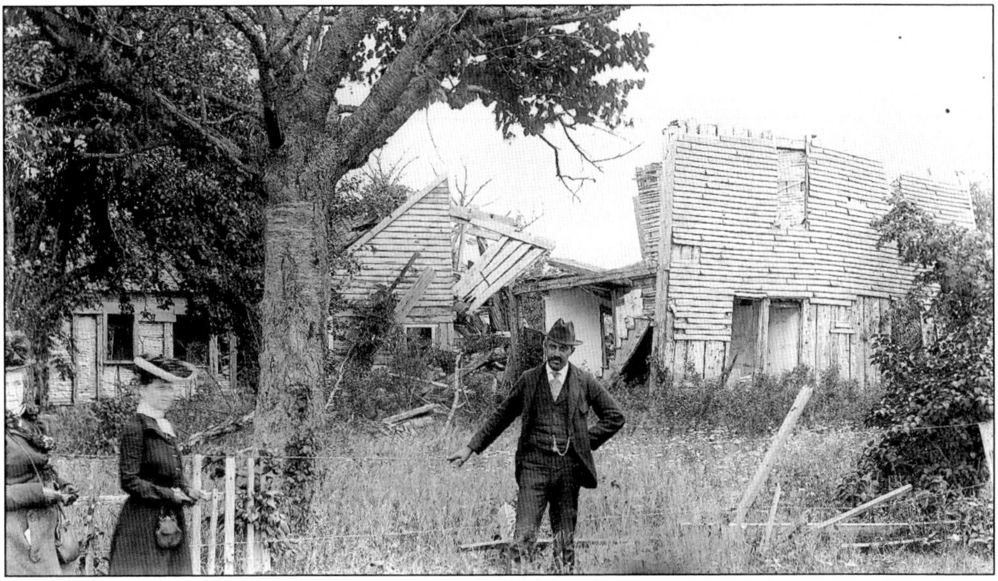

The Salt Box House was built on Beardsley Road in 1758 by Daniel Shelton, grandson of the Daniel Shelton who helped found Ripton Parish. Three generations of the Shelton family lived there.

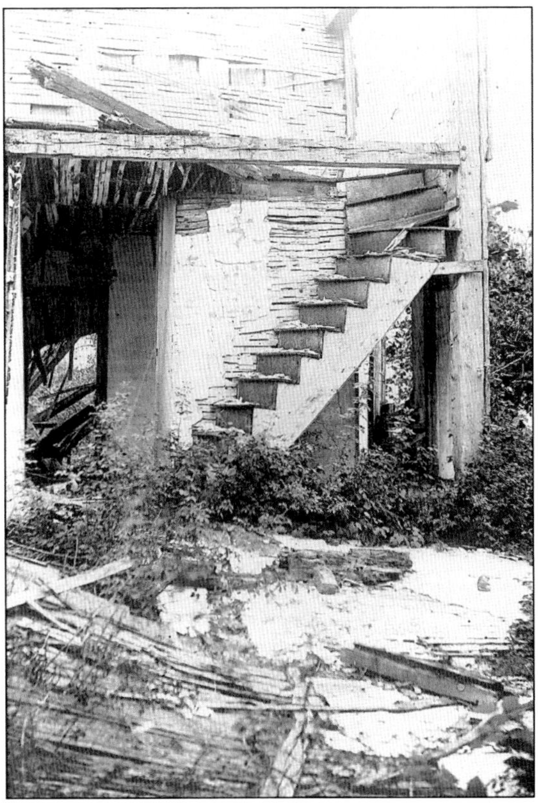

Published in 1900, *The Salt Box House, Eighteenth Century Life in a New England Hill Town*, written by Jane de Forest Shelton, fictionalized the lives of the occupants of the house. Although the house succumbed to neglect around the turn of the century, it is remembered through the book and is featured on the official seal of the city of Shelton. (Photograph by Miss Hubbard; courtesy of Philip Jones.)

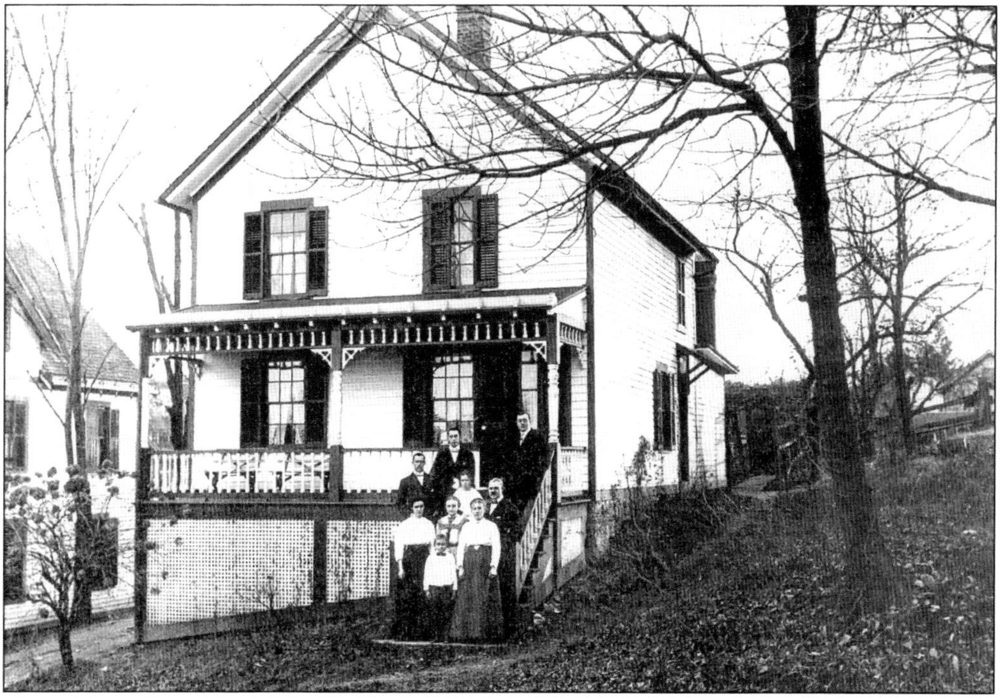

The pride of the Didsbury family comes through in this c. 1910 photograph in front of their 16 Perry Hill Road home. Robert Didsbury emigrated from England and worked at the International Silver Company at 6 Bridge Street. (Courtesy of Dorothy Didsbury Mills.)

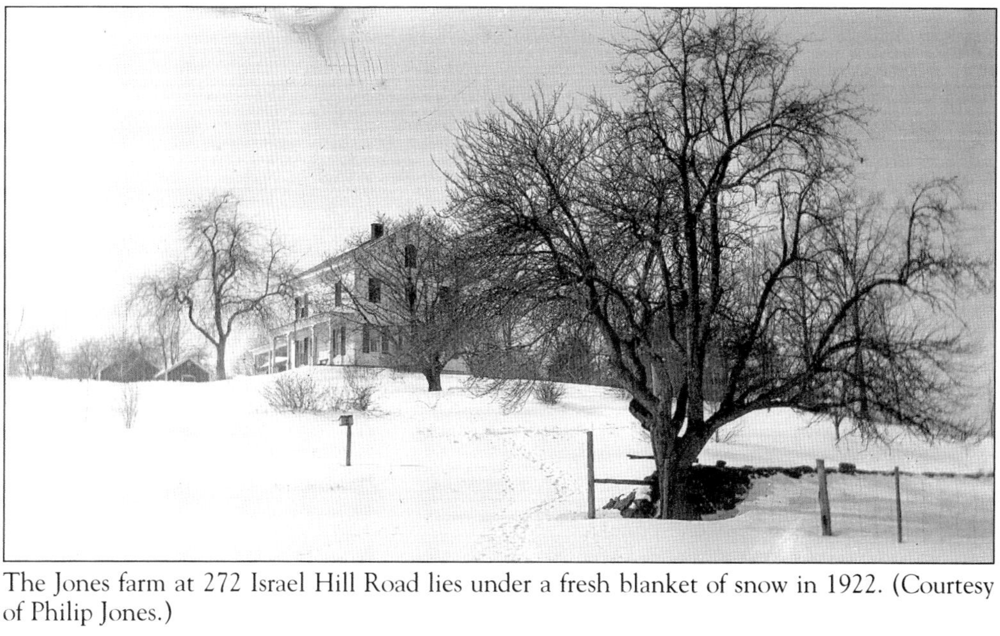

The Jones farm at 272 Israel Hill Road lies under a fresh blanket of snow in 1922. (Courtesy of Philip Jones.)

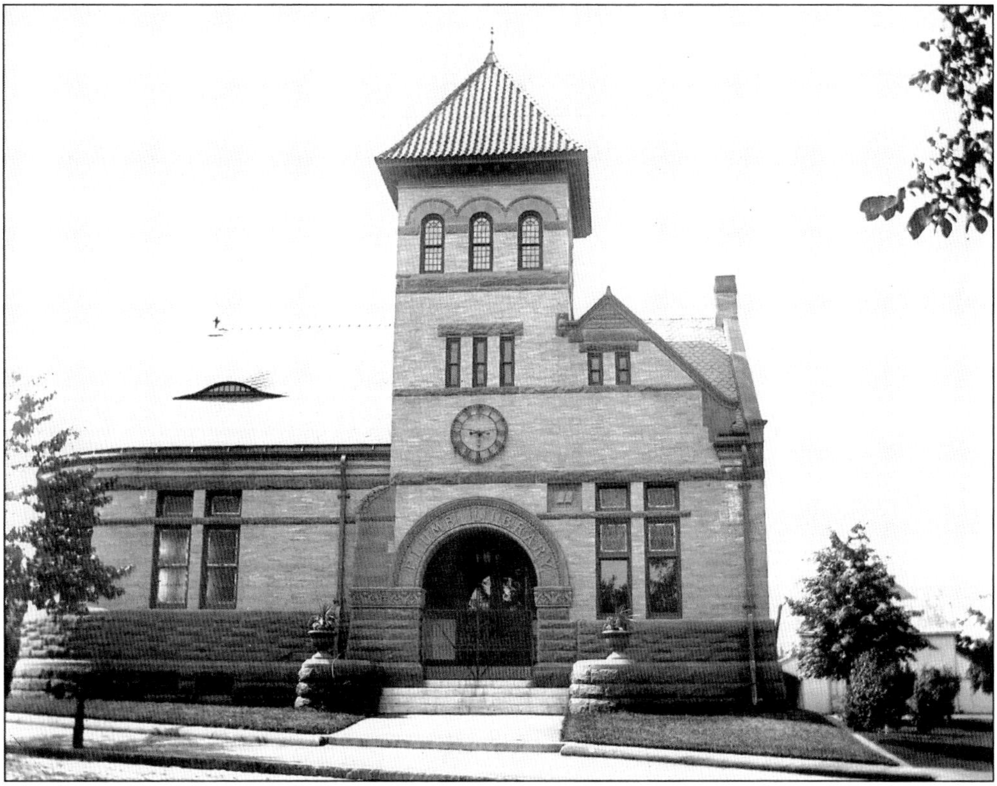

The first public library in Shelton opened on February 1, 1893. It was housed on the second floor of the Pierpont Block and contained around 1,000 books. David Wells Plumb, a founder of the library, was working toward a more permanent home when he died on June 29, 1893.

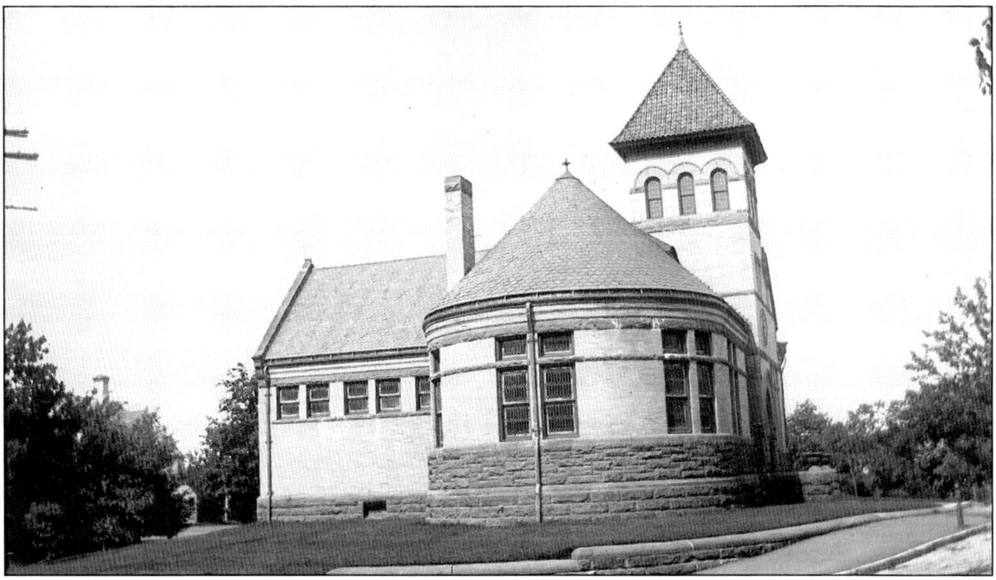

Plumb made no provisions for the library in his will. His brother and primary beneficiary, Horace S. Plumb, respected his wishes and donated money from the estate for the construction of a library. Louise W. Plumb, his widow, donated the lot at 65 Wooster Street.

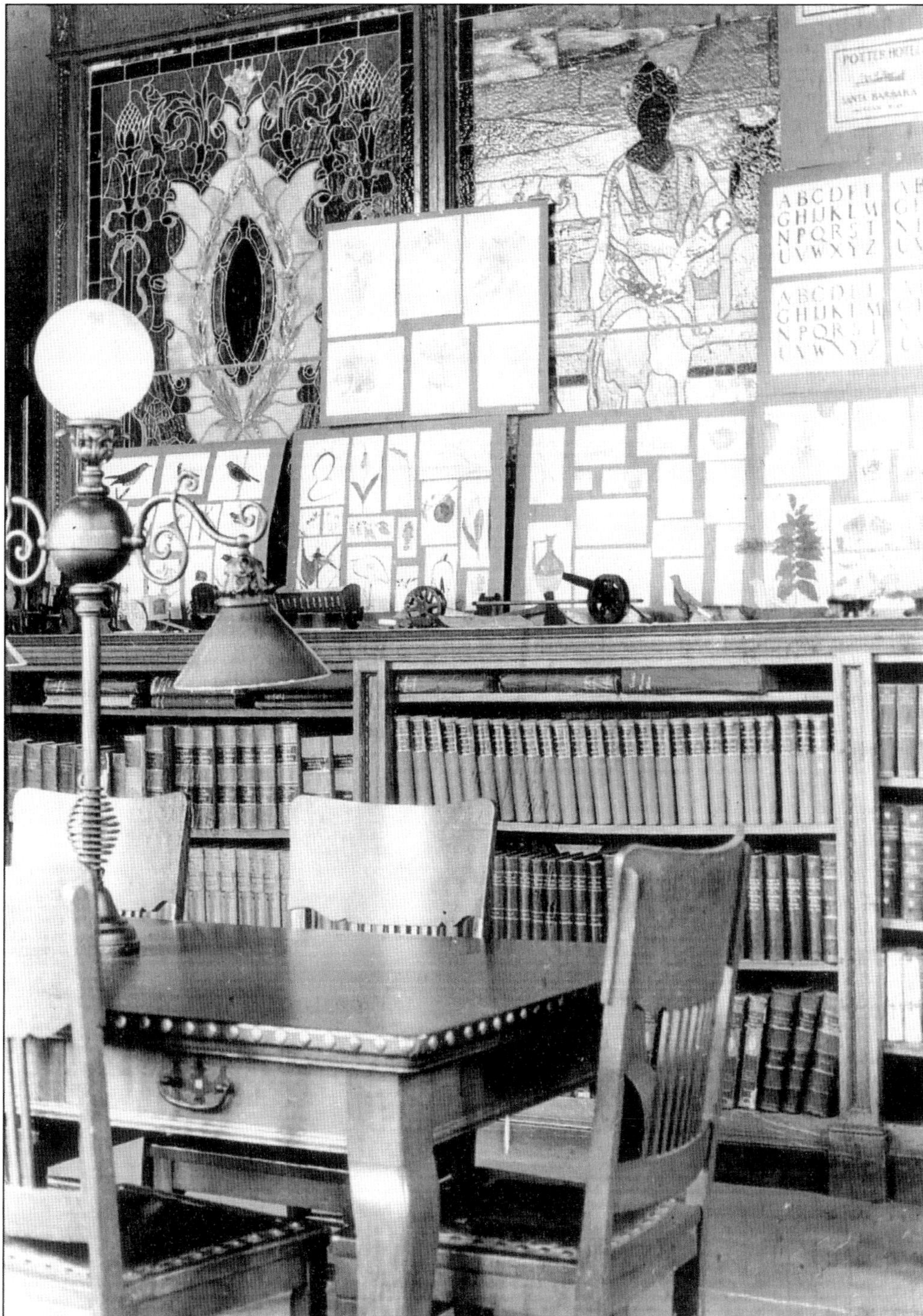

The official dedication of the Plumb Memorial Library was held on December 4, 1895. The building is a fine example of the Romanesque style and was designed by Charles T. Beardsley Jr. of Bridgeport. Seen here is the stained-glass partition that once shielded the reading room from front door drafts. (Courtesy of Bryan Lizotte.)

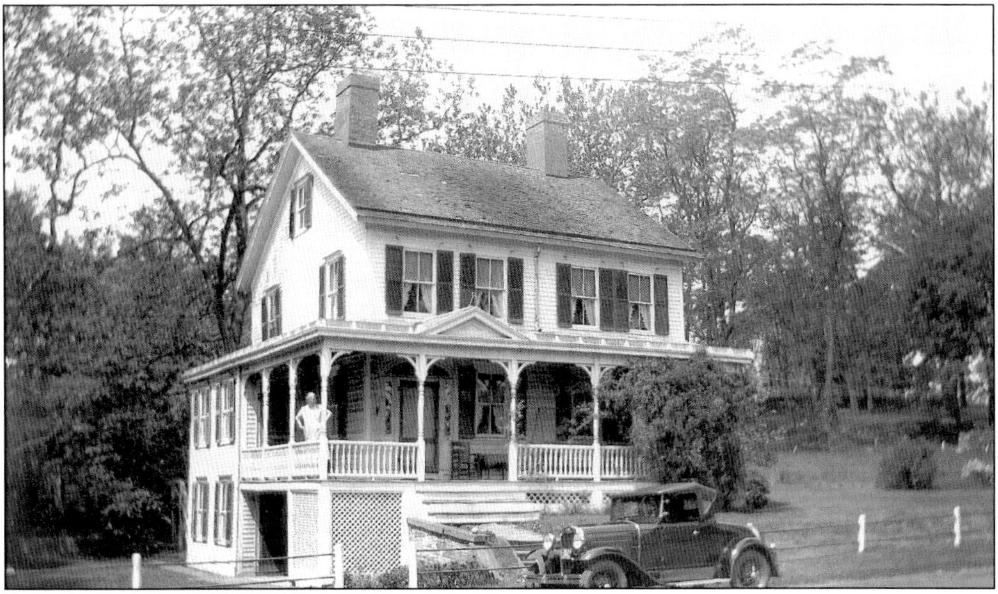

This *c.* 1935 view of 199 Huntington Street shows the porch that once graced the home. While the house is extant, only the side segment of the porch remains.

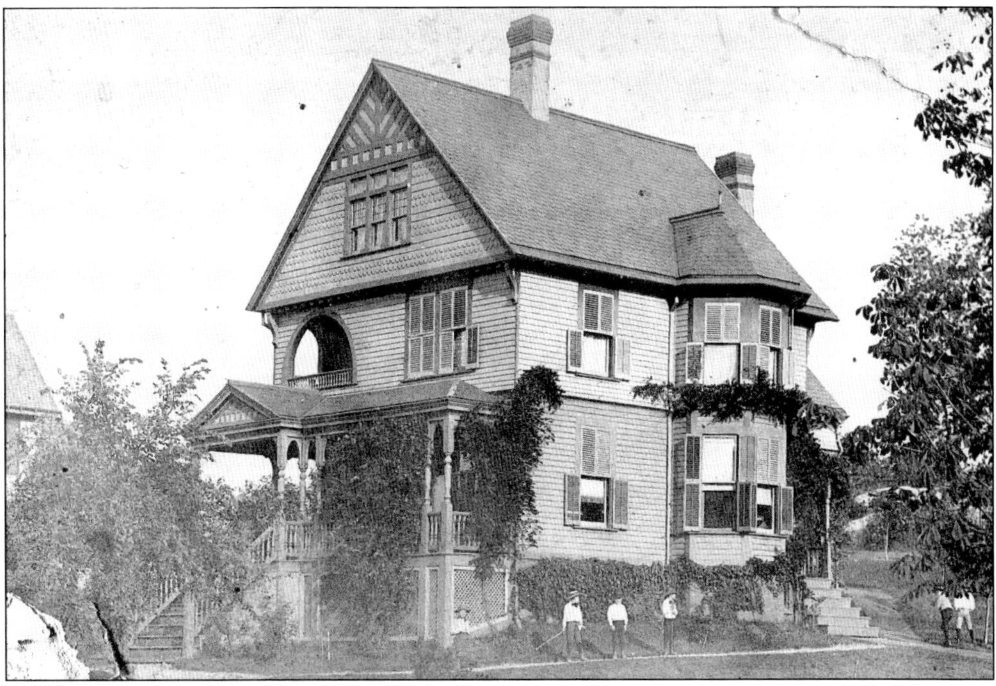

Downtown Shelton and Derby are full of Victorian-style houses. Factory owners and managers lined the streets with testaments to their success. The house of William Holmes at 120 Myrtle Street, *c.* 1900, is an excellent example of this trend. Holmes was a foreman in the plating department at the International Silver Company and the postmaster for Shelton.

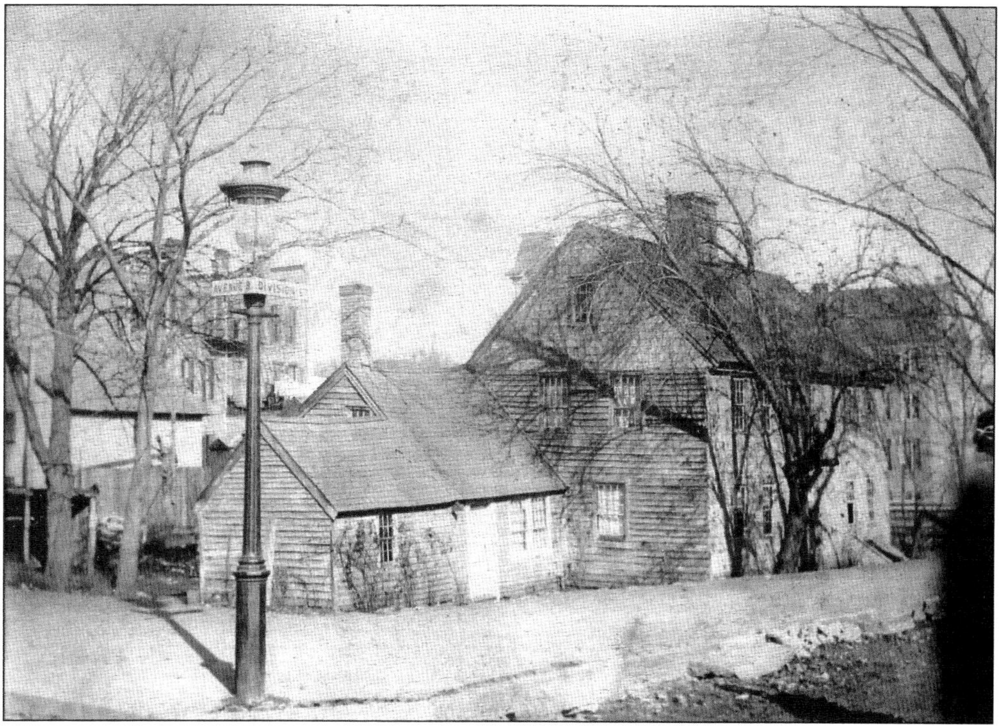

Issac Hull, hero of the War of 1812 and the USS *Constitution*, was born in Derby, but he spent his childhood in the Bennett Home, which was on Division Avenue. The house burned in 1890.

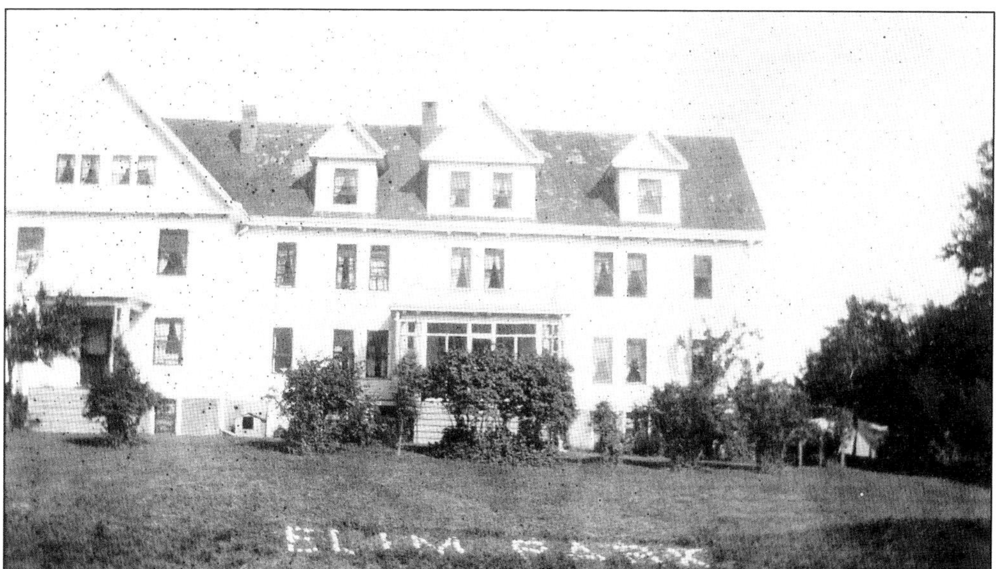

Elim Park was a Swedish Baptist retirement home on the Housatonic River, near what is now the city landfill. (Courtesy of Philip Jones.)

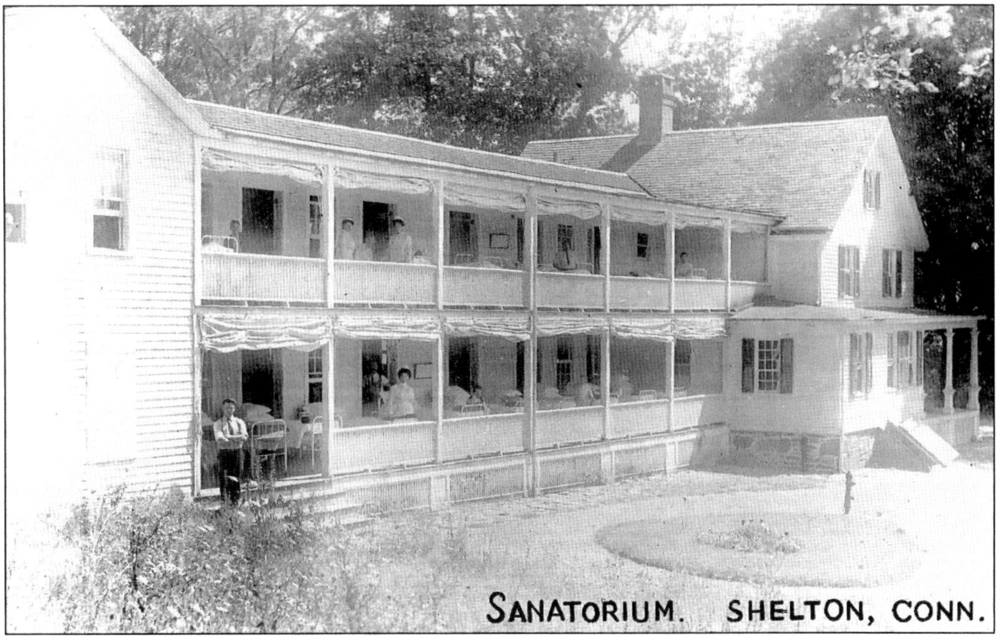

Laurel Heights originally opened in a converted farmhouse on River Road as the Fairfield County State Tuberculosis Sanatorium in 1910. In 1912, Eugene O'Neill (1888–1953) was a patient for 48 hours before transferring to a private facility. He would immortalize the facility as the Hilltown Sanitarium in his play *Long Day's Journey into Night*. (Courtesy of Bryan Lizotte.)

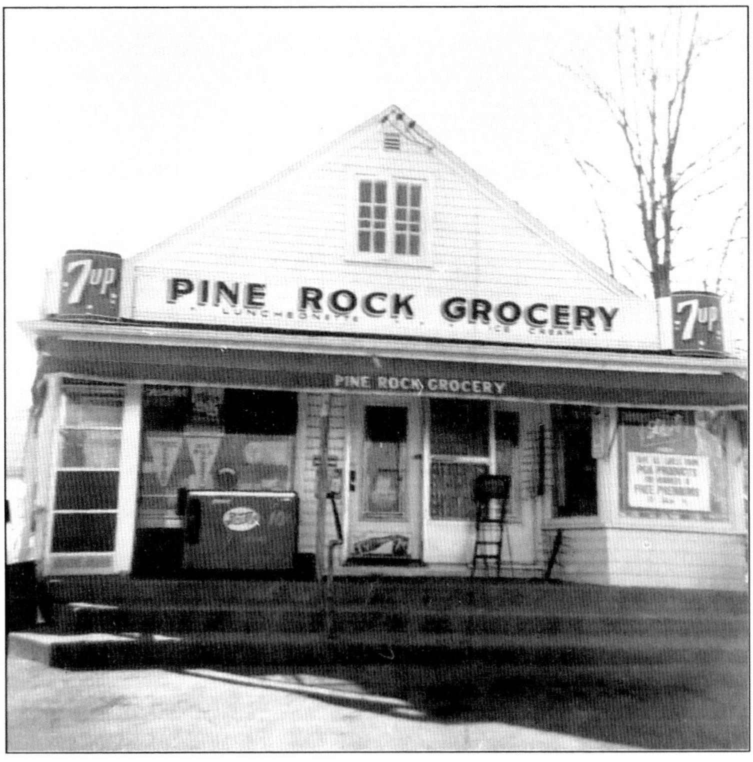

The Pine Rock Grocery, at 845 River Road, opened in the mid-1950s. Run for many years by Joseph and Anna Chulak, it is now known as the Pine Rock Deli.

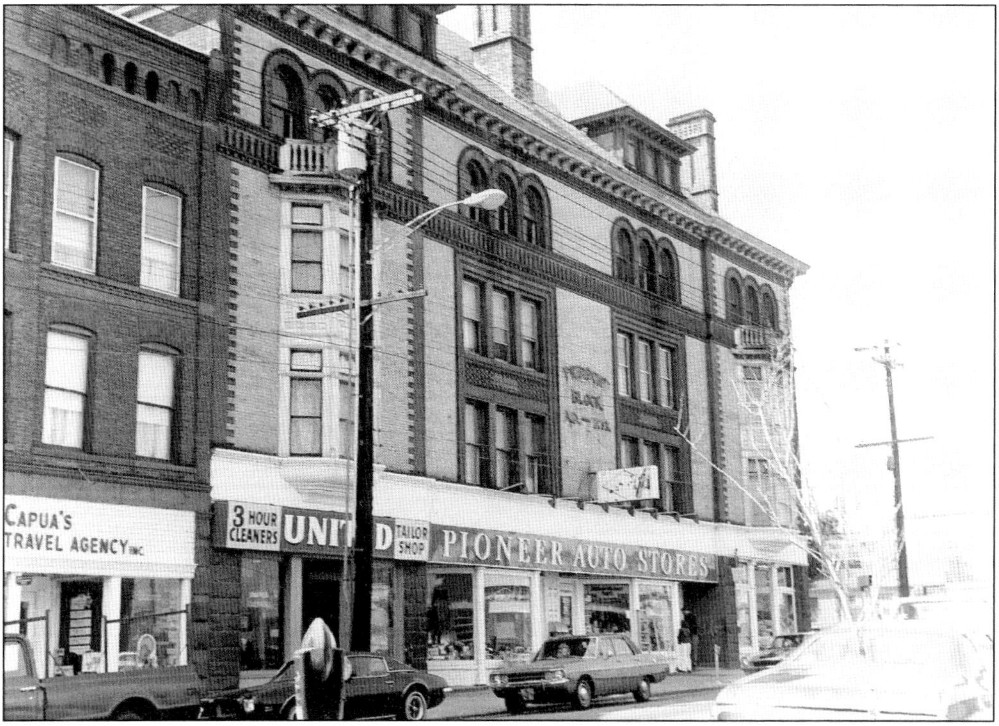

The Pierpont Block, pictured here *c.* 1975, is named in honor of J. Pierpont Morgan, one of the original investors in the building. (Photograph by Curt A. Scheibner.)

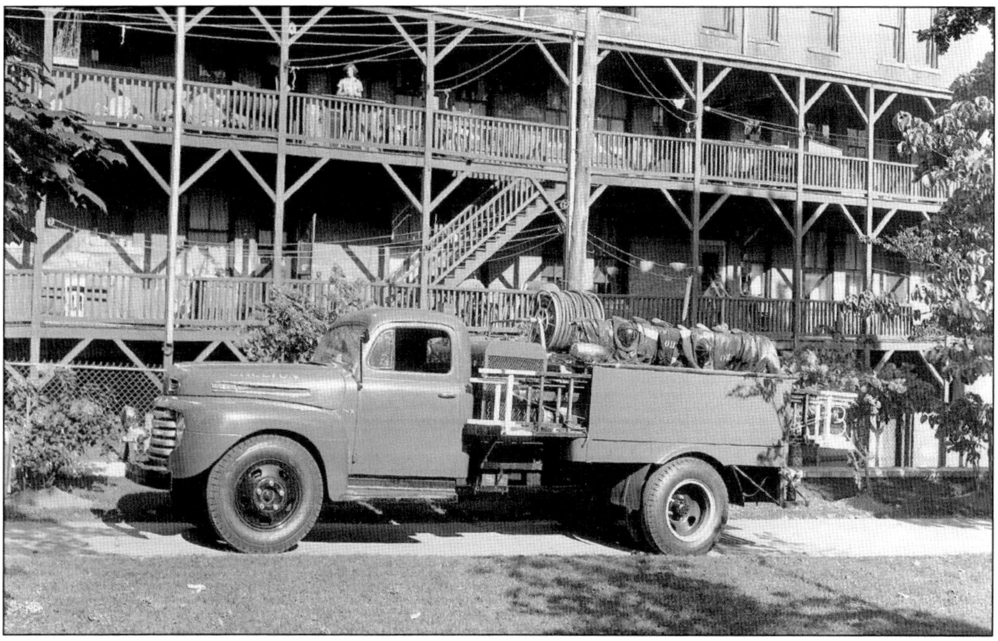

This *c.* 1950 photograph, taken to document a new fire truck for the Echo Hose Hook and Ladder Company No. 1, shows the back of the Pierpont Block building. The porches running from end to end and the profusion of clotheslines testify to the number of people who lived downtown. (Photograph by Anthony Zisek.)

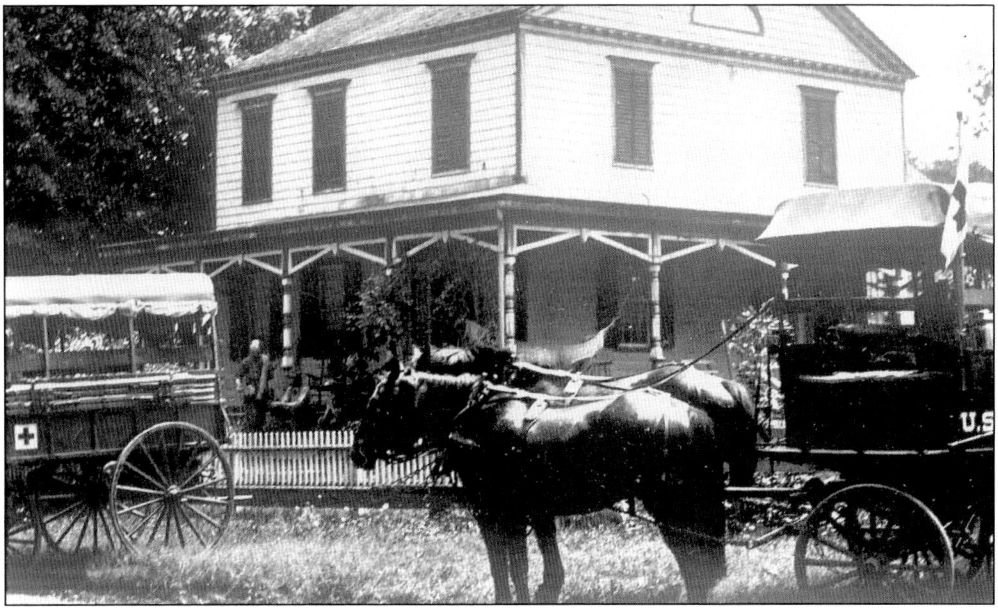

Built in the Greek Revival style around 1820 by Hezekiah Marks, the house at the corner of Shelton Avenue and Old Shelton Road had acquired a Victorian-style porch and color scheme by the August 1912 War Games when the ambulances rolled by. When this photograph was taken, it was the home of Harry and Gertrude Brownson and their son Sheldon.

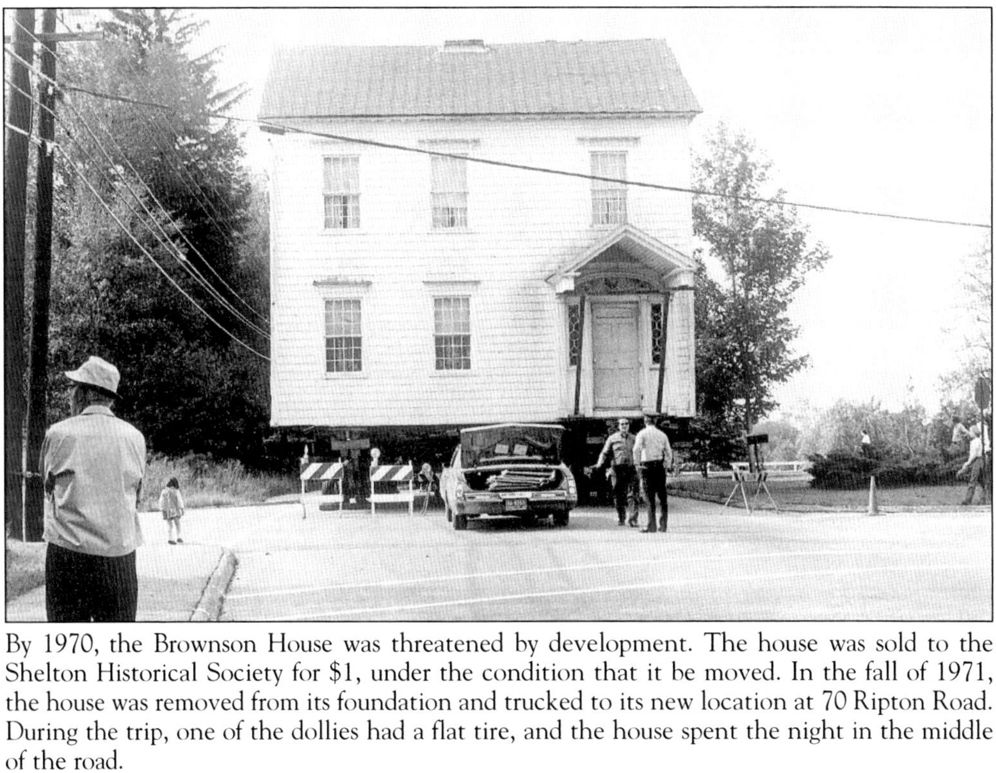

By 1970, the Brownson House was threatened by development. The house was sold to the Shelton Historical Society for $1, under the condition that it be moved. In the fall of 1971, the house was removed from its foundation and trucked to its new location at 70 Ripton Road. During the trip, one of the dollies had a flat tire, and the house spent the night in the middle of the road.

Eight

CELEBRATIONS

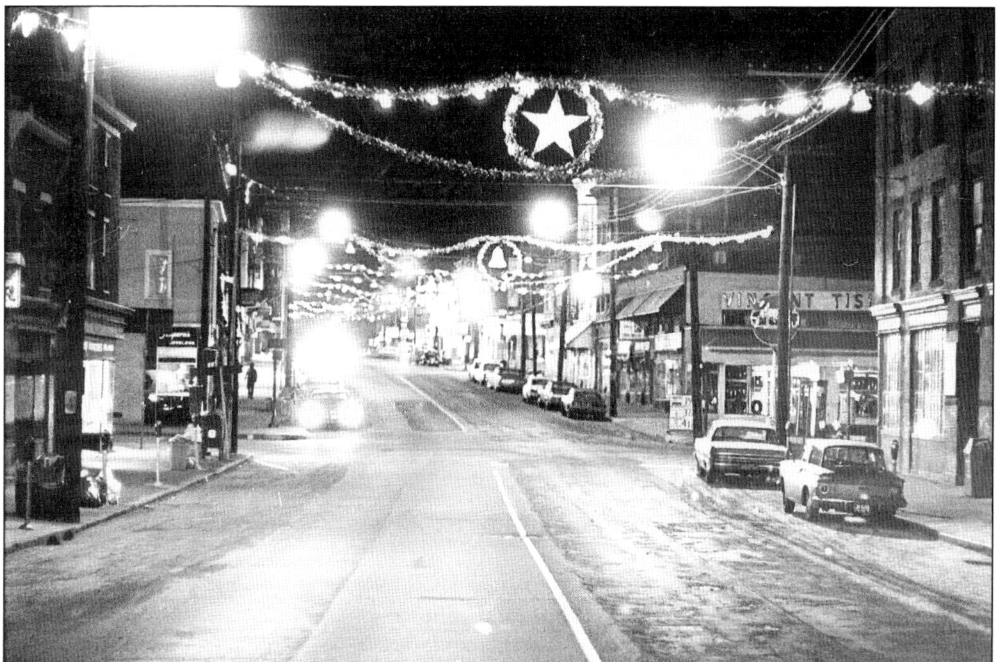

Howe Avenue is ready for Christmas on December 22, 1971. (Photograph by Fred M. Thomas; courtesy of the Shelton Economic Development Corporation.)

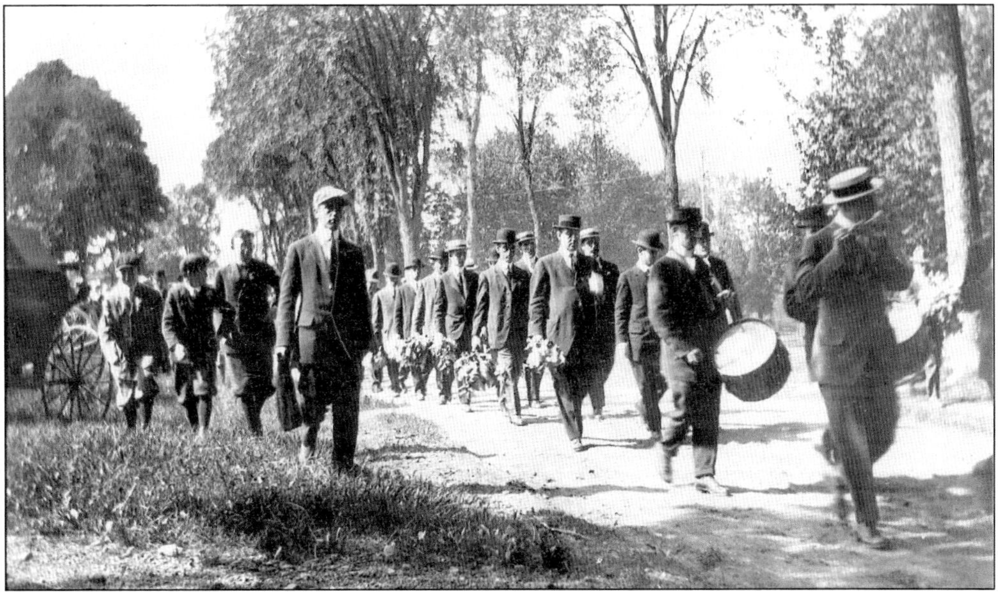

Gentlemen march through Huntington c. 1910 on their way to the cemetery on the green to lay wreaths on Memorial Day.

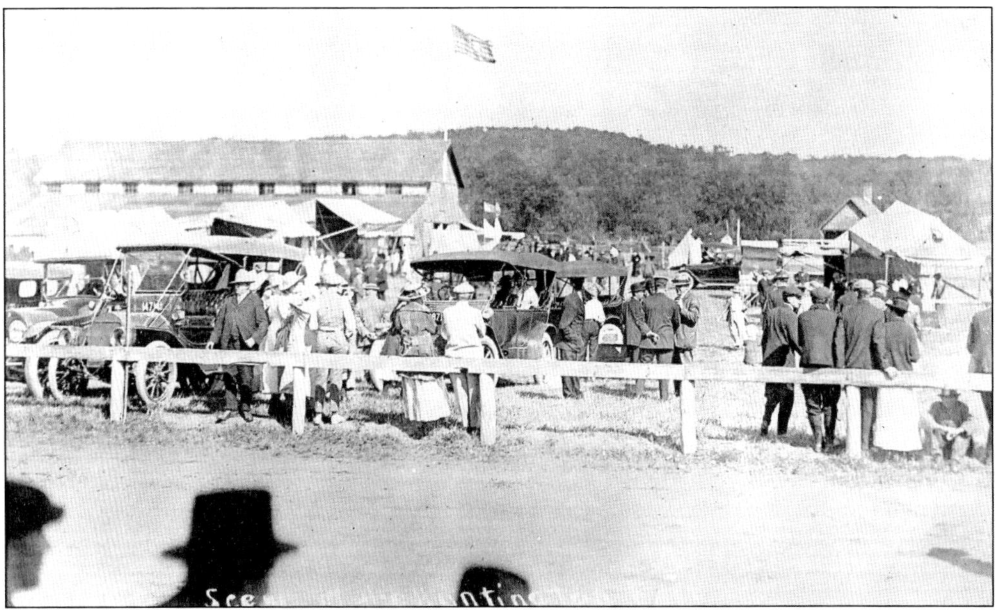

The Huntington Fair was held by the Huntington Agricultural Society on Mohegan Road, east of Booth Hill Road. The fair ran for several days in September from 1846 until World War I. This c. 1910 photograph shows people lined up around the racetrack. Races were a very popular event.

This Christmas tree at the Jones farm in 1919 or 1920 was a cedar. Brothers Newell (left) and Philip Jr. are enjoying their presents. (Photograph by Helen Jones; courtesy of Philip Jones.)

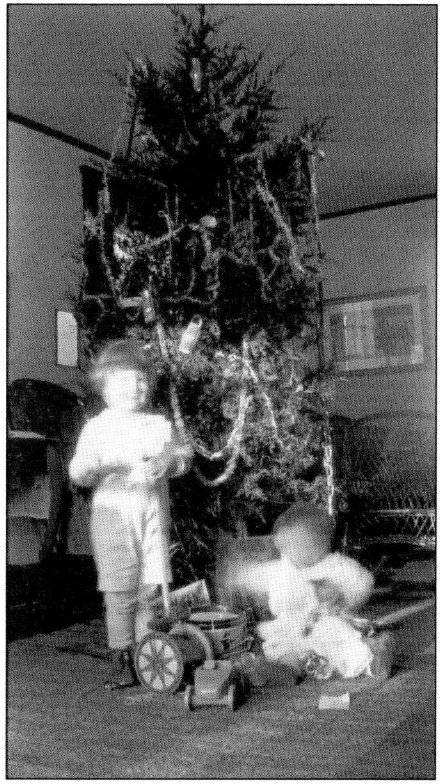

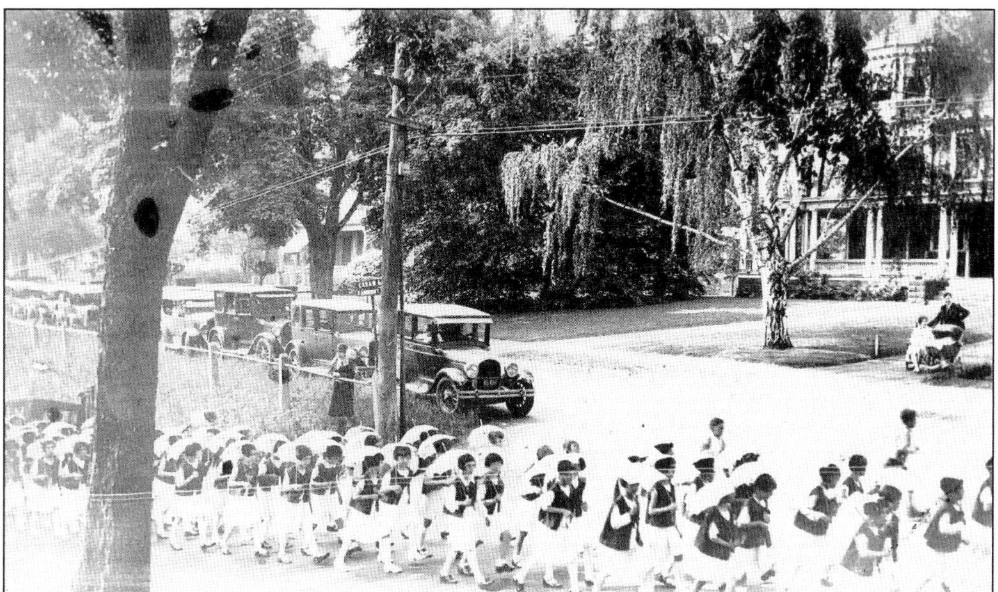

Marchers gather for the Memorial Day parade at Coram Avenue and Fairmont Place *c.* 1930. (Courtesy of Dorothy Didsbury Mills.)

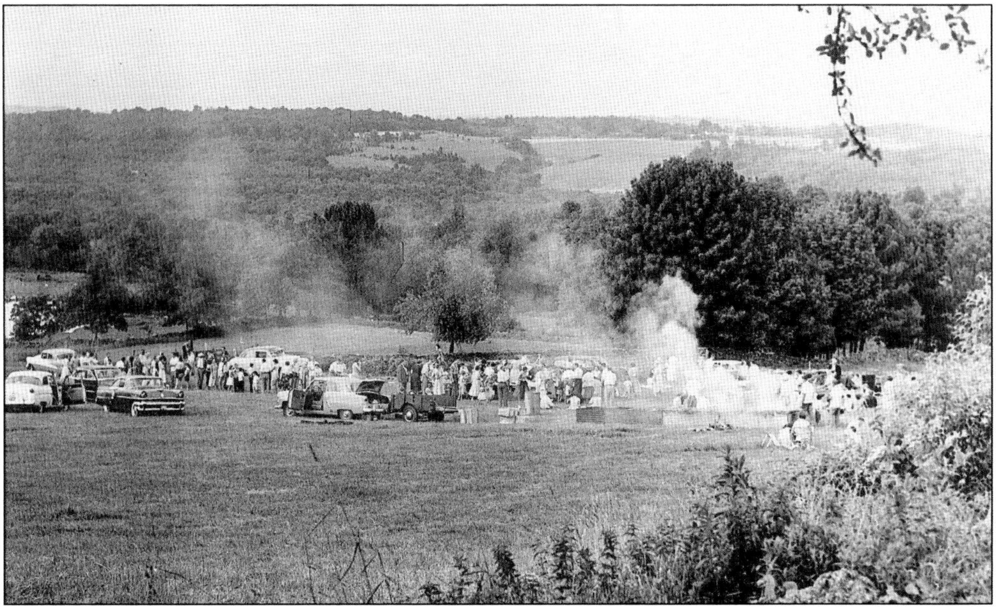

More than 500 people attended the Chicken Bar-B-Q sponsored by the Huntington Congregational Church at the Jones farm on June 23, 1956. Tickets were $1.75 a person, with milk and dessert costing an extra 25¢. (Photograph by Jack Stock; courtesy of Philip Jones.)

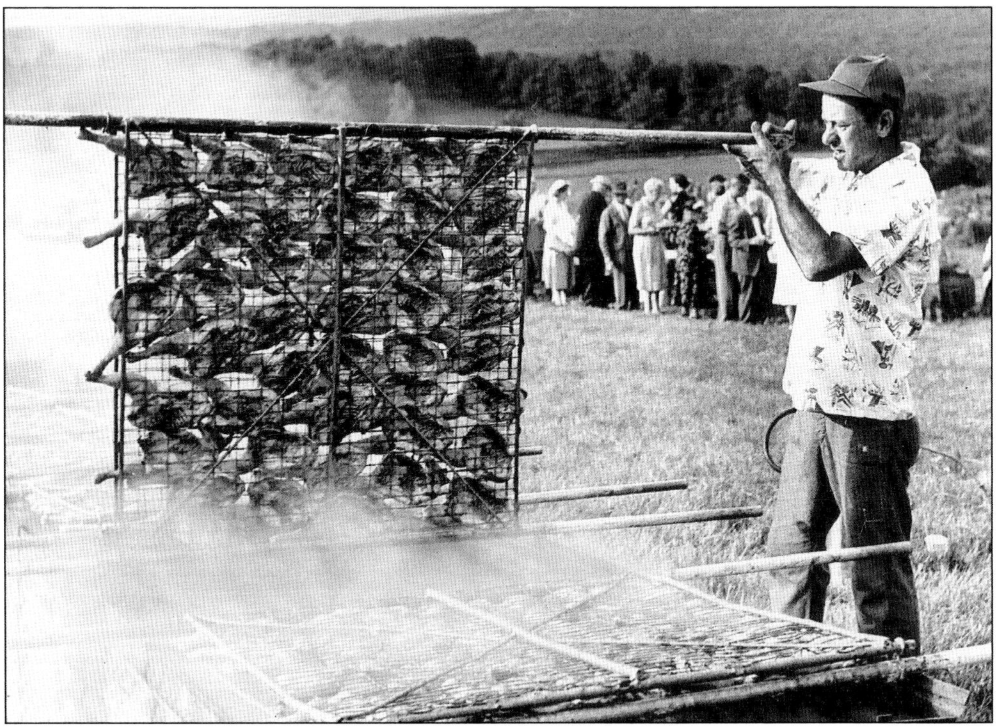

Here, Milton Heyse is turning the half-chicken portions, each weighing over one pound. Potato chips, spring salad, rolls and butter, coffee or milk, and strawberry ice-cream sundaes were also served. (Photograph by Jack Stock; courtesy of Philip Jones.)

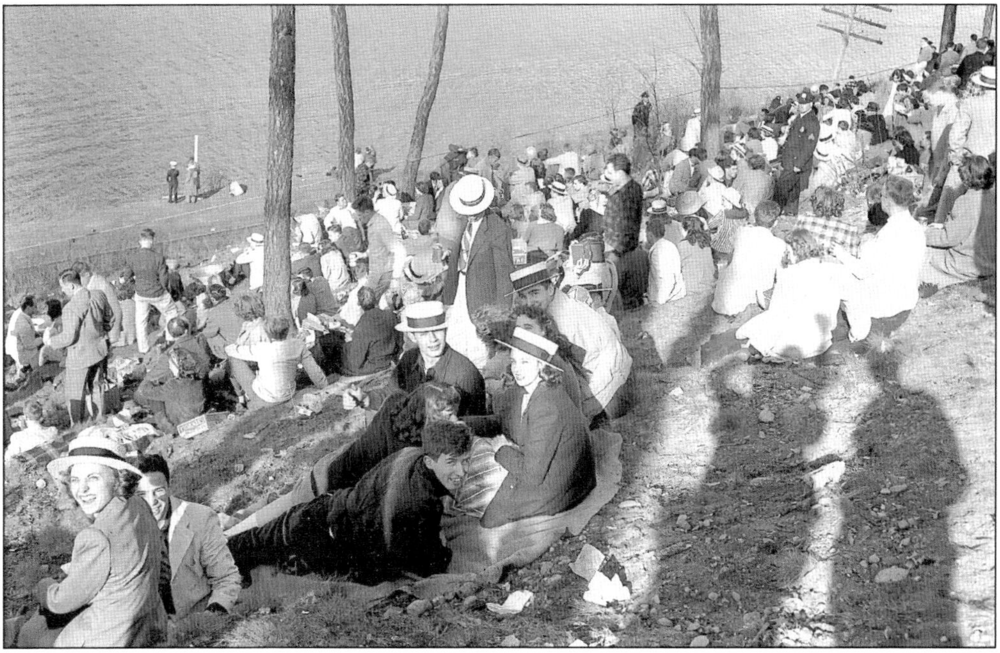

Yale University began racing sculls on the Housatonic River in 1918. During the first half of the 20th century, the Derby Day Regatta was held every spring. As seen in this *c.* 1950 photograph, hundreds of people would gather along the banks of the river to celebrate the races. (Photograph by Anthony Ziesek.)

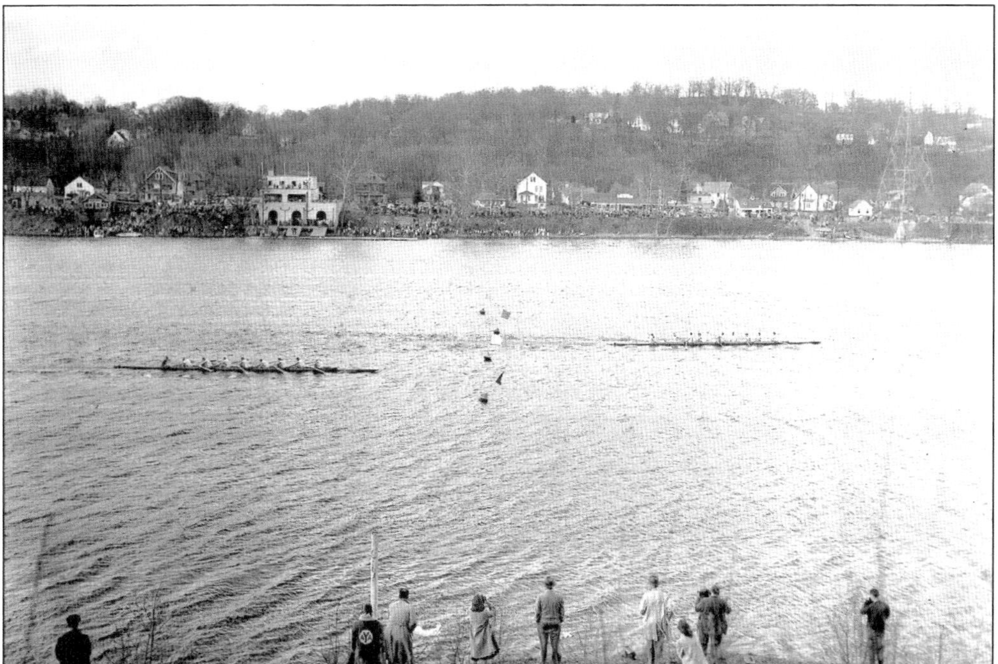

The Bob Cook Boathouse, belonging to Yale University, is seen from the Shelton side of the river in this *c.* 1950 photograph. It has since been replaced by the Gilder Boathouse, which is more than double the size of the original. (Photograph by Anthony Ziesek.)

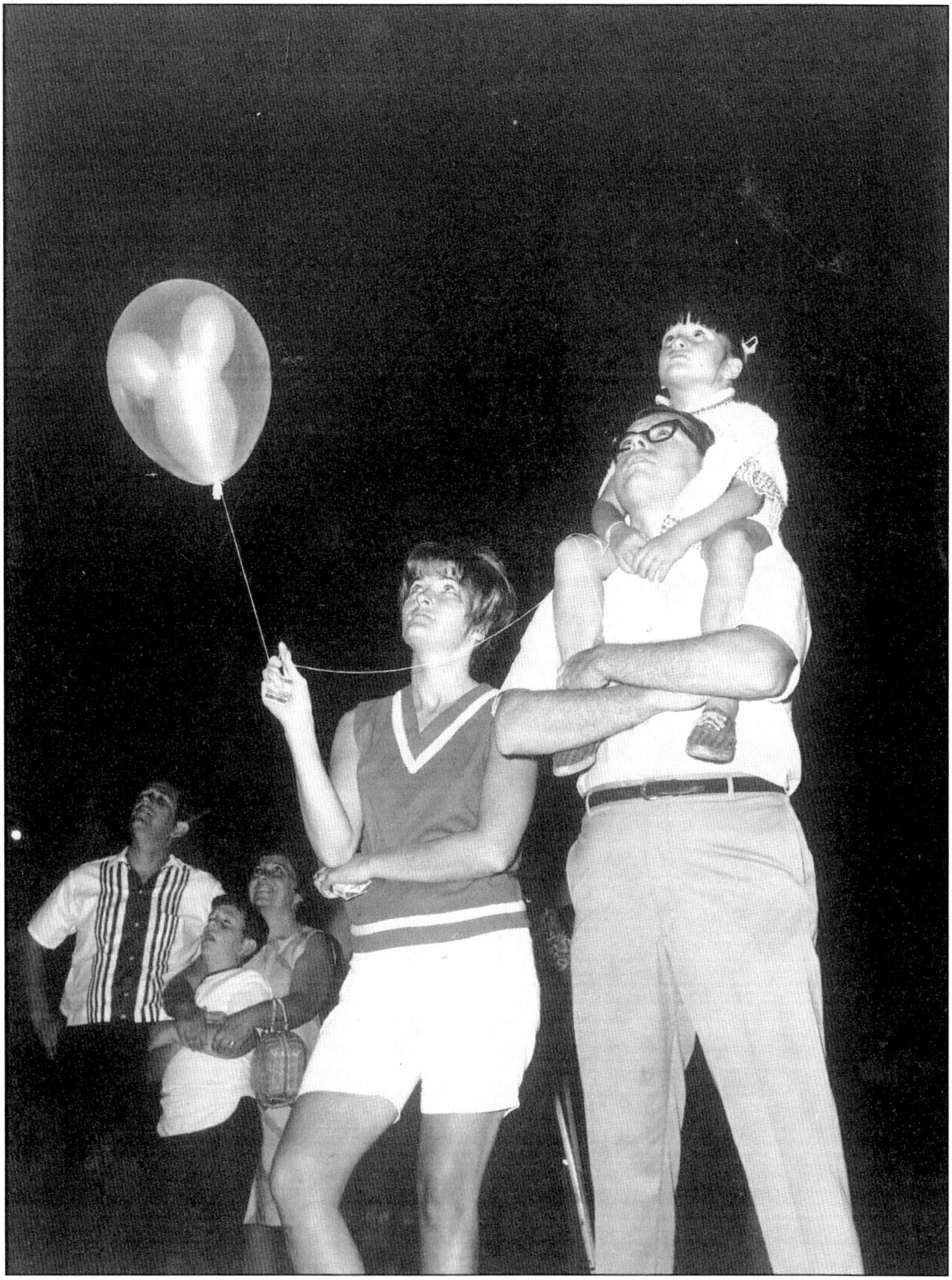

Carol (left), Dean, and Kim Taylor view the fireworks at Lafayette Field on July 3, 1964. Simonetti Cleaners donated the balloons. (Photograph by Curt Scheibner.)

Nine

FACES

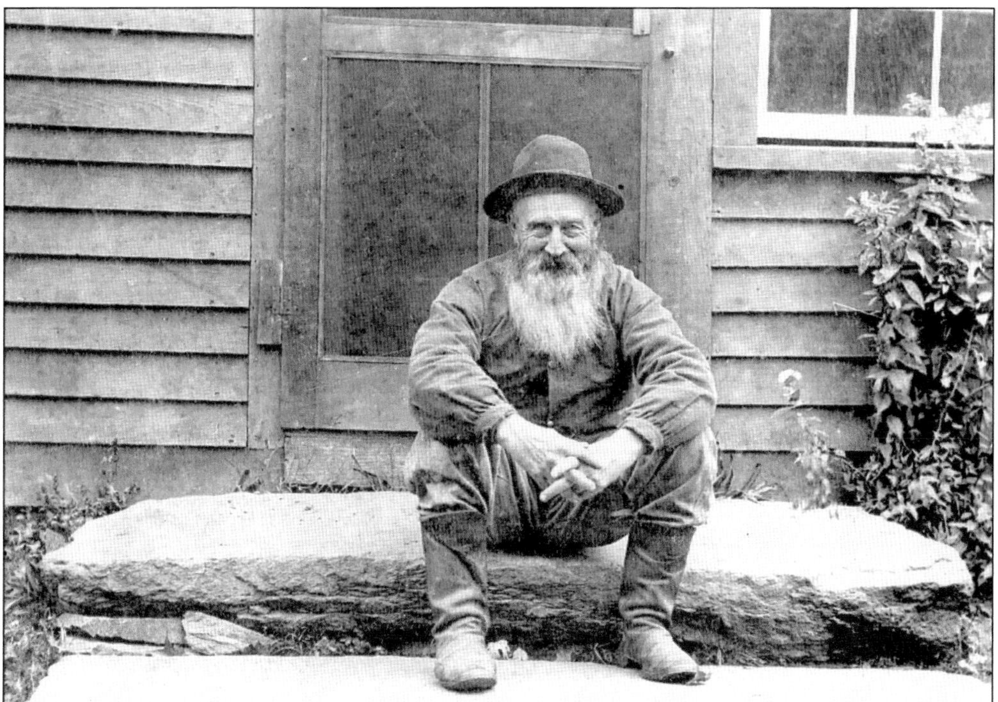

Charles Richard Hubbell of White Hills enjoys a rest on the side stoop in 1899. (Photograph by H.B.T.)

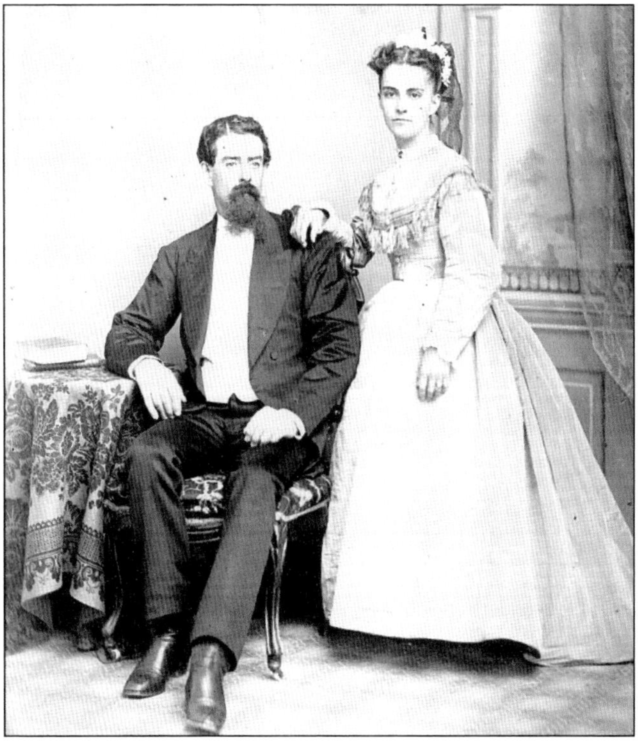

This October 1869 wedding portrait of Henry I. Brownson and Anna Maria Booth presents an interesting question. Brownson was a Shelton farmer, and Booth was from Newtown. Why then was this portrait taken in Baltimore? Perhaps they were there on their honeymoon.

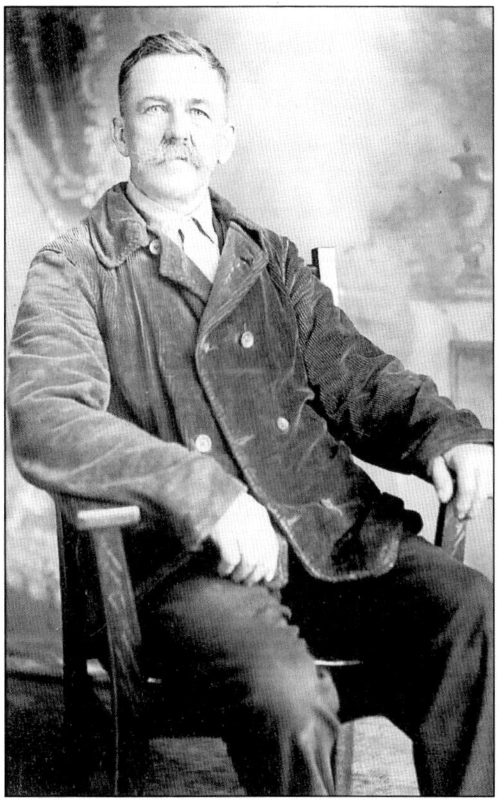

Samuel Thomas Buckingham was a farmer on Shelton Avenue. He supplemented his income by painting houses.

James Beardsley Wheeler of Thompson Street was a dedicated nonconformist. During the Civil War, when he was in his 20s, he was a conscientious objector. He had his own printing press, which he used to publish his own tracts, books, and the Funny Graphics, an odd collection of 19th-century philosophy. The great love of his life was a Monroe schoolteacher, Sarah Hack, whom he wooed with letters, which she returned. Many years later, Wheeler attended her funeral and tossed the letters into her grave.

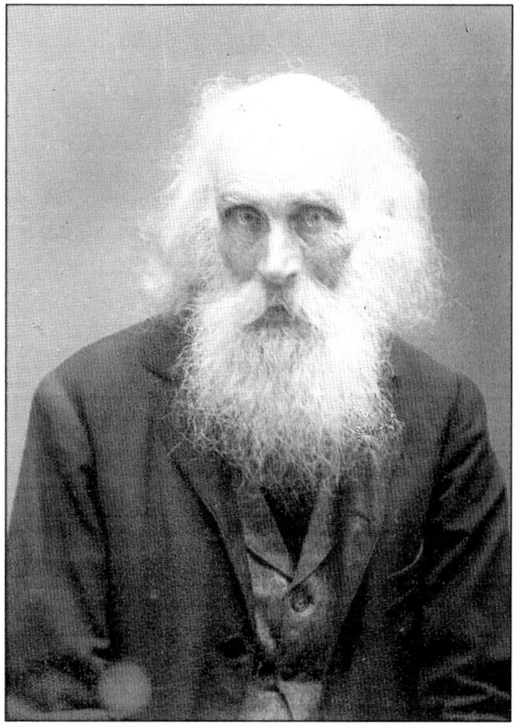

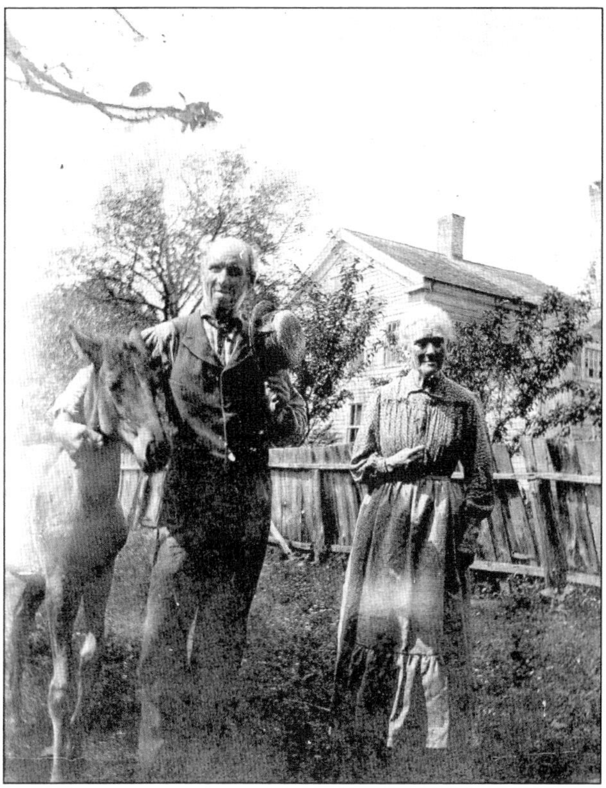

Amos and Wilhelmina Wheeler farmed on Willoughby Road. He is remembered as a very religious man and was a Sunday school teacher at the Huntington Congregational Church. One year, after a church picnic in Stratford, Wheeler realized that he had driven all the way home in the horse and buggy but had forgotten his wife.

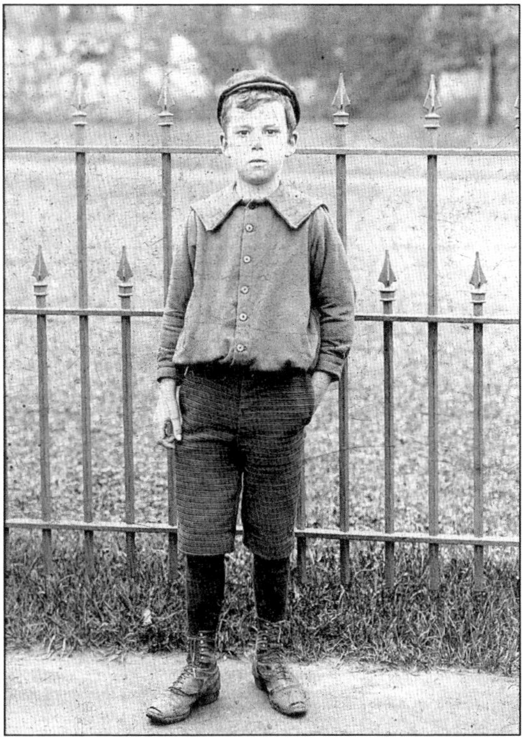

Ernest W. Ledger is standing at the fence in front of Ferry School *c.* 1900. (Courtesy of Ruth and Rod Kneen.)

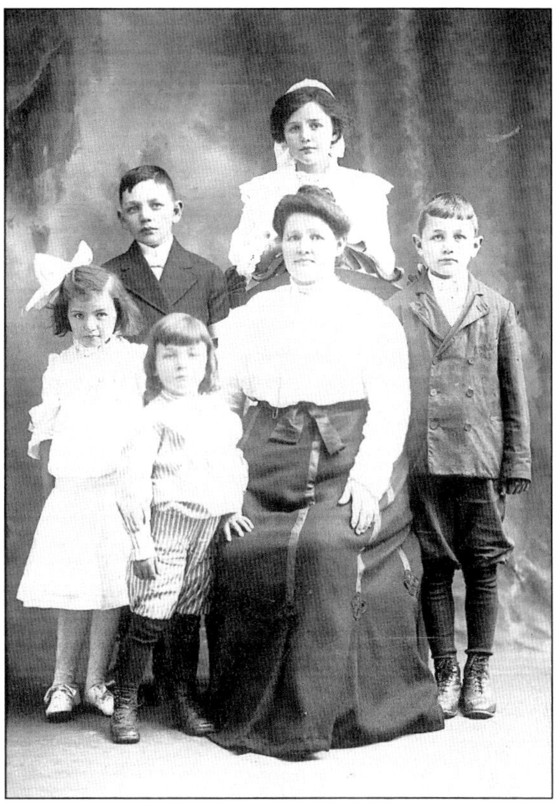

Frances Munster Kassheimer and her children sat for this formal portrait in 1908. The family is identified, from left to right, as follows: (front row) Gertrude, Charles, Frances, and Frank; (back row) Joseph and Frances. Kassheimer and her husband, Frank, were employees of the Sidney Blumenthal Company. (Courtesy of Randy Ritter.)

Edward William Kneen (1875–1951) served as the first mayor of the city of Shelton from 1917 to 1919. (Courtesy of Ruth and Rod Kneen.)

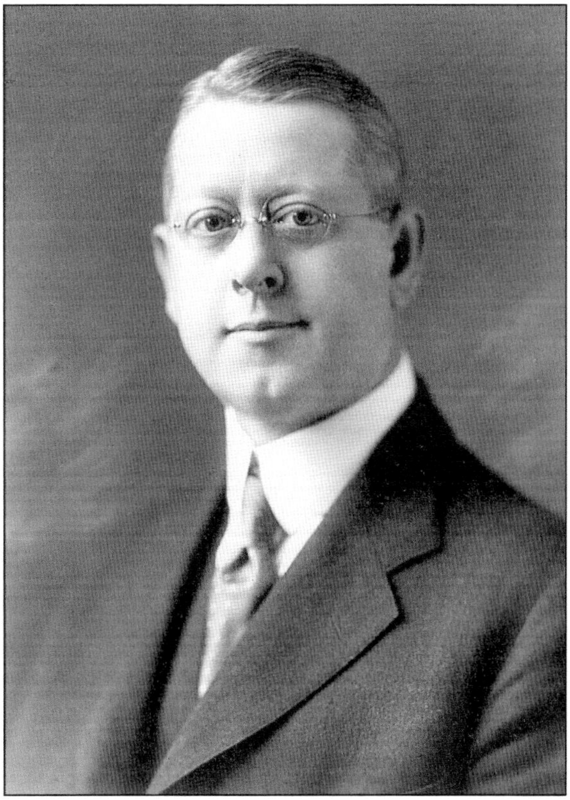

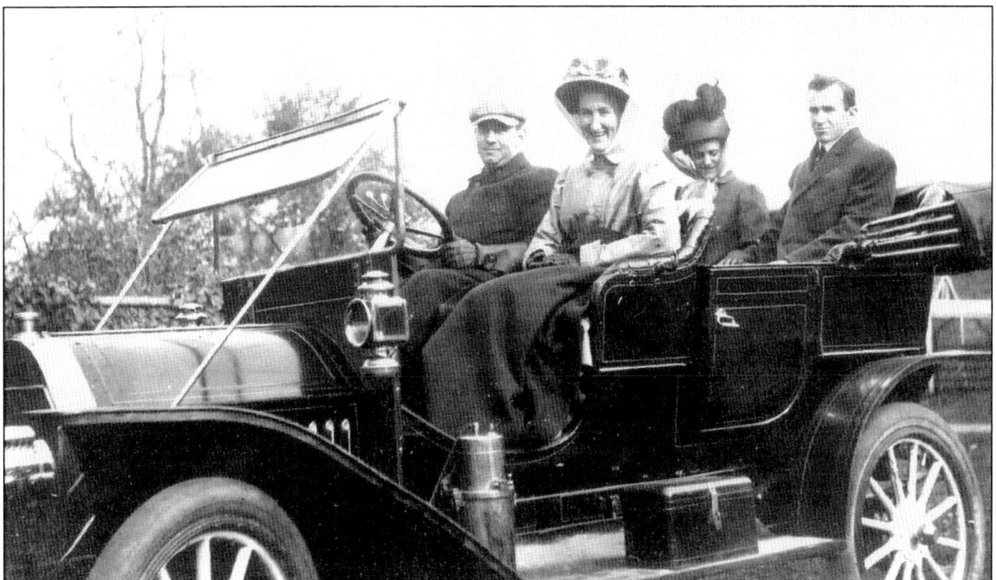

Mr. Lines (of Peck & Lines Auto Company), Helen Jones, Jessie Schand, and Philip Jones are pictured here on their first auto ride in 1910. On their way back from Newtown, they were caught in a thunderstorm in Monroe and had to take shelter in the Masonic Hall horse shed to put the top up. (Courtesy of Philip Jones.)

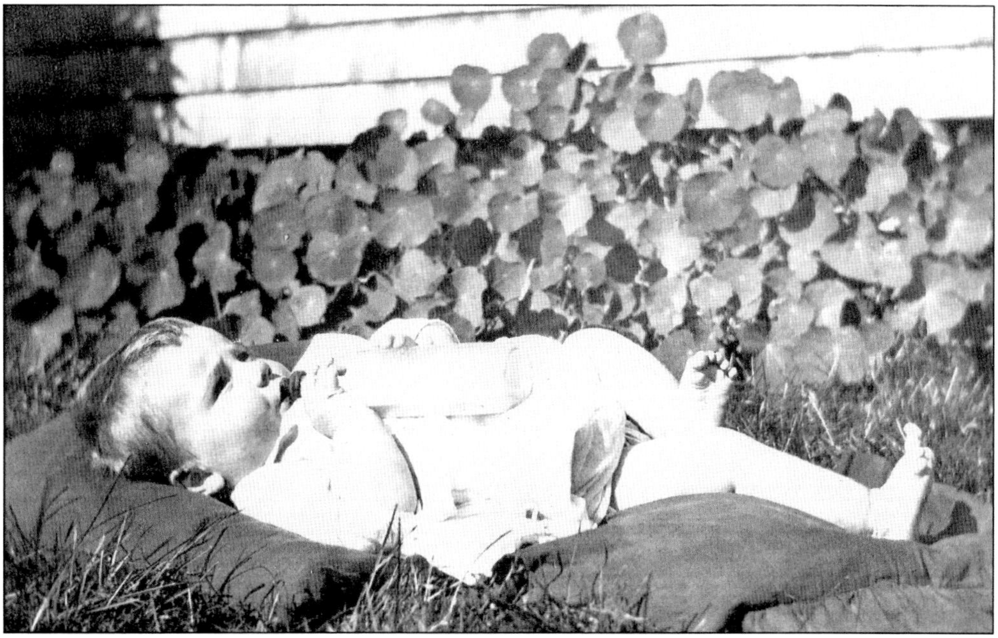

Philip Jones Jr. enjoys a bottle in the nasturtium bed on a visit to grandmother's house in 1919. (Photograph by Helen Jones; courtesy of Philip Jones.)

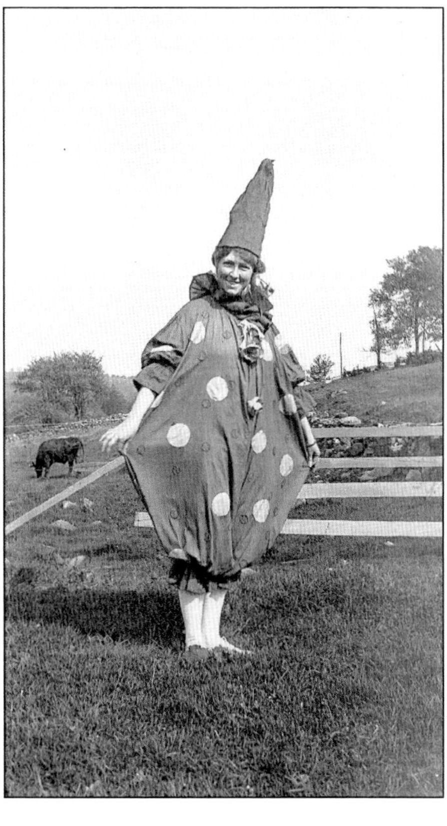

Joan Newell Jones enjoyed collecting costumes and would loan them to neighbors and friends who needed one for a party. Here, she is modeling a clown costume c. 1920. (Photograph by Helen Jones; courtesy of Philip Jones.)

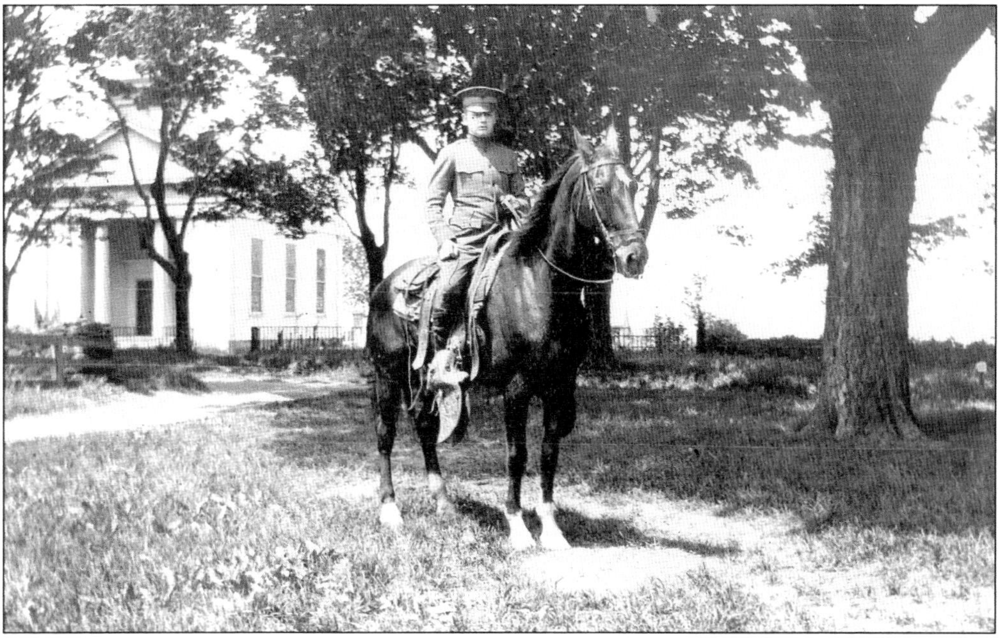

Harold A. Thompson was a member of the National Guard and is shown here *c.* 1920 on former cavalry horse Dan. Dan was not an easy mount and was difficult to control. The White Hills Baptist Church can be seen in the background. (Courtesy of Jeanette LaMacchia.)

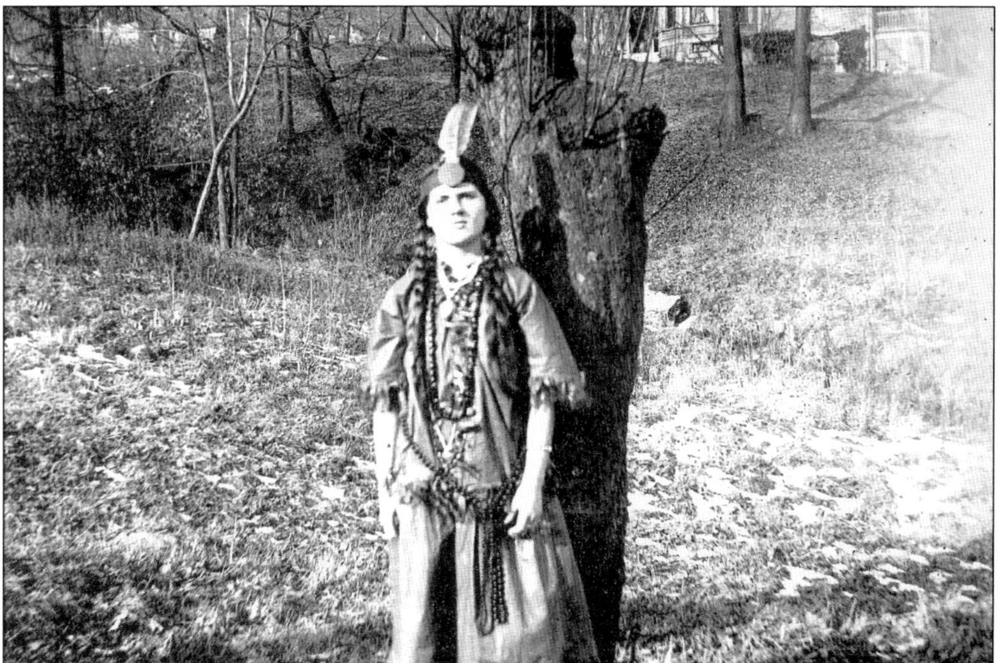

This photograph shows Lucy Little wearing an Indian costume behind the J.W. Perry House. This is an excellent example of how the history of a photograph can be easily lost. Even though it was labeled, there was not enough information included as to the location of the house (other than that it was in Shelton), why Little was in costume, or a date.

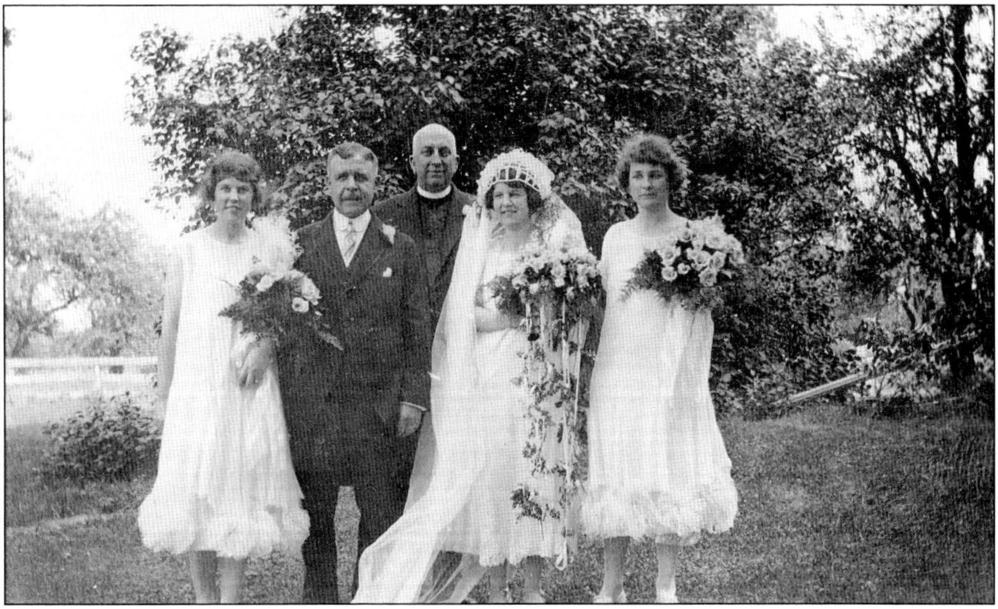

Bridesmaid Sue Beardsley, bridegroom Robert Aberdeen, the minister, bride Marion Beardsley, and bridesmaid Jennette Beardsley pose for a formal wedding portrait on June 10, 1925.

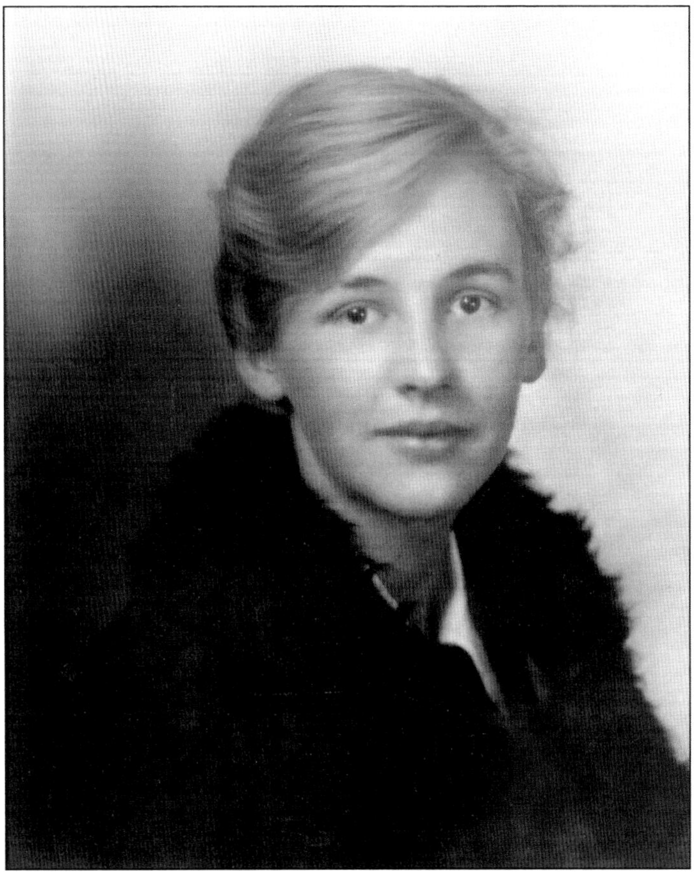

This formal portrait of Guila Hawley (1907–1989) was taken *c.* 1930. Hawley was from an old Shelton family and farmed vegetables and raised chickens at her home on Huntington Street. She was known as a storehouse of historical information and donated land to the Land Trust to help preserve the rural character of Shelton.

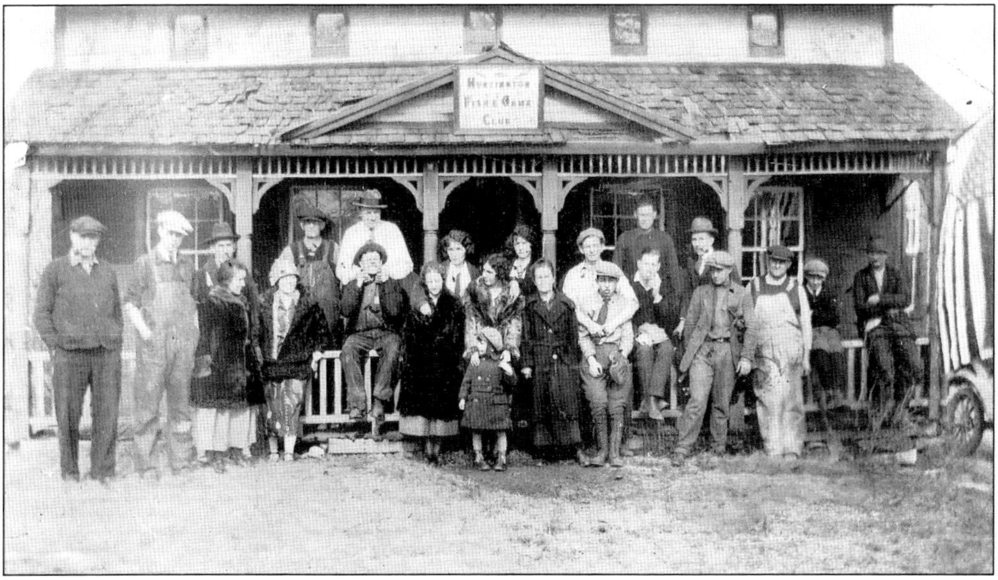

The Huntington Fish and Game Club was located off Far Mill Street, near Mohegan Road. Here, the members gather for a group portrait c. 1920. (Courtesy of the George G. Boehm family.)

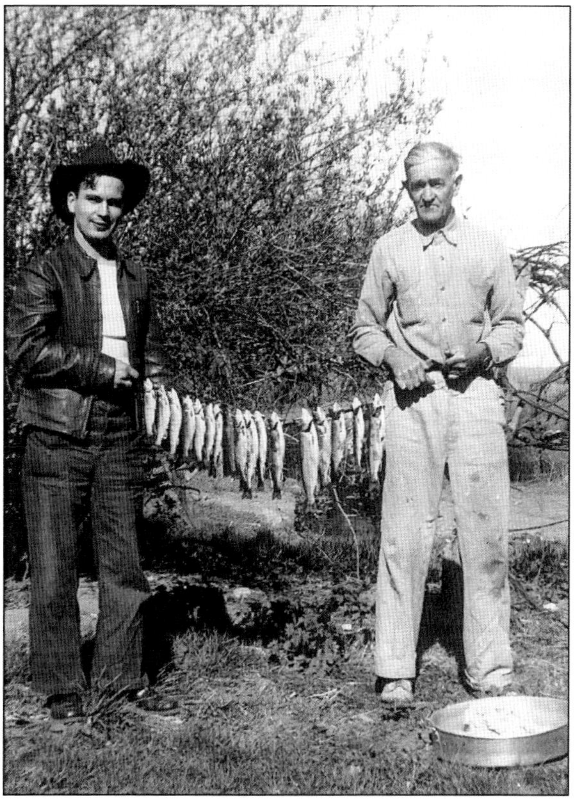

Clifford Paulson and Edward Jackson Beardsley display a good day's catch of freshwater fish c. 1940. (Courtesy of Elma Jean Wiacek.)

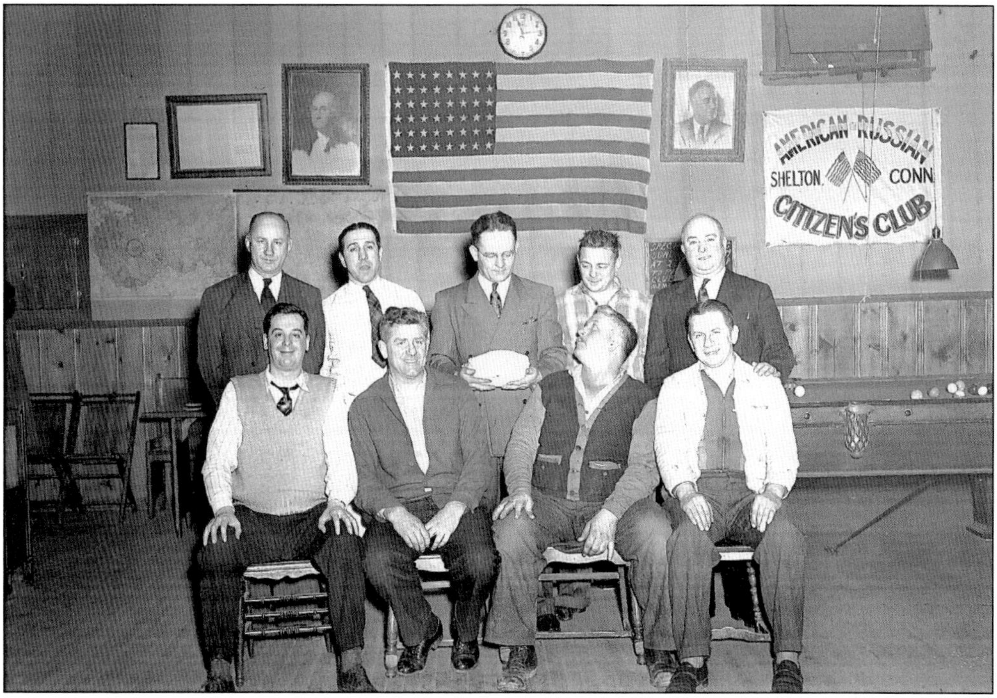

Civic, recreational, religious, and community service clubs abounded in Shelton. In this *c.* 1945 view, the members of the American Russian Citizen's Club sit for photographer Anthony Zisek. The first man on the left in the front row is Walter Clark, and the man on the right in the back row is Frank Pagliaro Sr.

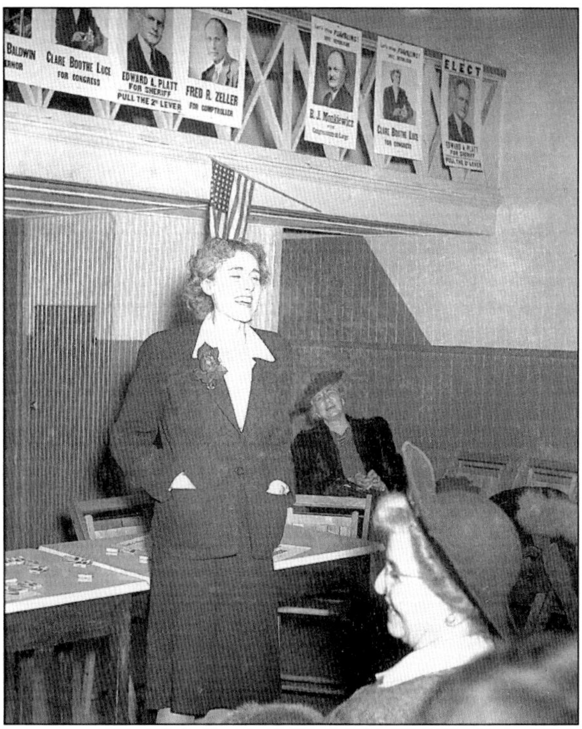

Clare Booth Luce (1903–1987) served as the congressional representative for the Fourth Congressional District from 1943 to 1947. Here, she is speaking at the Shelton Republican Rally *c.* 1945. (Photograph by Anthony Zisek.)

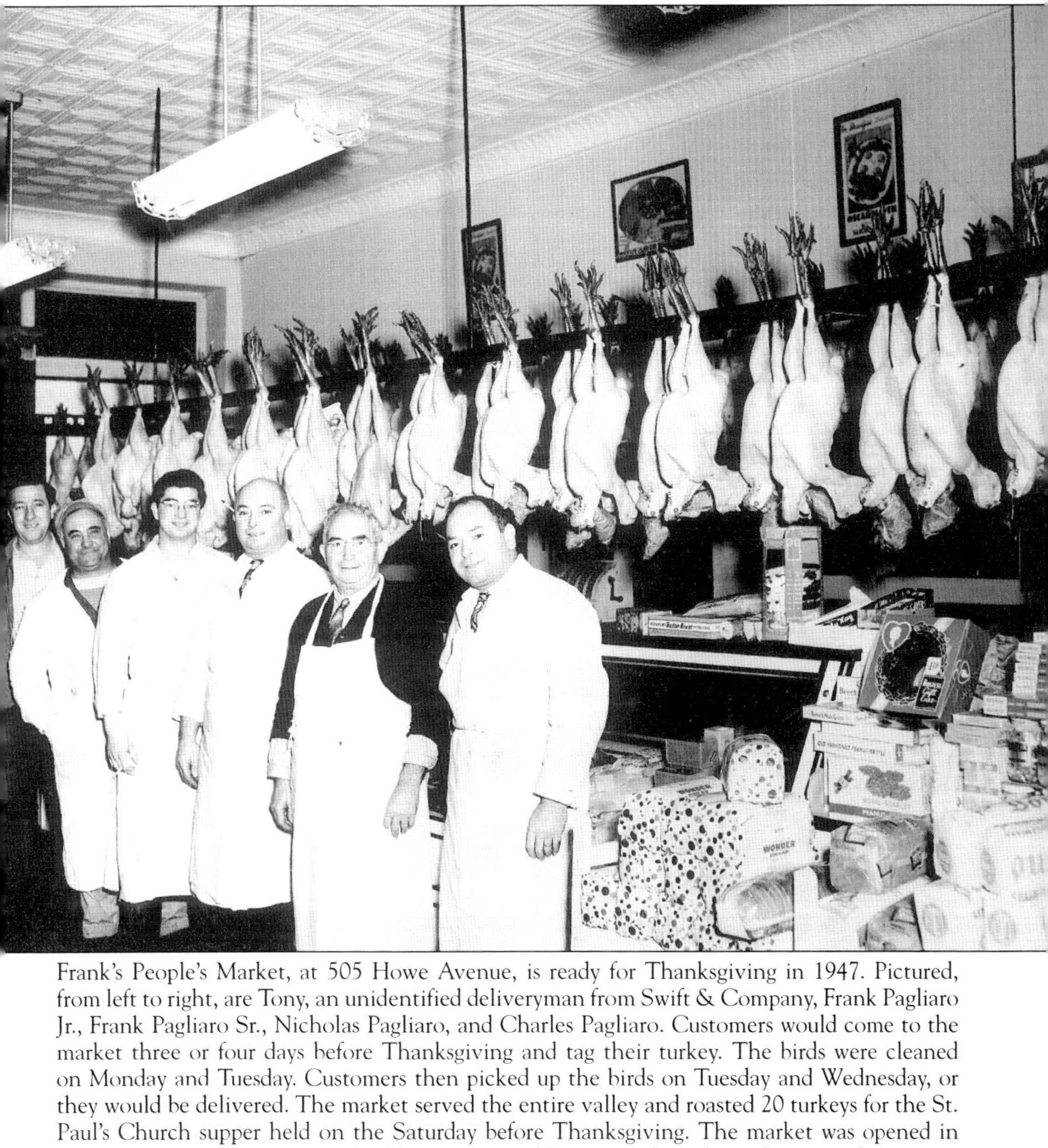

Frank's People's Market, at 505 Howe Avenue, is ready for Thanksgiving in 1947. Pictured, from left to right, are Tony, an unidentified deliveryman from Swift & Company, Frank Pagliaro Jr., Frank Pagliaro Sr., Nicholas Pagliaro, and Charles Pagliaro. Customers would come to the market three or four days before Thanksgiving and tag their turkey. The birds were cleaned on Monday and Tuesday. Customers then picked up the birds on Tuesday and Wednesday, or they would be delivered. The market served the entire valley and roasted 20 turkeys for the St. Paul's Church supper held on the Saturday before Thanksgiving. The market was opened in 1927 by Frank Pagliaro Sr. and sold fruits, vegetables, canned goods, and meats. There was a daily delivery route throughout the valley. The market also catered food for local clubs on the weekends. (Courtesy of Frank C. Pagliaro Jr.)

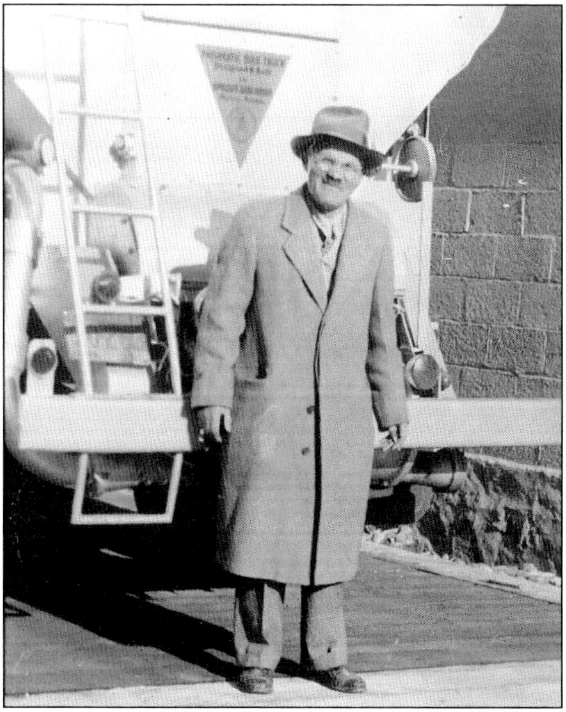

Wolf Savitsky, shown at his feed store and mill in 1956, was an enterprising businessman. At various points, he owned a package store, grocery market, and a farm equipment and feed store. (Courtesy of Rosalind and Linda Savitsky.)

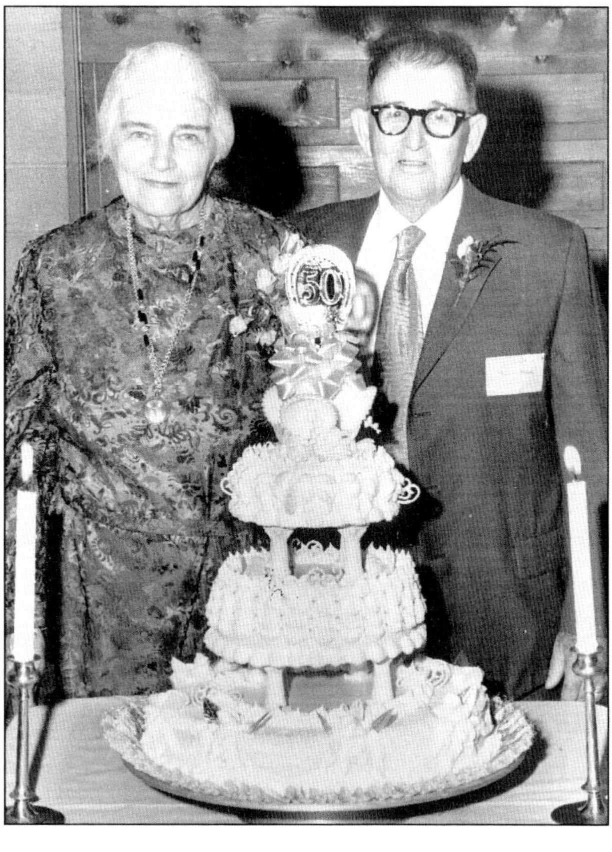

Dorothy and Wisner Wilson, well remembered for their farm stand on Ripton Road, celebrated their 50th wedding anniversary on October 29, 1970.

Ten

CHANGES

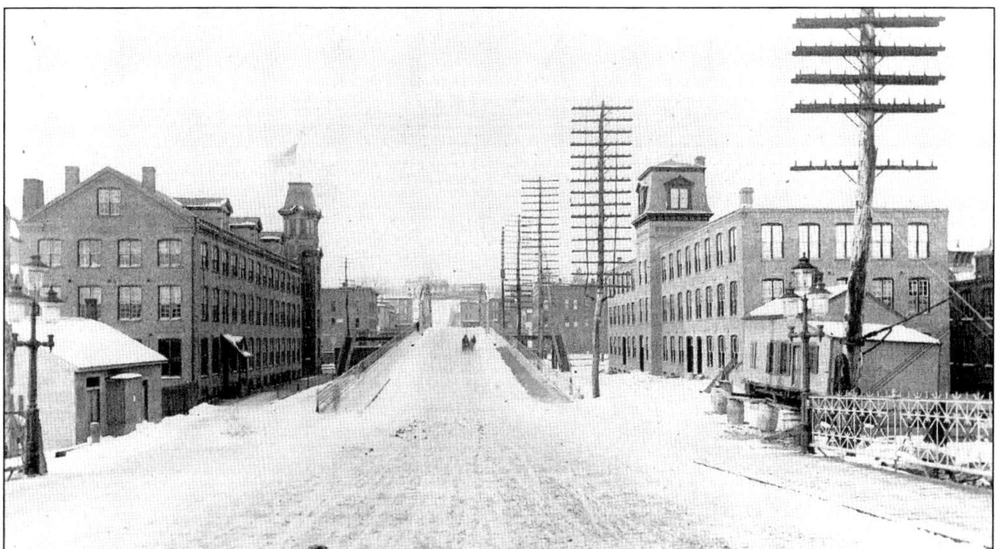

A wagon and team of horses travel over the Viaduct Bridge into Shelton *c.* 1895. The gaslights and utility poles testify to the borough's burgeoning growth.

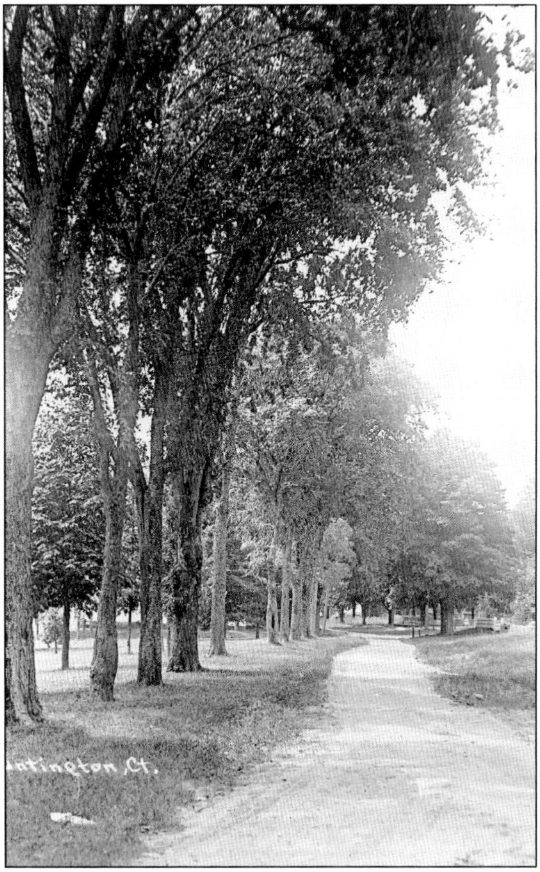

Elm trees once lined the Huntington Green. This photograph was taken at the junction of what is now Route 108 and Ripton Road. Ripton Road is on the right side of the image. (Courtesy of Philip Jones.)

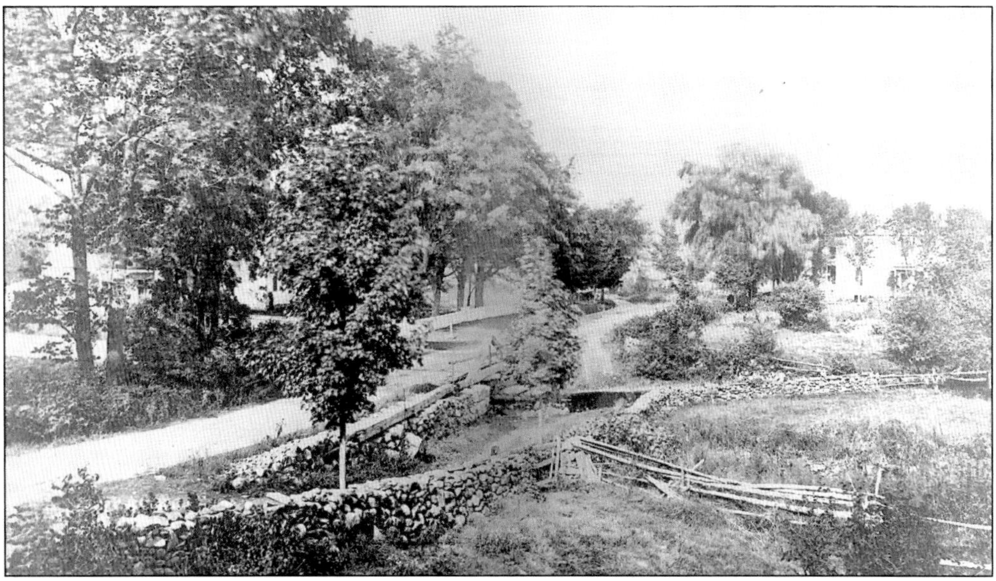

Shelton Avenue near Means Brook in Huntington center was once in the quiet countryside. The Brownson House is seen in its original location at the corner of Shelton Avenue and Old Shelton Road. Horses could drink from the brook. There was a path below the bridge for access.

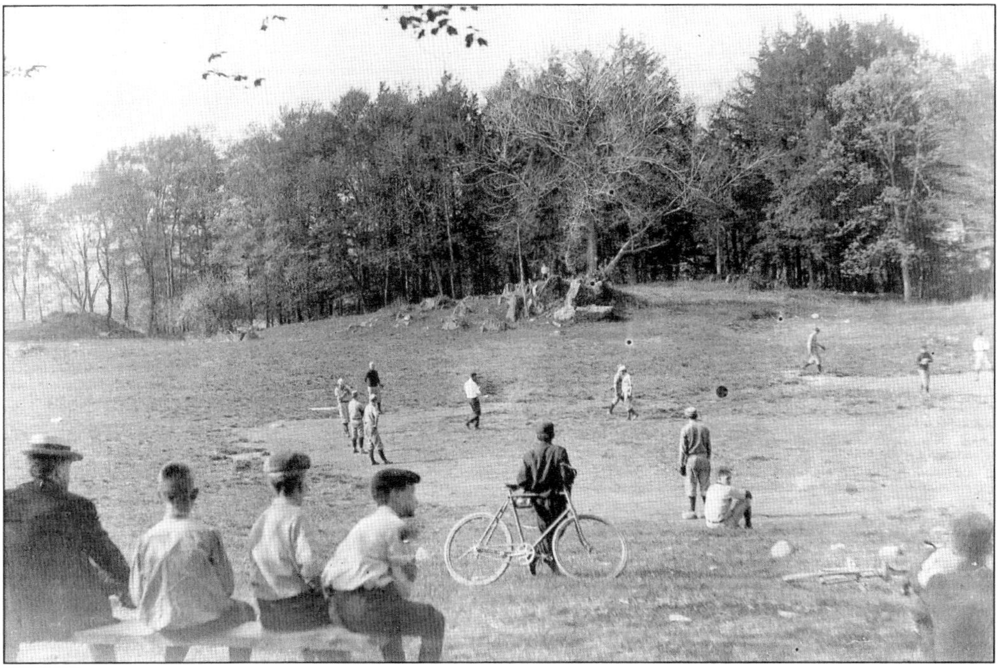

The Frederick Meyer baseball team plays a game at a Shelton park c. 1905. Meyer owned a foundry on Wooster Street that specialized in small castings. (Courtesy of the Frederick W. Ziegler family.)

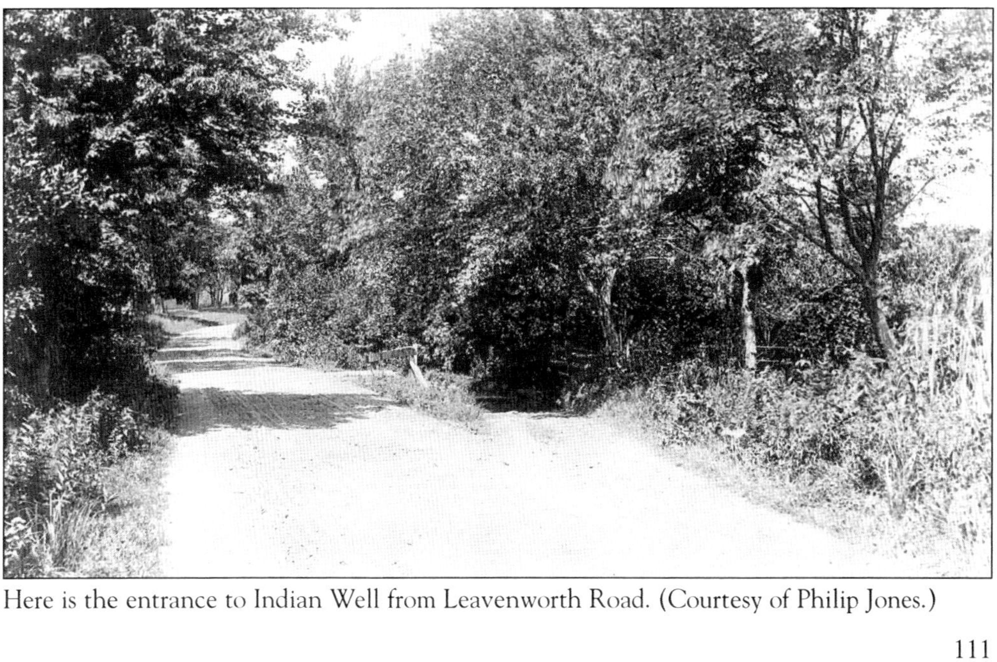

Here is the entrance to Indian Well from Leavenworth Road. (Courtesy of Philip Jones.)

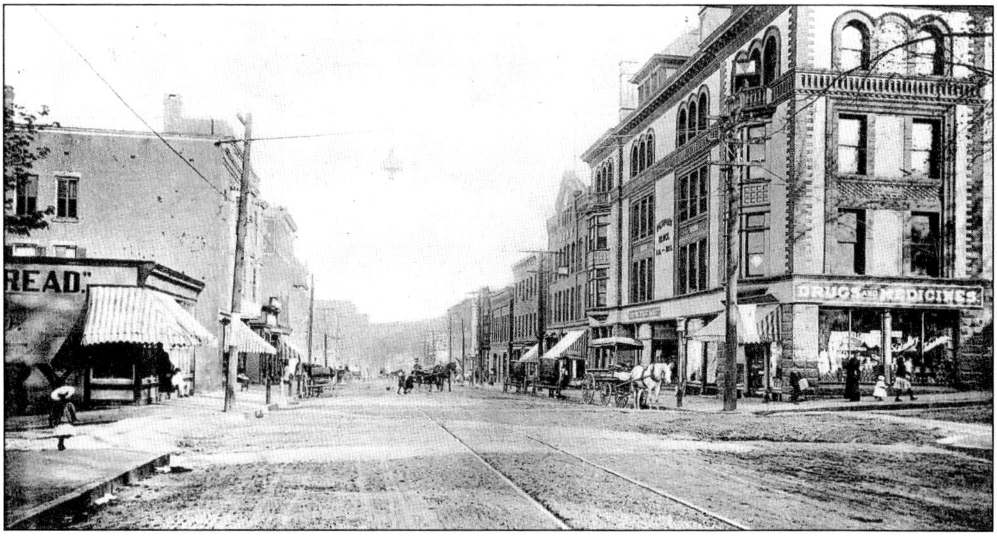

Here is a view of Howe Avenue and the Pierpont Block from a 1906 postcard. (Courtesy of Jean Mason.)

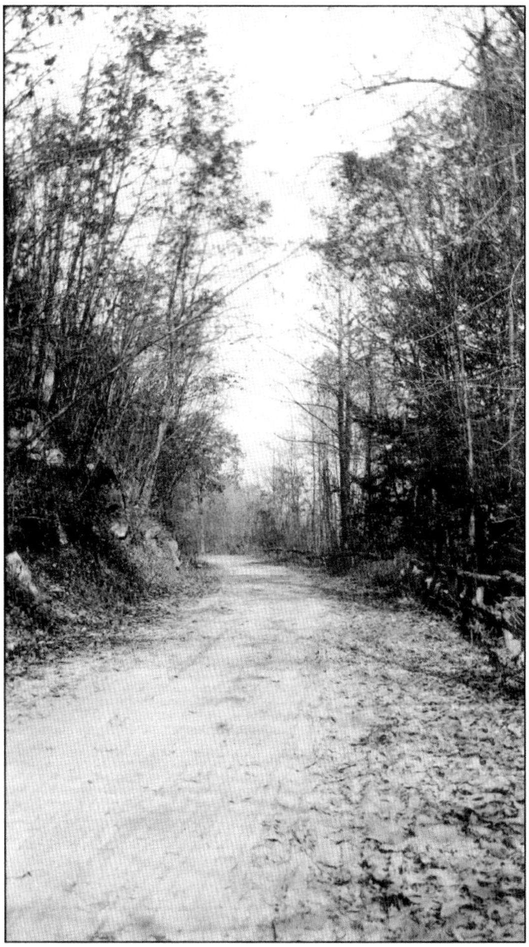

Leavenworth Road, with a log rail fence and unpaved surface, continues up toward Monroe. It is remembered as being dusty in the summer and muddy in the winter. (Courtesy of Philip Jones.)

Helen Jones stopped the family buggy to photograph this view of French's Hill on East Village Road *c.* 1910. (Courtesy of Philip Jones.)

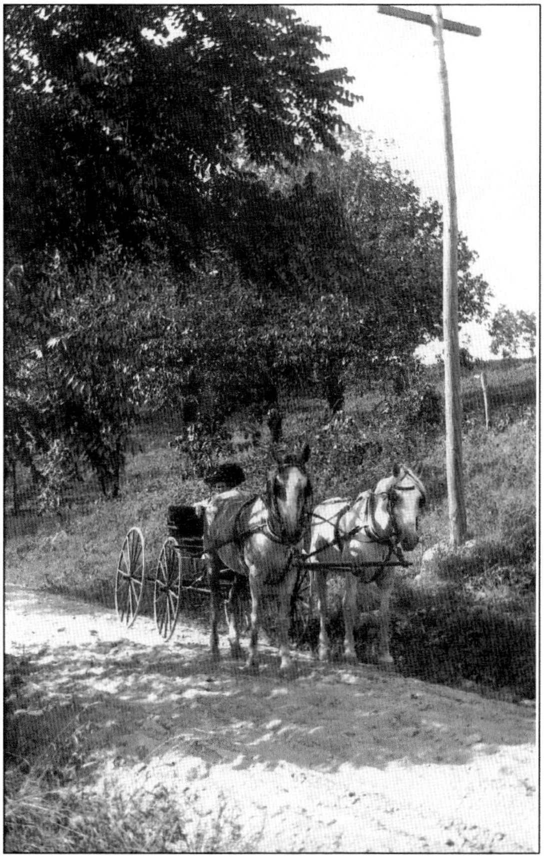

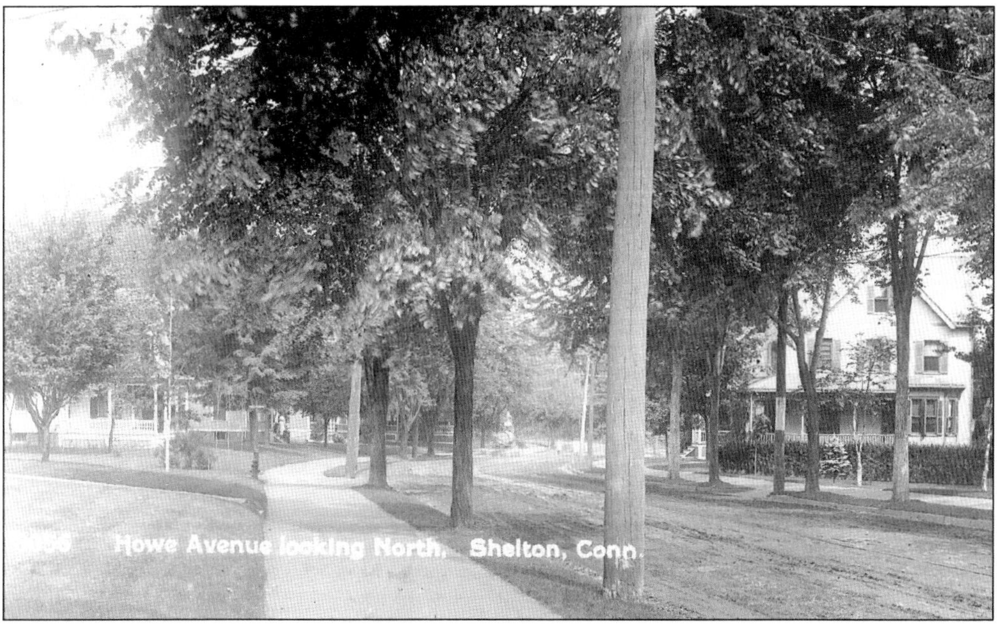

The photographer stood in front of 92 Howe Avenue looking north when this 1911 postcard was taken. (Courtesy of Philip Jones.)

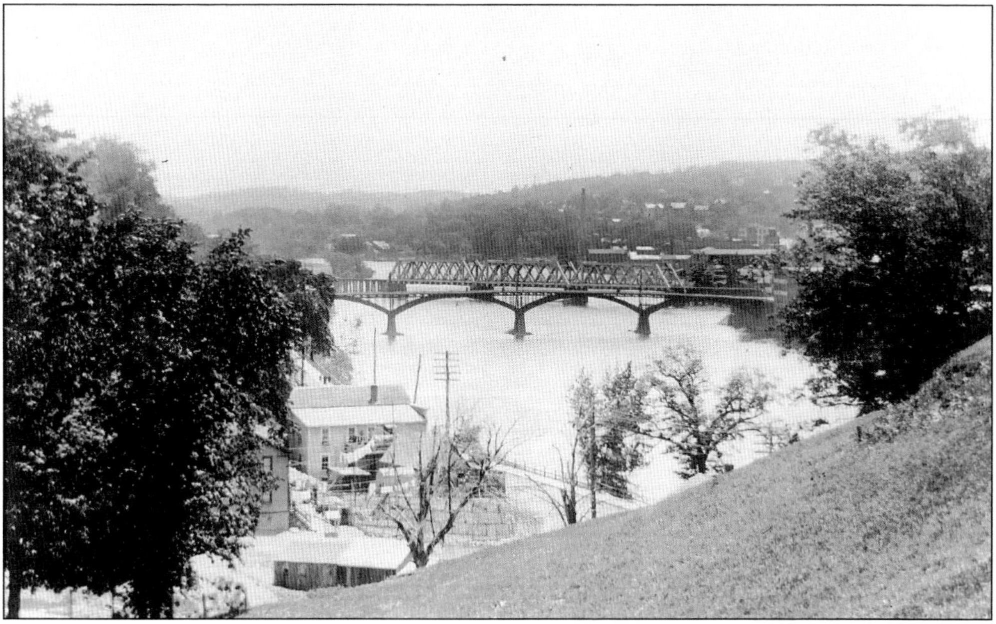

The iron Shelton-Derby Bridge and the railroad bridge can be seen from this photograph taken from a Derby hillside. (Courtesy of Philip Jones.)

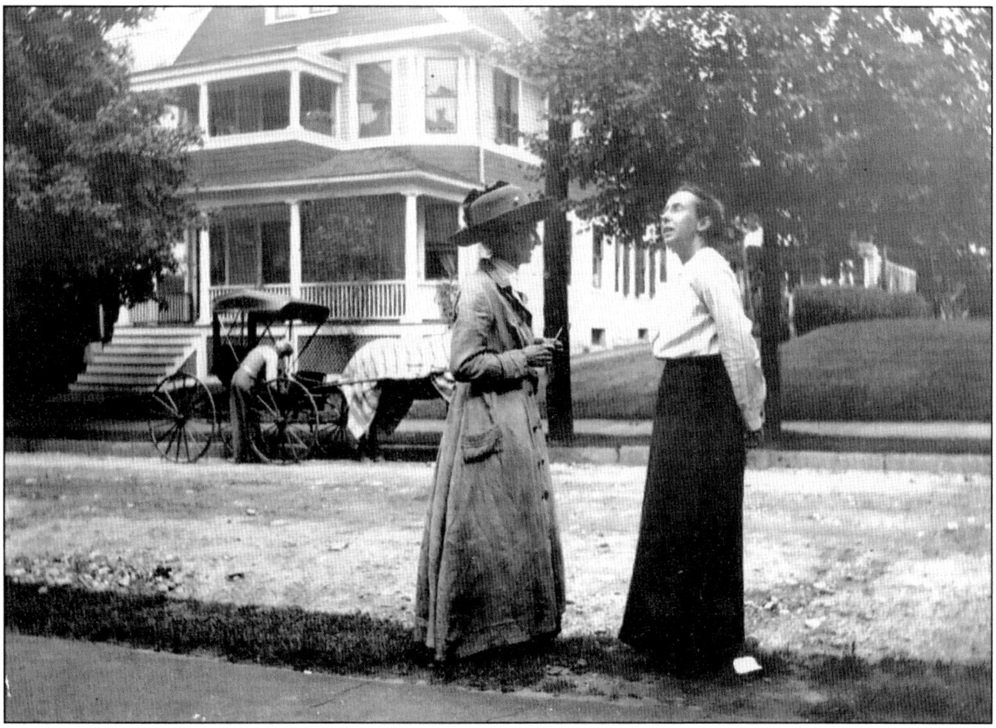

An unidentified woman and Linda Diedrichsen enjoy a chat on Kneen Street c. 1905. (Courtesy of Dorothy Didsbury Mills.)

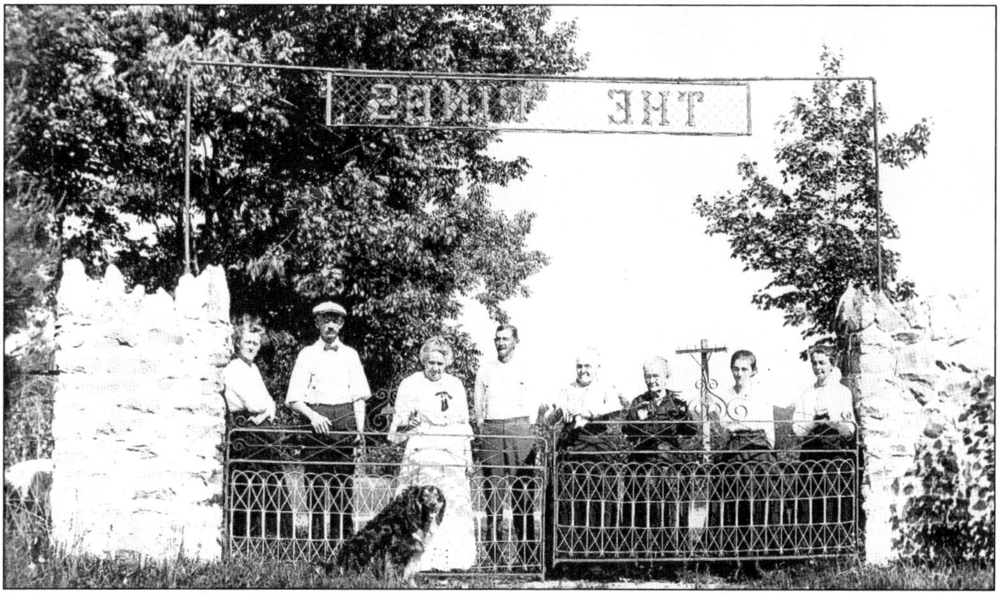

This early-20th-century photograph of the front gates of 54 Pine Street shows the sign of which only the columns remain. Pictured, from left to right, are Mr. and Mrs. Nicholas Wakelee and Mr. and Mrs. Elret Stone; the remaining people are unidentified. (Courtesy of the Willoughby family.)

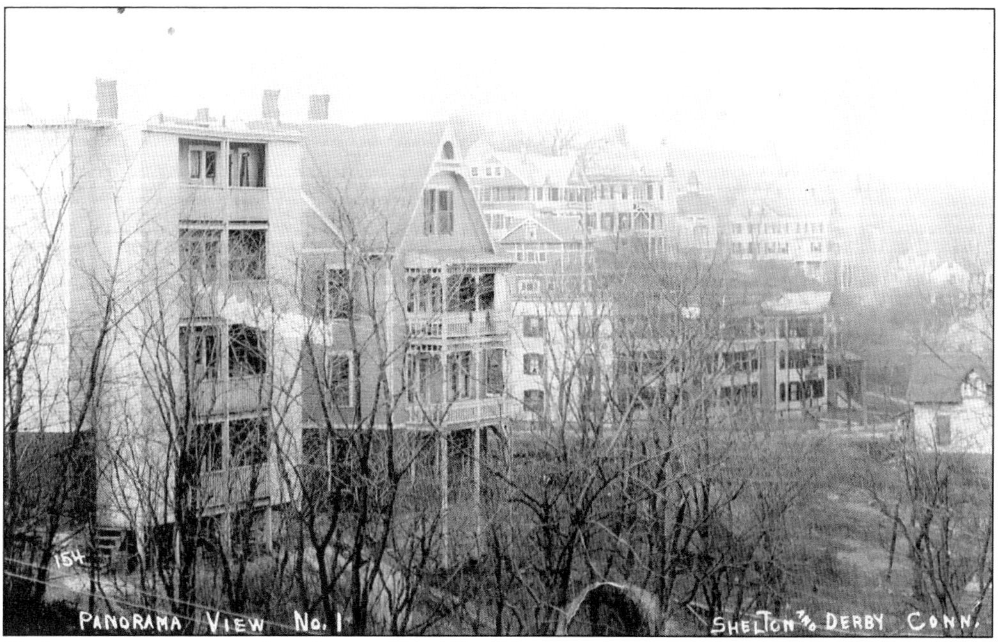

Shelton was once very densely populated downtown. This view of Howe Avenue was taken from what is now Route 8. The third house from the left is 248-250 Howe Avenue and is extant. (Courtesy of Bryan Lizotte.)

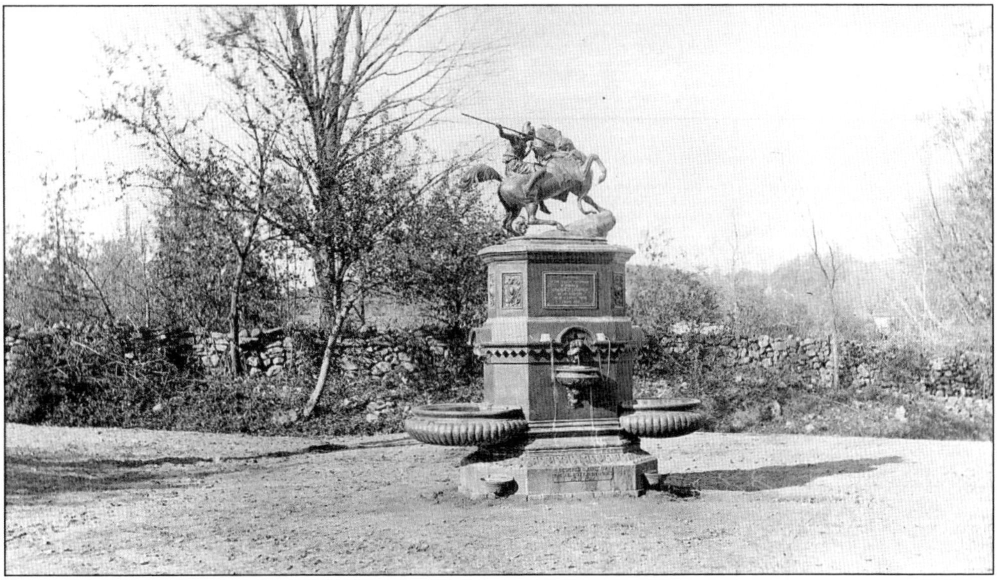

The Curtiss Memorial Fountain was installed on the Huntington Green in 1895 by Julia DeForest Nash, in memory of her father, Charles Curtiss. The fountain, shown here before 1900, originally stood in the road where Huntington Street and Shelton Avenue meet.

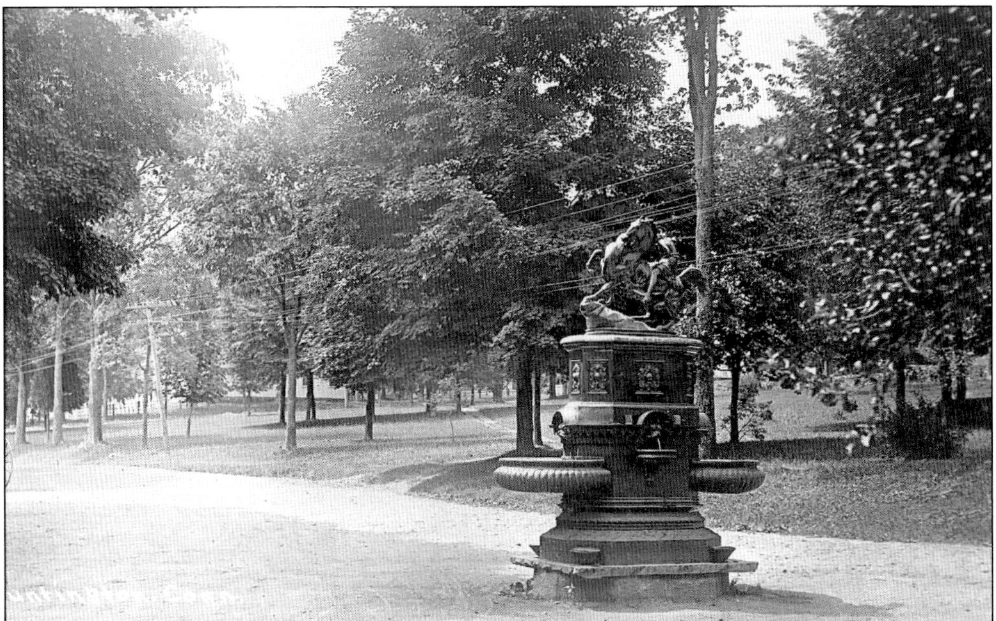

Sometime around the turn of the century, the base of the fountain was modified. The central column was shortened, and the large basins were moved from the bottom of the column to the middle.

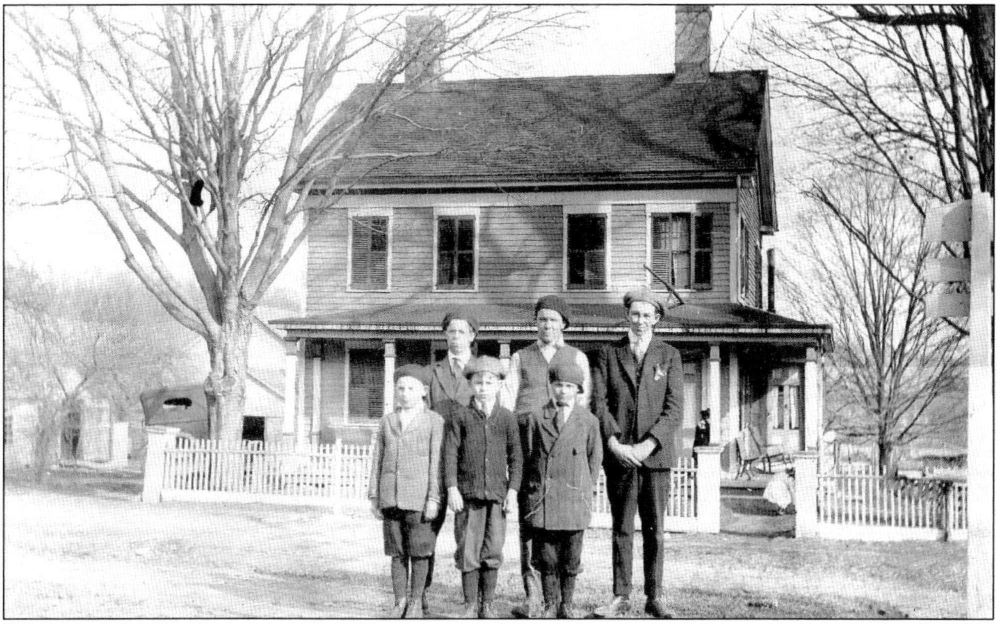

Six neighborhood boys gather in 1917 in front of 656 Bridgeport Avenue. In the back row, from left to right, are Henry Shelton Wells, Ben Wells, and Wallace Milford. The sign to their right reads, "All Roads Lead to Howland's," which was a dry goods store in Bridgeport. (Courtesy of the Wells family.)

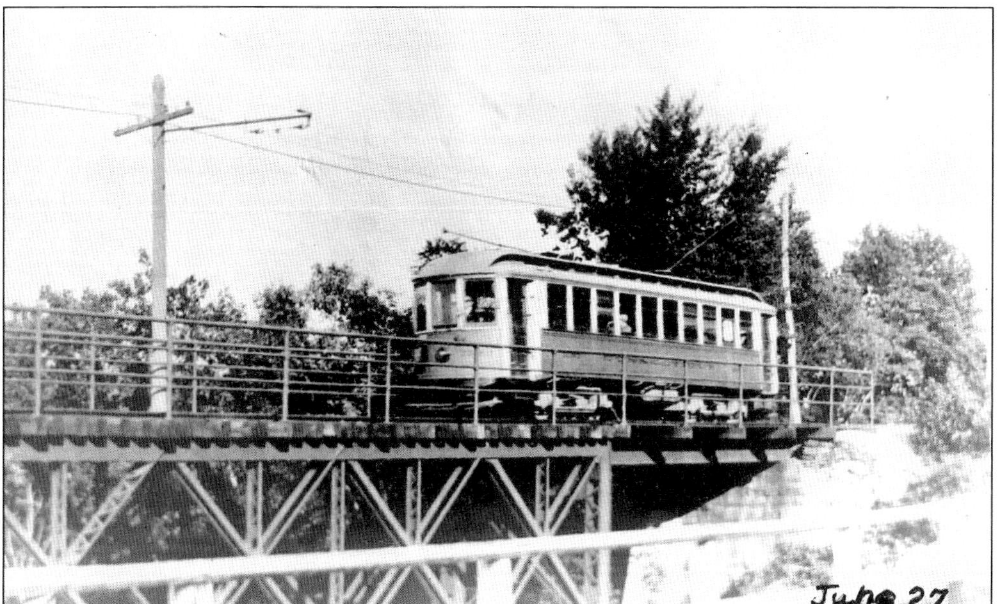

The final trolley ran through Shelton on June 27, 1928. Here, one of the last cars travels over the bridge south of Grove Street, on the Shelton-Bridgeport line.

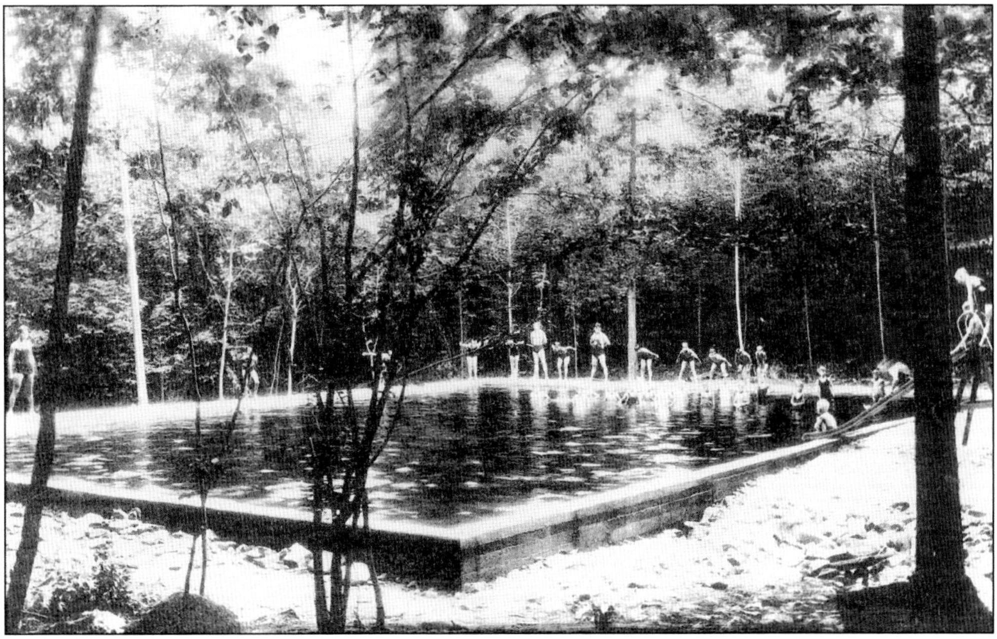

Camp Huntington was located at Park and Soundview Avenues. The private overnight camp operated from the 1930s into the 1950s. (Courtesy of Bryan Lizotte.)

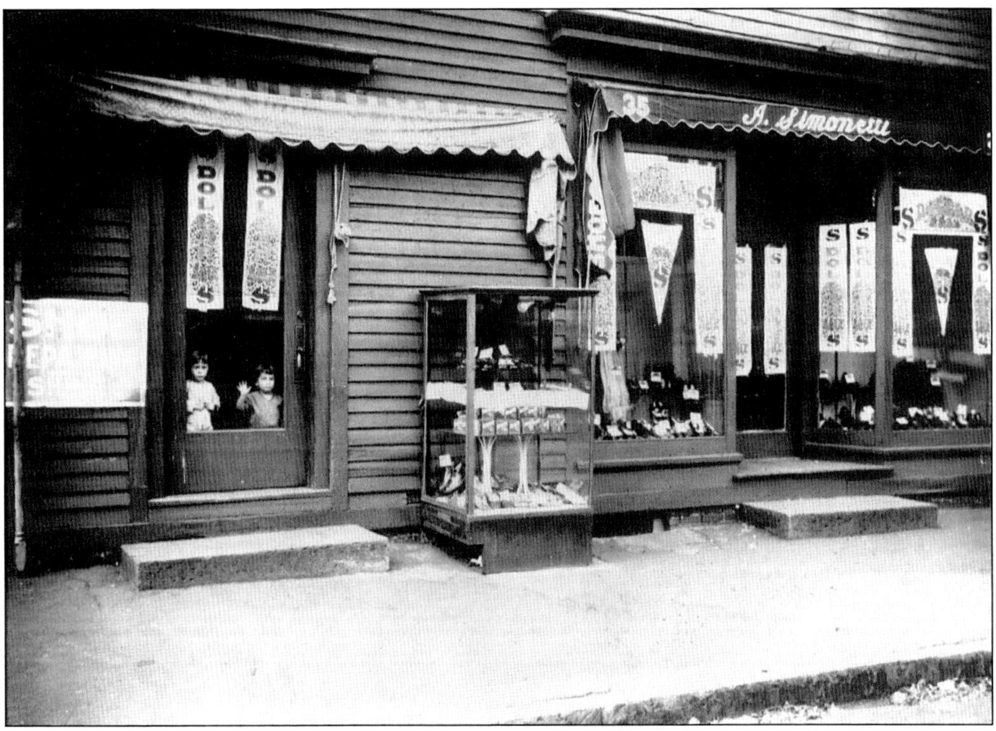

John and Tom Simonetti look out the window of their father's shoe-repair shop at 35 Center Street c. 1935. (Courtesy of the Simonetti family.)

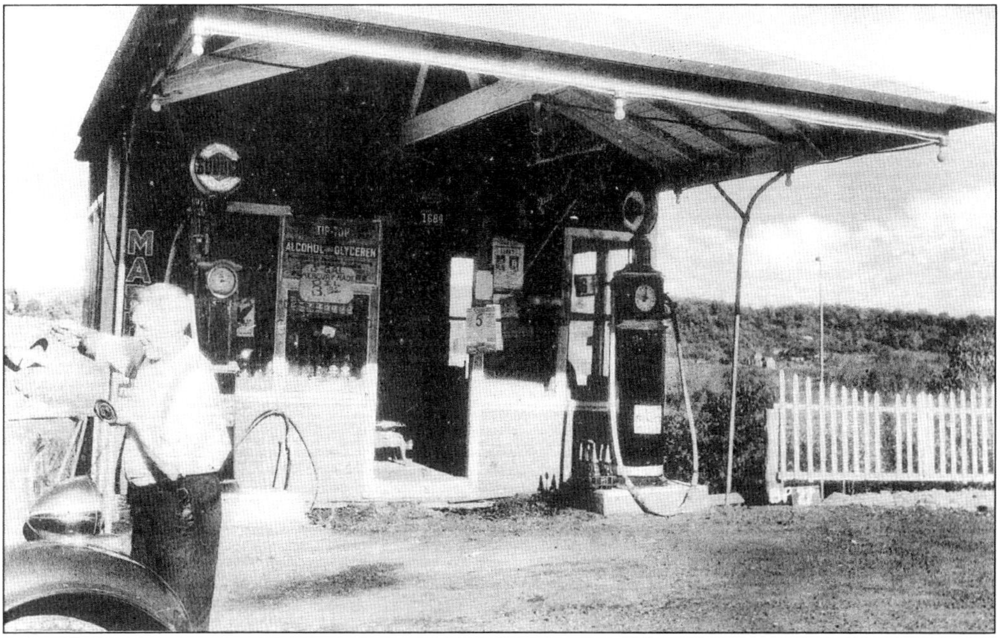

Diedrichsen's Filling Station served the public at 1684 River Road for many years. This image has been reproduced from an advertising postcard from *c.* 1935. (Courtesy of Dorothy Didsbury Mills.)

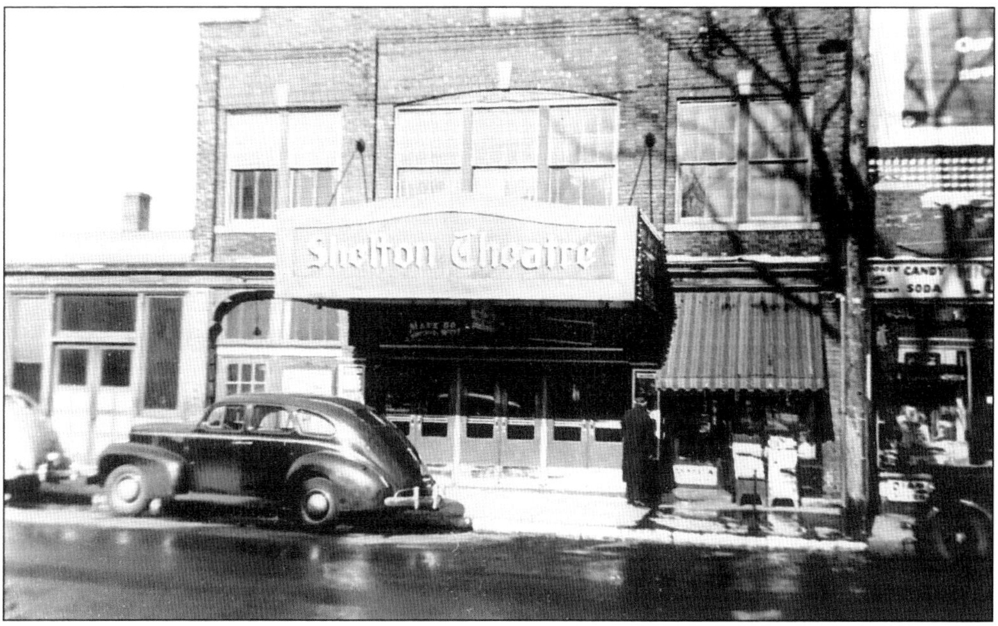

The Shelton Theatre, at 509 Howe Avenue, entertained valley residents from 1915 to the 1970s. This photograph of the theater was taken in 1941. (Courtesy of Dorothy Didsbury Mills.)

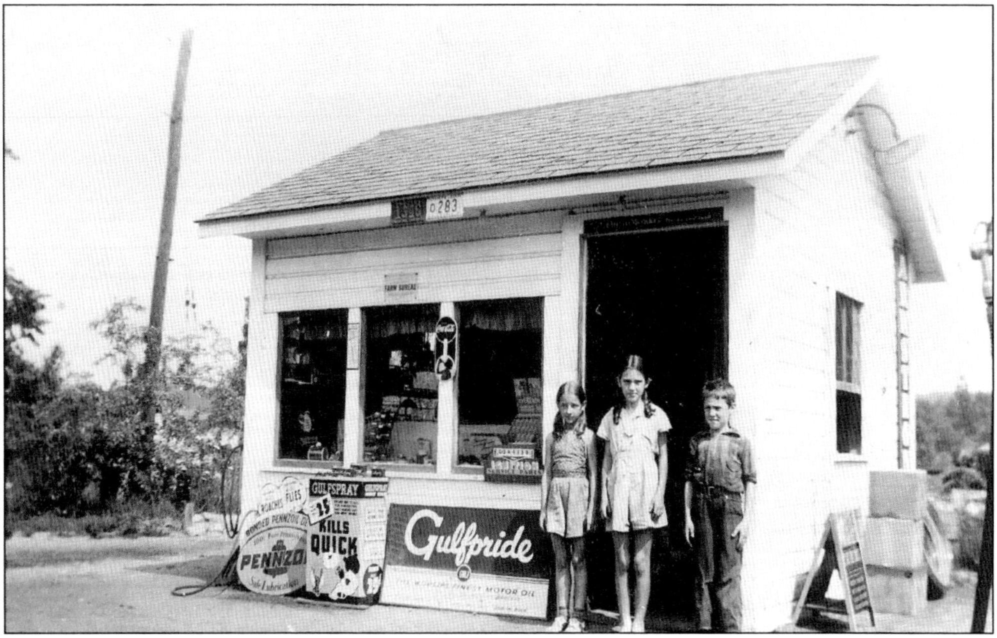

Josie and Willard Nicholas opened this filling station at 429 Shelton Avenue *c.* 1932. Their children Jean, Dorothy, and Bill stood for their portrait *c.* 1936. This site is now the Buck Stop. (Courtesy of Jean N. Vollaro, Dorothy N. Sutton, and Willard Nicholas.)

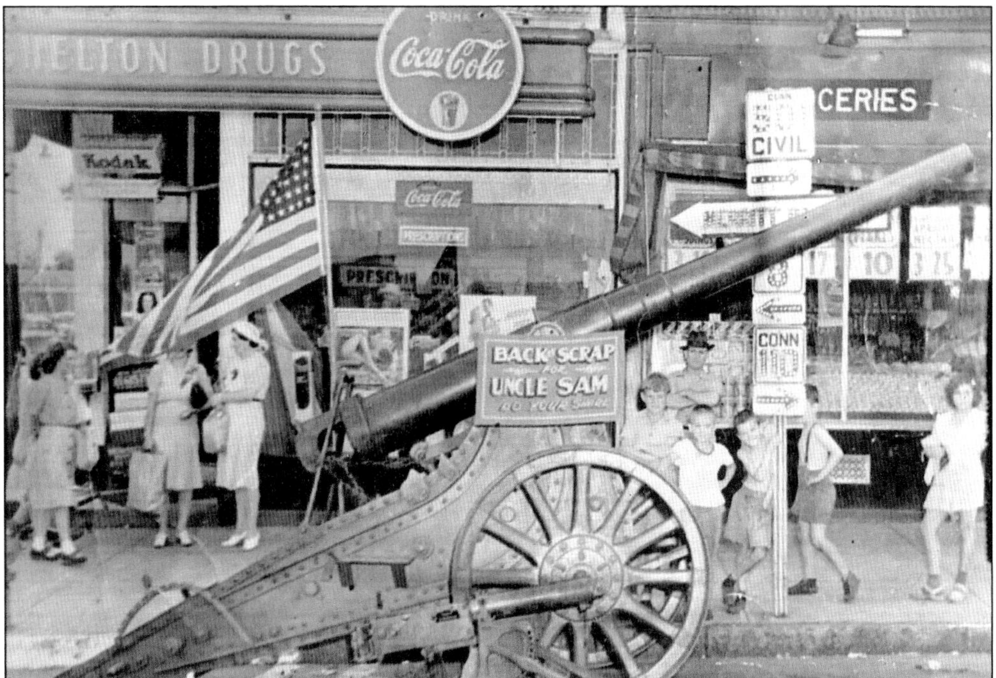

In 1942, World War II mobilized everyone and everything. Even the World War I cannon, formerly on display at Riverview Park, was melted down to serve the war effort.

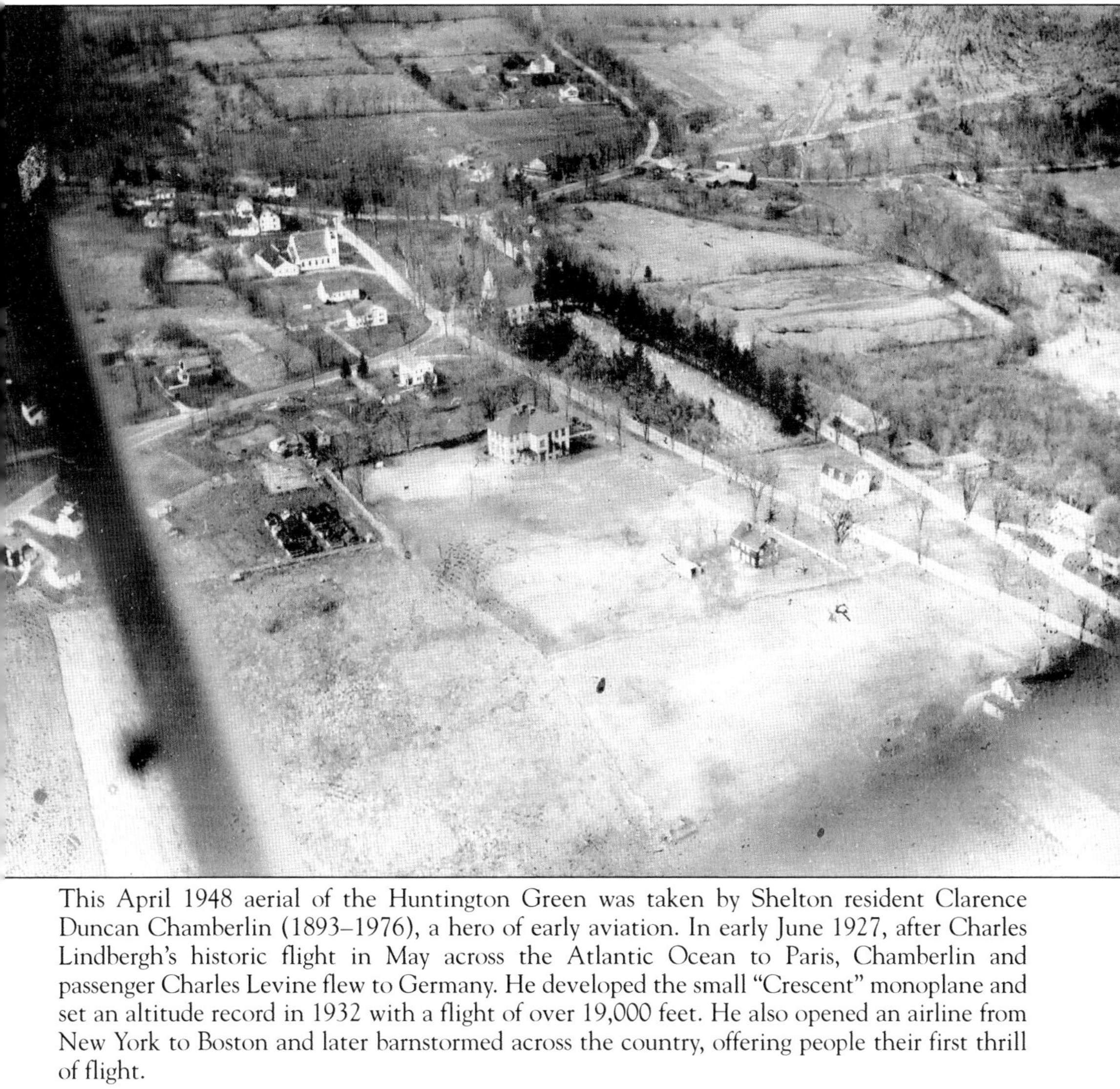

This April 1948 aerial of the Huntington Green was taken by Shelton resident Clarence Duncan Chamberlin (1893–1976), a hero of early aviation. In early June 1927, after Charles Lindbergh's historic flight in May across the Atlantic Ocean to Paris, Chamberlin and passenger Charles Levine flew to Germany. He developed the small "Crescent" monoplane and set an altitude record in 1932 with a flight of over 19,000 feet. He also opened an airline from New York to Boston and later barnstormed across the country, offering people their first thrill of flight.

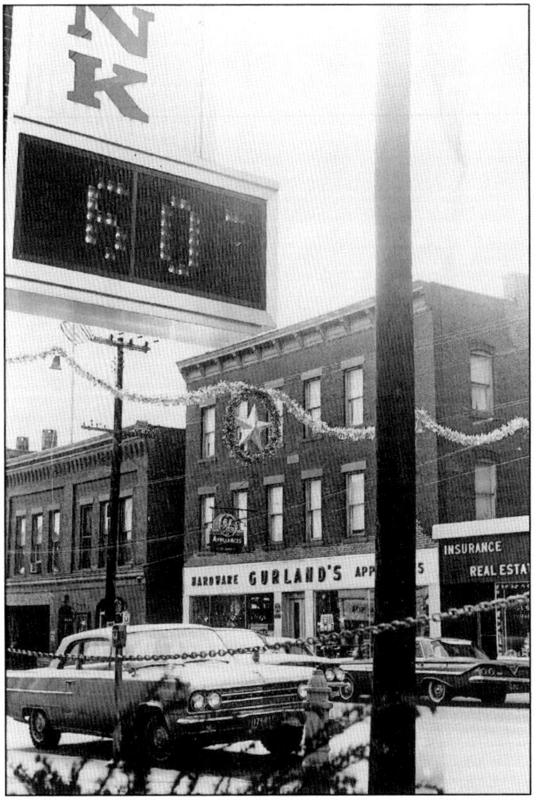

In December 1956, when this photograph was taken, Gurland's Hardware and Appliance Store, at 474-478 Howe Avenue, was selling hardware, paints, window and auto glass, housewares, and General Electric appliances. (Courtesy of the Shelton Economic Development Corporation.)

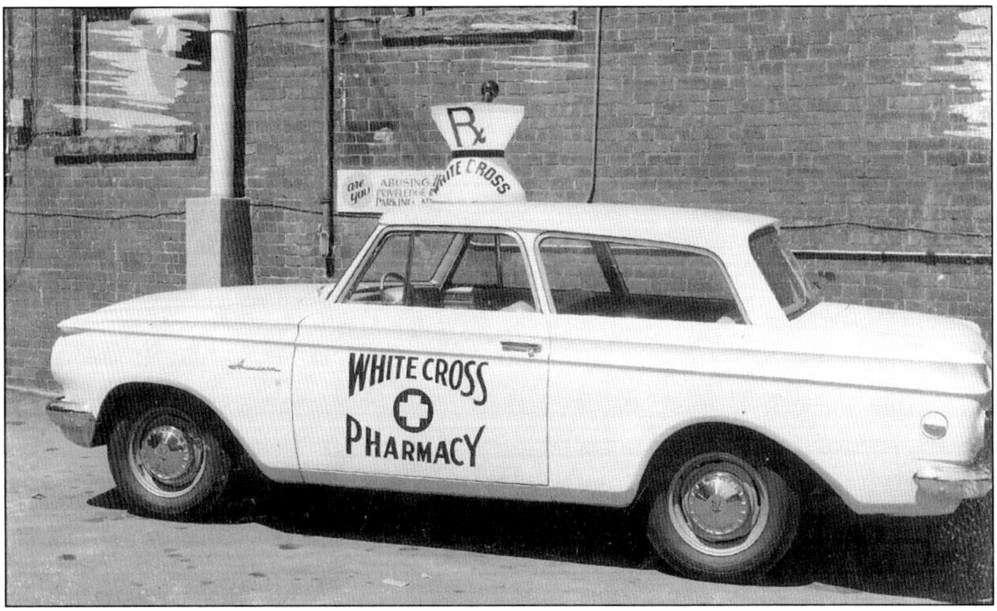

John Simonetti opened the White Cross Pharmacy at 73 Center Street in 1959. It made deliveries throughout Shelton. It changed ownership in 1994, when it was sold to Arrow Drug. (Courtesy of the Simonetti family.)

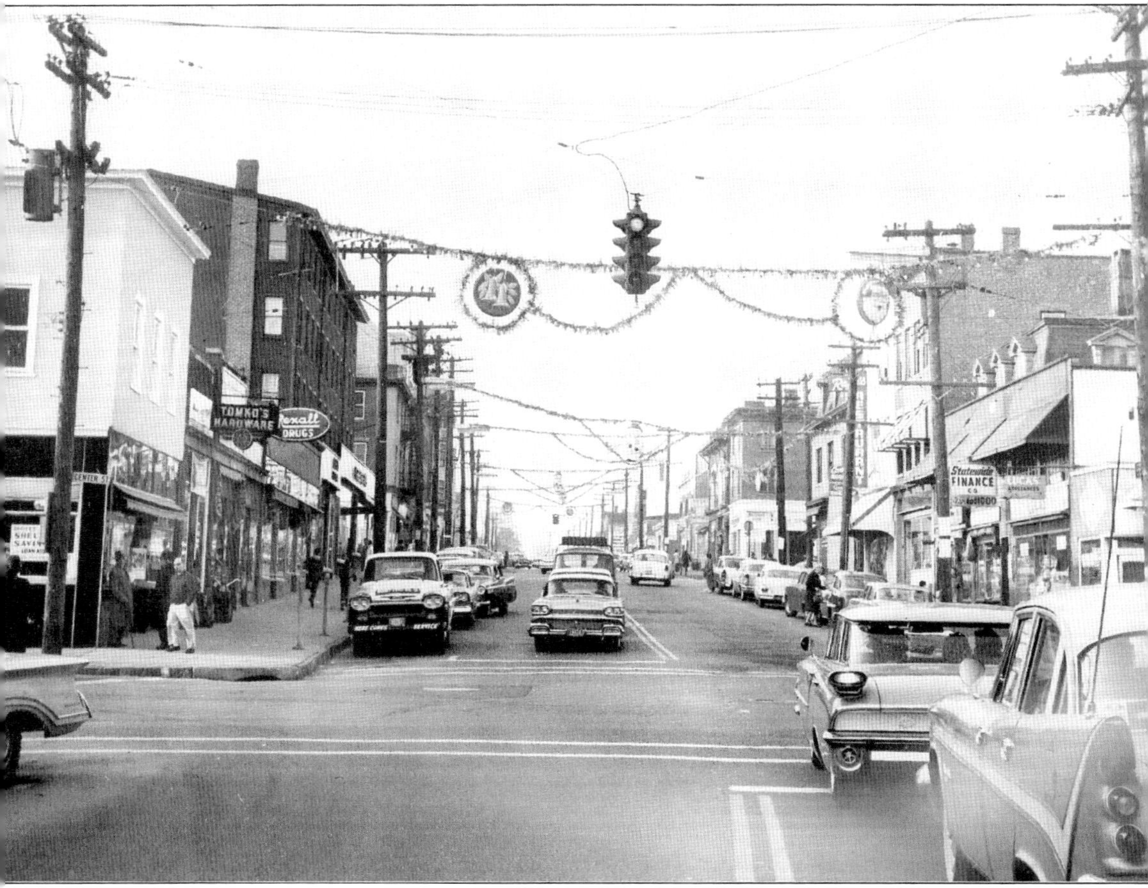

The businesses and signs seen in this *c.* 1960 view of Howe Avenue include the Shelton Savings and Loan Association, Tomko's Hardware, Rexall Drugs, Rapp's Restaurant, Statewide Finance, Lucas Appliances, and the Sheehy Insurance Agency. (Courtesy of the Shelton Economic Development Corporation.)

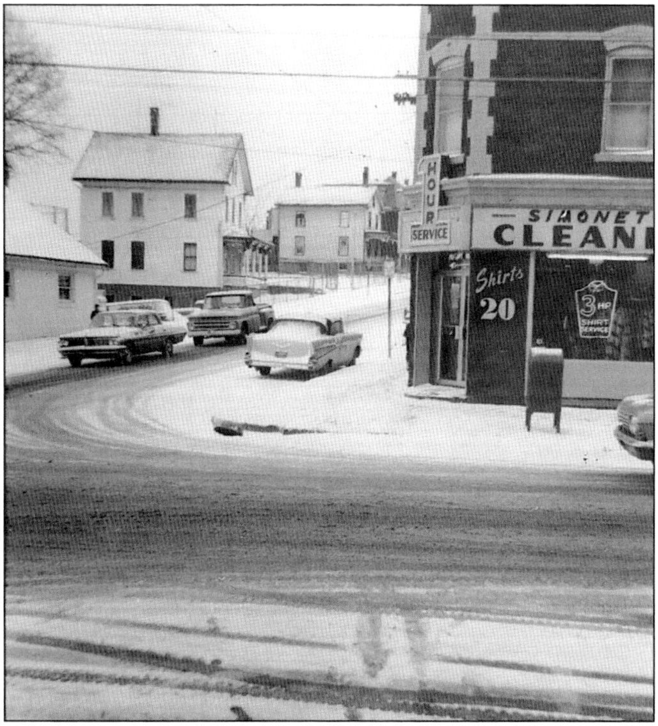

The building housing Simonetti's Dry Cleaners, on the corner of Coram Avenue and Center Street, has changed little since this photograph was taken during an ice storm on January 22, 1964. (Courtesy of the Simonetti family.)

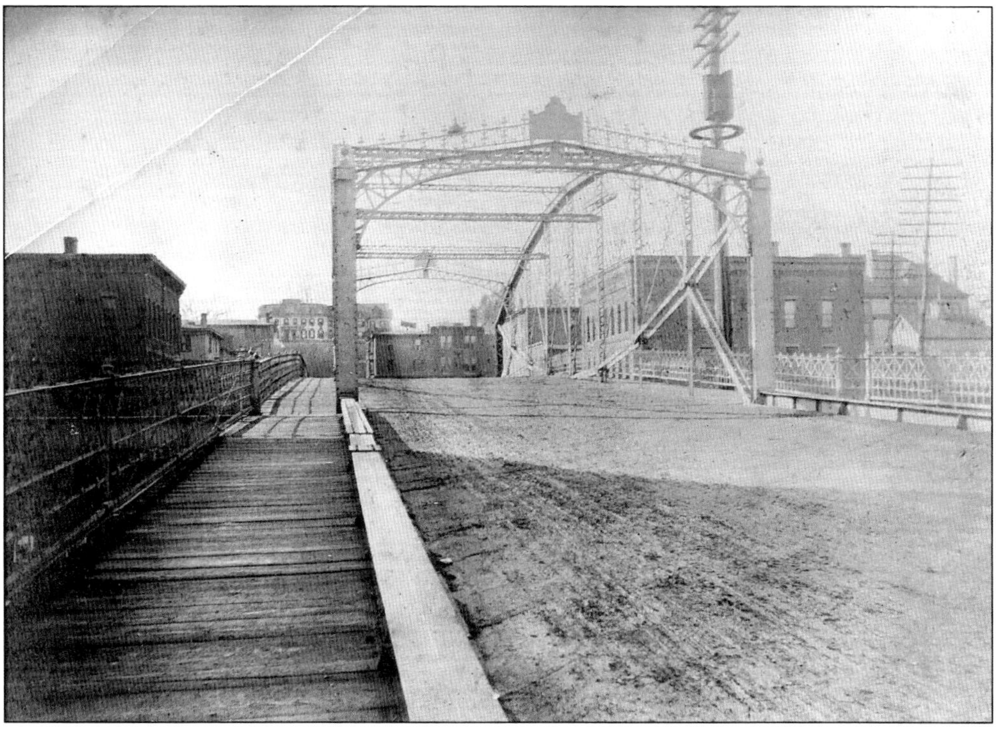

Originally constructed in 1888, the Viaduct Bridge had a wooden substructure, which needed to be replaced on a regular basis. This *c.* 1900 photograph clearly shows the wooden sidewalk and roadbed over the bridge. (Courtesy of the Frederick W. Ziegler family.)

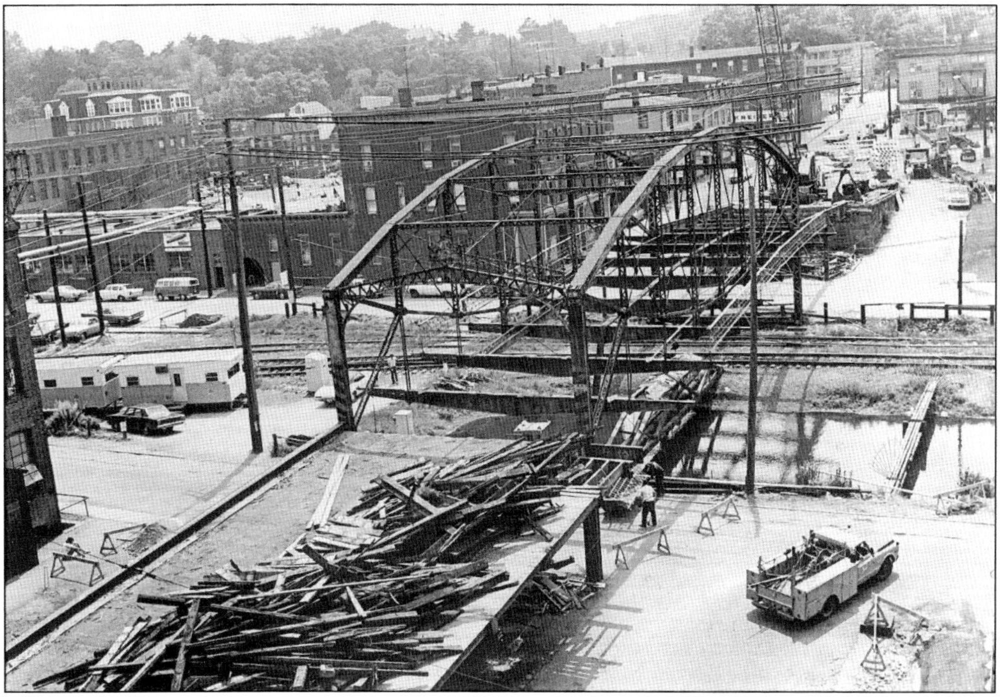

By June 28, 1973, the time had come to replace the old iron Viaduct Bridge. Here, the wooden substructure has been removed and is piled on the road. (Courtesy of the Shelton Economic Development Corporation.)

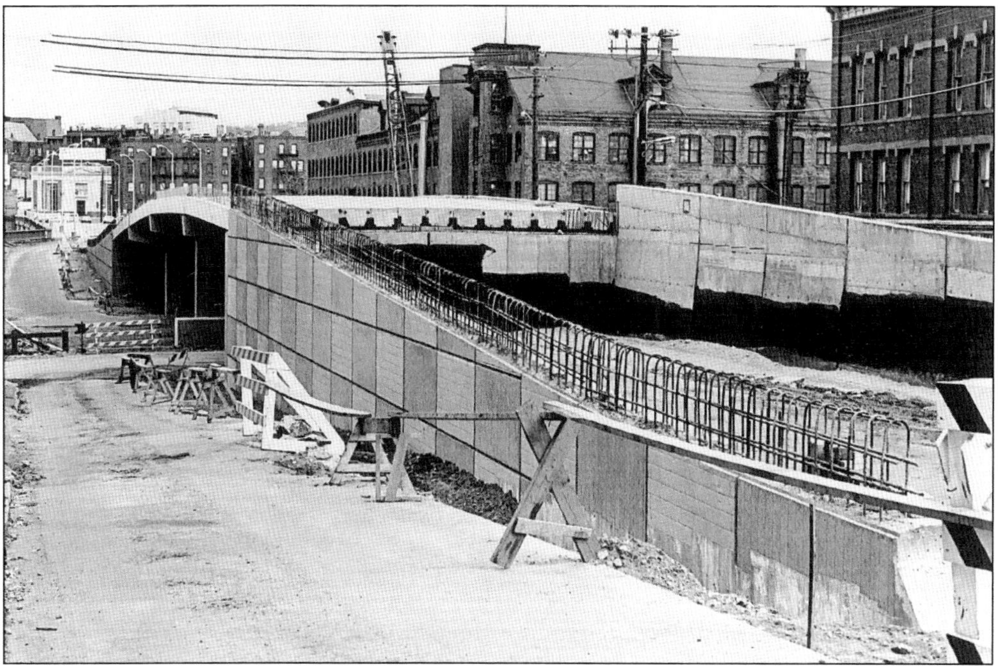

The new bridge was near completion by November 20, 1973. Until it was finished, traffic had to traverse the railroad tracks or use the Commodore Hull Bridge on Route 8 to cross the river. (Courtesy of the Shelton Economic Development Corporation.)

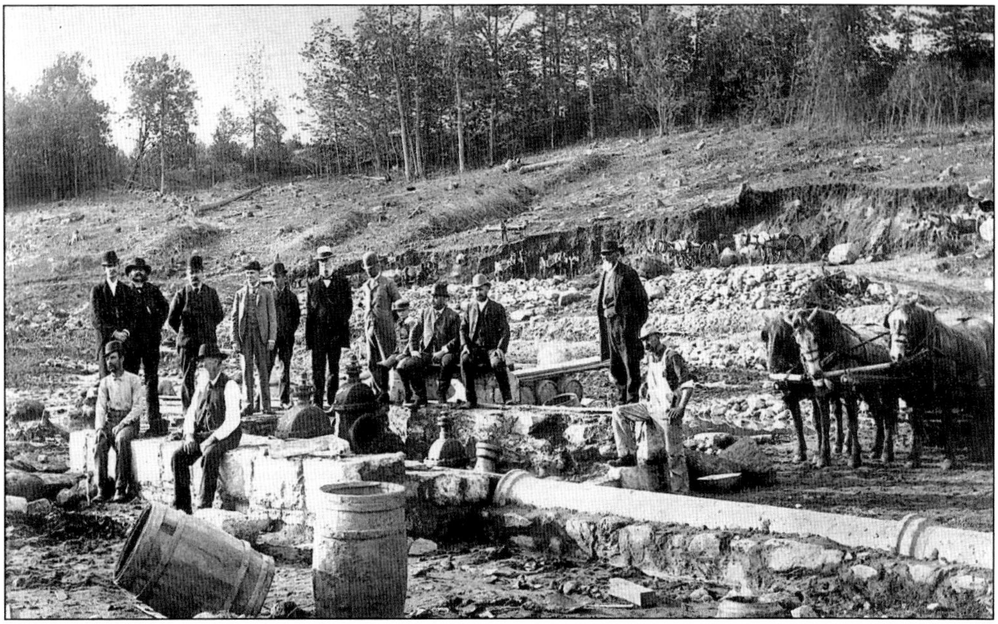

Formed in 1857, the Bridgeport Hydraulic Company has long utilized Shelton as a source of water. In this *c.* 1900 view, pipes are being laid from the Far Mill River collecting reservoir to the Trap Falls distributing reservoir. (Courtesy of the Aquarion Water Company.)

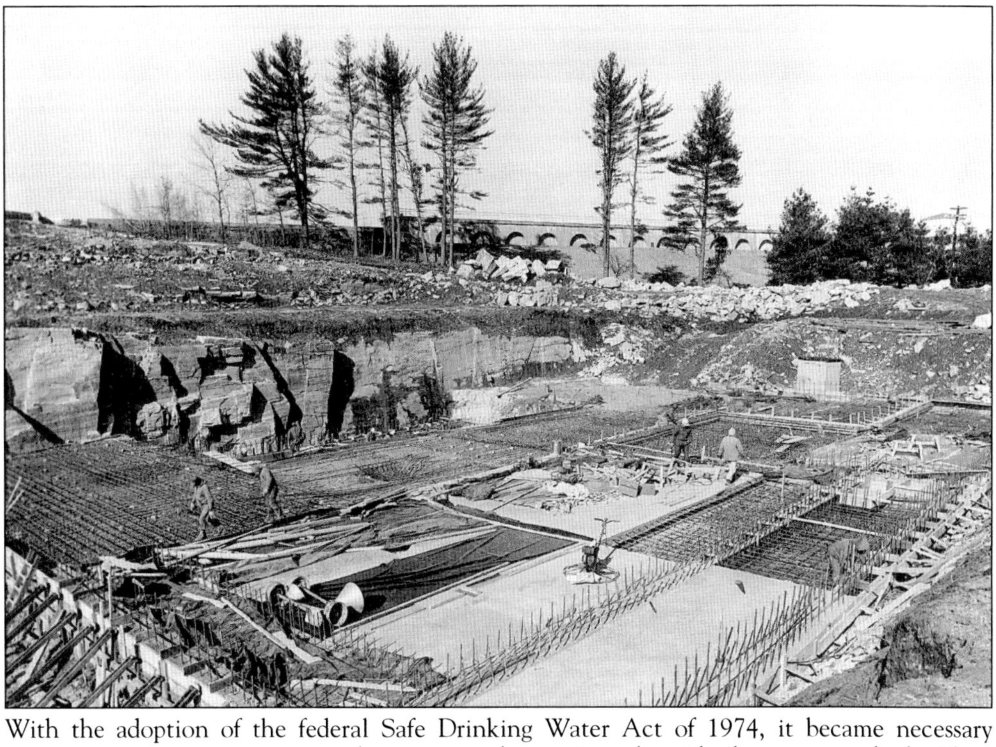

With the adoption of the federal Safe Drinking Water Act of 1974, it became necessary to construct a water-treatment plant to comply consistently with the new standards. Plant construction, on 10 acres near the Trap Falls Reservoir, took three years to complete. (Courtesy of the Aquarion Water Company.)

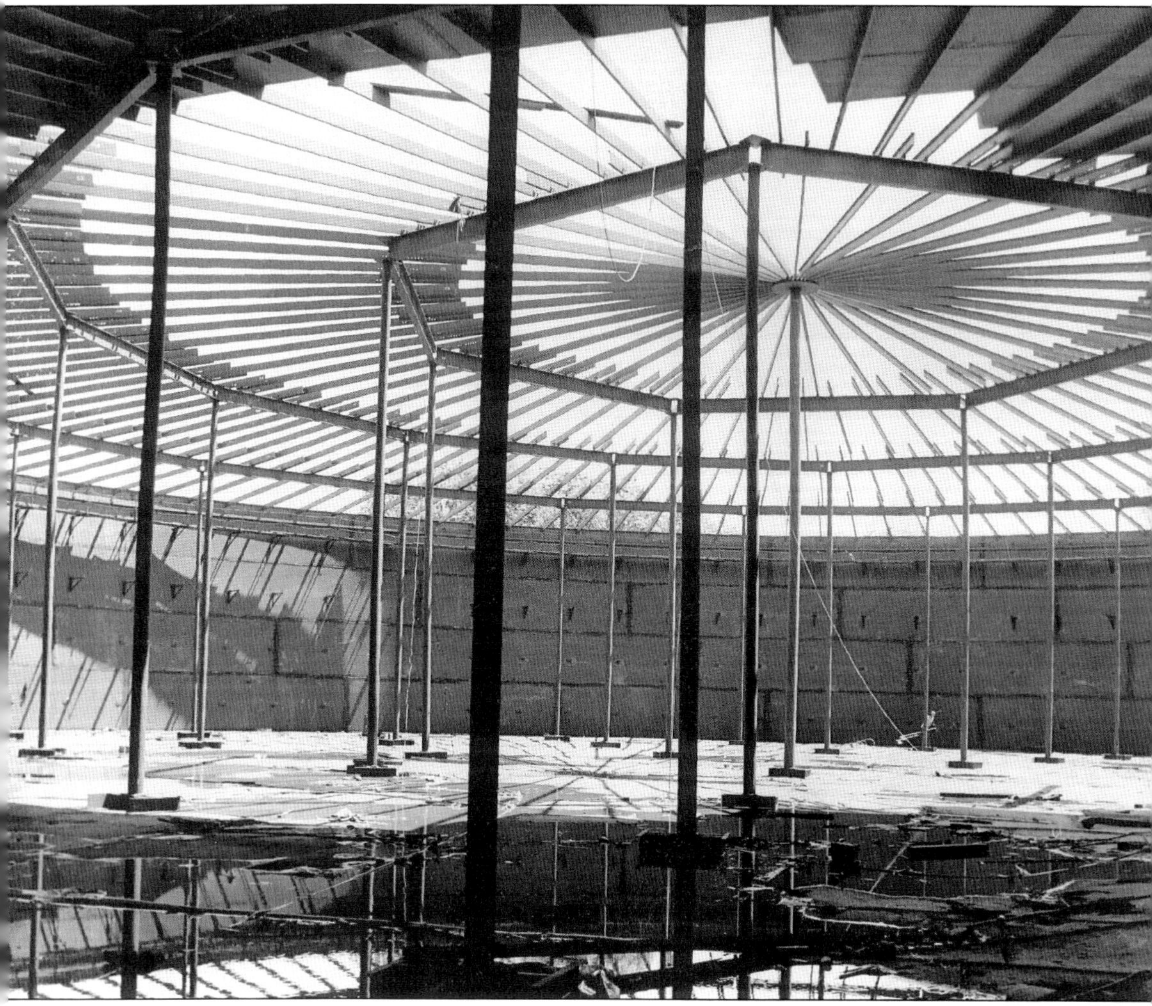

Upon completion in January 1981, the 10-million-gallon water-storage tank was the largest of its kind in New England. Here, it is seen under construction. The Trap Falls project cost $18 million. At that time, it was the most expensive capital improvement project for the Bridgeport Hydraulic Company. (Courtesy of the Aquarion Water Company.)

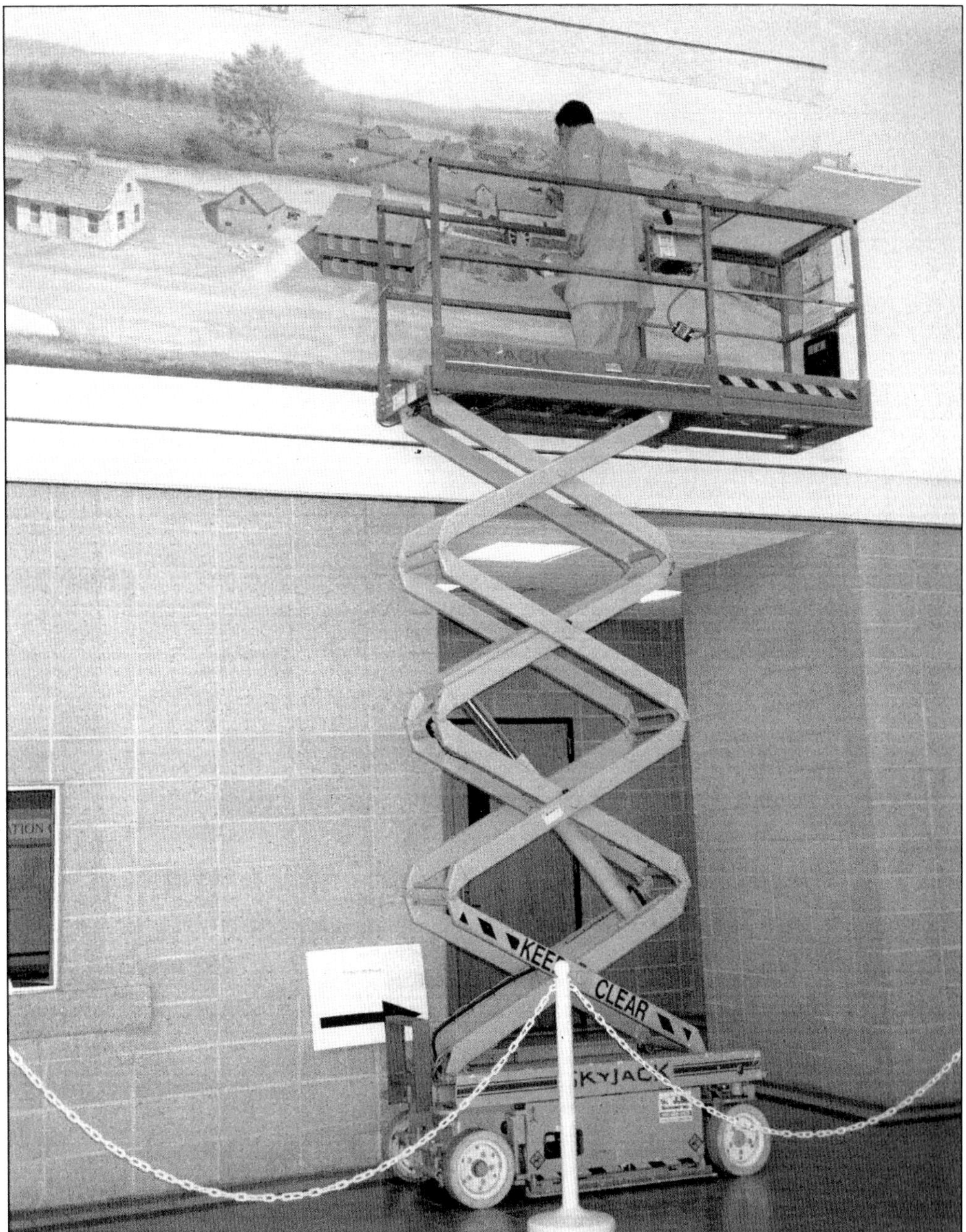

Shelton is a rapidly expanding city in the 21st century. With the growth in light industries and corporate headquarters has come an increase in population. To accommodate this growth, a new intermediate school opened to its first students in the fall of 2001. To celebrate the history of the area and educate the students of the school, the Jones family commissioned the artist David Merrill to paint a mural of the history of the site in the school's lobby. The mural is 68 feet long and 8 feet high. Following a seasonal theme as well as a chronological one, the mural begins with a depiction of the Native Americans in a summer setting. The mural will be a daily reminder of Shelton's history for generations of schoolchildren to come. (Photograph by D.G. Rossi.)